CAMBRIDGE LIBRARY COLLECTION

Books of enduring scholarly value

History of Printing, Publishing and Libraries

The interface between authors and their readers is a fascinating subject in its own right, revealing a great deal about social attitudes, technological progress, aesthetic values, fashionable interests, political positions, economic constraints, and individual personalities. This part of the Cambridge Library Collection reissues classic studies in the area of printing and publishing history that shed light on developments in typography and book design, printing and binding, the rise and fall of publishing houses and periodicals, and the roles of authors and illustrators. It documents the ebb and flow of the book trade supplying a wide range of customers with products from almanacs to novels, bibles to erotica, and poetry to statistics.

Prices of Books

A prolific author and bibliographer, Henry Benjamin Wheatley (1838–1917) wrote or edited dozens of works during a distinguished literary career. First published in 1898 as the fourth volume in Richard Garnett's 'Library Series', *Prices of Books* traces the market value of books in England from the seventeenth century to the late nineteenth century. Wheatley recounts the history of booksellers, and manuscript and book pricing in England, providing detailed analyses of significant auction sales over three centuries. He also devotes chapters to the pricing history of Shakespeare's works and other notable English publications. Serving as a fascinating micro-history of England's reading and book-collecting habits, this work will appeal to those interested in antiquarian culture and the history of the book. Several other works by Wheatley are also reissued in the Cambridge Library Collection, including the delightful *Literary Blunders* (1893).

T0370602

Cambridge University Press has long been a pioneer in the reissuing of out-of-print titles from its own backlist, producing digital reprints of books that are still sought after by scholars and students but could not be reprinted economically using traditional technology. The Cambridge Library Collection extends this activity to a wider range of books which are still of importance to researchers and professionals, either for the source material they contain, or as landmarks in the history of their academic discipline.

Drawing from the world-renowned collections in the Cambridge University Library and other partner libraries, and guided by the advice of experts in each subject area, Cambridge University Press is using state-of-the-art scanning machines in its own Printing House to capture the content of each book selected for inclusion. The files are processed to give a consistently clear, crisp image, and the books finished to the high quality standard for which the Press is recognised around the world. The latest print-on-demand technology ensures that the books will remain available indefinitely, and that orders for single or multiple copies can quickly be supplied.

The Cambridge Library Collection brings back to life books of enduring scholarly value (including out-of-copyright works originally issued by other publishers) across a wide range of disciplines in the humanities and social sciences and in science and technology.

Prices of Books

An Inquiry into the Changes in the Price of Books
which Have Occurred in England at Different Periods

HENRY BENJAMIN WHEATLEY

CAMBRIDGE
UNIVERSITY PRESS

University Printing House, Cambridge, CB2 8BS, United Kingdom

Cambridge University Press is part of the University of Cambridge.
It furthers the University's mission by disseminating knowledge in the pursuit of
education, learning and research at the highest international levels of excellence.

www.cambridge.org
Information on this title: www.cambridge.org/9781108078009

© in this compilation Cambridge University Press 2015

This edition first published 1898
This digitally printed version 2015

ISBN 978-1-108-07800-9 Paperback

This book reproduces the text of the original edition. The content and language reflect
the beliefs, practices and terminology of their time, and have not been updated.

Cambridge University Press wishes to make clear that the book, unless originally published
by Cambridge, is not being republished by, in association or collaboration with,
or with the endorsement or approval of, the original publisher or its successors in title.

𝔗𝔥𝔢 𝔏𝔦𝔟𝔯𝔞𝔯𝔶 𝔖𝔢𝔯𝔦𝔢𝔰

EDITED BY

DR. RICHARD GARNETT

IV

PRICES OF BOOKS

PRICES OF BOOKS

AN INQUIRY INTO THE CHANGES IN THE PRICE
OF BOOKS WHICH HAVE OCCURRED IN
ENGLAND AT DIFFERENT PERIODS

BY

HENRY B. WHEATLEY, F.S.A.

LONDON
GEORGE ALLEN, 156, CHARING CROSS ROAD
1898

Printed by BALLANTYNE, HANSON & Co.
At the Ballantyne Press

EDITOR'S INTRODUCTION

THE history of prices is one of the most interesting subjects that can engage research. As language has been called fossil poetry, from which the primitive workings of the mind of man may be elicited, so the story of his progress in material well-being lies enfolded in the history of the prices which have at various periods been procurable for commodities, whether of prime necessity, of general utility, or simply ornamental. The prices of books, so ably investigated and recorded by Mr. WHEATLEY in the following pages, are a small but significant department of a great subject. If we had no record of the price of any other article of commerce, we should still perceive in them an index to the world's advance in wealth, taste, and general intelligence. With every allowance for the fall in the value of money, it would yet be manifest that prices could now be afforded for books which at an earlier period would have been out of the question ; and not less so that while some classes of books had risen in worth with the enhanced standard of wealth, others had accommodated themselves to the requirements of the poor. We should trace the effect of mechanical improvements in diminishing the prices of things, and of fashion and curiosity in augmenting them. We should see the enormous influence of scarcity in forcing up the value of products, while we should learn at the same time that this was not the sole agent, but that intrinsic merit must usually to some extent co-operate with it, and that prices must bear some relation to the inherent reason of things. It must, for instance, have been entirely unforeseen by the early printers that the books which they advertised with such exultation as cheaper than the manuscripts they were superseding would in process of time become dearer, but we can discern this metamorphosis of relative value to have been rational and inevitable. Finally, the fluctuations of price would afford a clue to the intellectual condition of the age. Observing, for example, the great decline which, as a rule, has taken place in the value of early editions of the classics, we should conclude that either the classical writers were less generally esteemed than formerly, or that such progress had been made in their study that the old editions had become inadequate; and both conclusions would be well founded.

Books occupy a middle position between ordinary products and works of art. Like the latter, they are in theory the offspring of an exceptional talent. The humblest bookman views himself as in some measure the superior of his readers for the time being; he would have no excuse for addressing them if he did not suppose himself able to convey to them some pleasure which they could not have attained without him, or to inform them

of something, however insignificant, which but for
him would have remained unknown. But whereas
in the arts price is usually in the ratio of the real or
supposed intellectual merit of the production, in
books it may almost be said that the reverse rule
obtains. The fine picture or statue cannot be re-
produced as an original work; copies may be made
to any extent, but no amount of copying impairs
the value of the unique original. Again, such a
work, whether absolutely perfect or not, once
finished is complete for all time, and allows of no
further improvement. But the book admits of in-
definite multiplication, and the extent to which this
proceeds is commonly in the ratio of its intellectual
worth. It is the very greatest authors, the Homers,
the Shakespeares, that are usually the easiest and
cheapest to procure.

It appears, therefore, that, although great books
unquestionably demand more intellectual power
for their production than great works of art, their
very superiority tends to cheapen them in comparison by encouraging their dissemination. There
could not be a stronger instance of the power of
scarcity in determining price ; and, in fact, the
rarity of a book is the most important element in
its commercial worth. Yet intrinsic desert plays
its part, though an inferior one. There are some
cases in which it utterly fails. The commercial
value of the productions of the Dutch prototypo-
graphers, for example, would probably not be augmented in the least if they could be transformed
from fragments of dull lesson-books into leaves from

sages and poets. The Papal Bulls relating to the Turks in Cyprus, which have the honour to be the first documents to have issued complete from an European press, would hardly gain in commercial value if they were briefs announcing the foundation of the Vatican Library, or official announcements of the fall of Constantinople. On the other hand, the first edition of Virgil, one of the rarest of books, would assuredly be less valued if, while equally rare, it were the *editio princeps* of a Latin author of inferior reputation. In general, the celebrity of an author will be found a considerable factor in determining the value of a book; but while rarity without celebrity will effect much, celebrity without rarity, or some other adventitious circumstance devoid of relation to the intellectual value of the book, will effect very little.

Many other circumstances besides scarcity will contribute to render a book highly prized, and consequently dear. Some of these are obvious at once, such as fine paper, fine print, fine binding, or the autograph of a celebrated man. A book will be valued because it has been the subject of a judicial condemnation, or because it is a copy containing a plate in general deficient or mutilated, or perhaps only because it has an erratum corrected in other copies. Mr. Sidney Lee's recent discovery of a unique peculiarity in the Baroness Burdett-Coutts' Shakespeare folio may probably have doubled the value of the book. Sometimes such causes are very singular. King Charles the First dropped a pamphlet into the mud; the stain remains to this

day, and centuples the value of a tract which would
have been only deteriorated if it had slipped from
the fingers of a lord-in-waiting. Such a fact intro-
duces the element of sentiment, a powerful factor,
and one of far-reaching influence; for the Quaker
or Freemason who collects literature interesting to
his society, or the local patriot who buys up the
books printed in his native town, sets others upon
collecting them too, and raises the value all round.
Next to scarcity and great beauty, nothing, perhaps,
imparts such stability to the worth of a book as to
be addressed to a small but well-defined circle of
readers. Books on chess and angling are familiar
instances. They are not too numerous to dismay
a collector, and every one differs from the rest in
some feature sufficient to make it indispensable to
a collector ambitious of completeness.

A certain description of books would excite lively
interest if they could be identified with certainty,
those which are not valuable now, but which are
about to be. It may probably be considered that
almost any book which can manage to exist for
five hundred years will find itself augmented in
value at the end of this period, but some classes
will have proved much better investments than
others. Two may be signalised with considerable
confidence—illustrated books, which portray the
fashions and humours of the age for posterity, and
newspapers. Nothing grows in value like a newspaper ; the sheets of to-day, which, perhaps, contain nothing of interest to any contemporary reader,
will be priceless to the historian and antiquary of

the centuries to come. They fructify in silence,
and imperceptibly make their possessor rich. Their
intellectual as well as their pecuniary value aug-
ments by lying still. Nothing so faithfully depicts
an age for its successors; they are worth all the
histories and all the novels. Their preservation—
which involves their assemblage in one place for
the sake of accessibility and of comparison with
each other and with books—is a momentous trust,
neglect of which would strike a heavy blow at historical, archæological, and sociological research, and
inflict a grievous injury upon the ages to come.

R. GARNETT.

March 1898.

PREFACE

THE subject of the prices of books is one which always exercises a certain fascination over the minds of book-lovers, although some have expressed their objection to any discussion of it, lest this should have the effect of enhancing prices.

In a single volume it is impossible to deal with so large a subject in any fulness of detail, and I have therefore endeavoured to give a general view, merely instancing a few cases in illustration of the whole, but making an exception in respect of two of the most interesting and high-priced classes of books in literature, namely, the productions of the press of Caxton, and the original editions of Shakespeare's works.

It is necessary for the reader to bear two points in mind—

(1) That the value of money has changed during each century of our history to an extent not easy to calculate with precision, because the prices of all articles have not been equally affected. We can say generally that definite incomes a hundred years ago were equivalent in worth to twice their nominal

amount at the present day, and that those of two hundred years ago would be worth about five times as much. In the fifteenth and sixteenth centuries money was worth ten or twelve times what it is now, but there is some difficulty in calculating correctly the rates respectively of necessaries and luxuries. This is a matter for experts, and cannot be more than alluded to here, as a warning to the reader that he must always remember that a pound or a shilling in previous centuries was of more value than it is to-day, and possessed a much greater purchasing power.

(2) That in dealing with prices we are interested with rare and specially valuable books. Ordinary standard books, even in good editions, were never cheaper than at present.

A writer of a work of this kind must feel grateful to predecessors, who have made it possible for him to gather satisfactory material for his purpose. Special gratitude is due to Thomas Frognall Dibdin, Hartwell Horne, and William Clarke (author of the *Repertorium Bibliographicum*), who were all thorough workers in this field. The labours of Dibdin have been unjustly depreciated by many modern writers. His works, besides being among the most beautiful books produced in Europe, are mines of bibliographical anecdote and useful literary information. Objections may be made by some to his descriptions, but he certainly greatly influenced the bibliomania of a former age, and made many sales famous which otherwise would have been forgotten except by the few.

There is a gap in the literature of our subject between authors at the beginning of the century and the modern writers, who largely obtain their information from French sources.

H. B. W.

CONTENTS

CHAPTER VII

CHAPTER VIII

CHAPTER IX

CHAPTER X

CHAPTER XI

PRICES OF BOOKS

CHAPTER I

INTRODUCTION

THE treatment of such a subject as the Prices of Books necessarily obliges us to range over a wide field, for books have been bought and sold far back in the historical period, and to books, both manuscript and printed, we have to refer largely for records of the past. It is, however, only possible in the space at our disposal to take a very general view of the subject; and it is to be hoped that, in recording the main points in the vicissitudes of prices, the information may not be deemed too desultory to be serviceable.

We might go back to the earliest times, even to Job's famous exclamation, but for our present purpose there would not be much advantage in roaming in this early period, as the results to be recorded would partake more of an archæological, than of a practical character. There is very little chance of a copy of the first book of Martial's Epigrams (which, when first composed by the author, cost at Rome about three shillings and

A

sixpence of our money) coming to auction, so that
we are not likely to be able to record its present
value.

A consideration of the subject opens up a large
number of interesting subjects, which can only
casually be alluded to, such as the position of
authors, and their remuneration.

For several centuries monasteries were the chief
producers of literature, and it seems probable that
it was worth the while of the chiefs of some of
these literary manufactories to pay a poet such as
Chaucer something for a new Canterbury Tale,
which they could copy and distribute over the
country. We know by the number of manuscripts, and the different order in these, that
several establishments were employed in the production of the manuscripts, and we may guess
that there would probably be competition among
them, which would naturally result in a settlement
of some terms of payment.

In the early times it was only rich men who
could afford to collect books. Amongst these, one
of the most distinguished was Richard de Bury,
Bishop of Durham, Treasurer and Chancellor of
Edward III., who collected everything, and spared
no cost in the maintenance of a staff of copyists
and illuminators in his own household. Not only
was he a collector (whose books, however, have been
dispersed), but he was the author of an interesting
relic of that devotion to an ennobling pursuit, the
famous *Philobiblon*. This book had never been
satisfactorily produced until the late Mr. Ernest

Thomas issued in 1888 an admirable edition, founded on a collation of many manuscripts, and a spirited translation.[1] This work occupied Mr. Thomas several years, and before he completed it he saw reason to doubt the high literary position which had been universally accorded to the author; and his opinion was confirmed by an unpublished passage in a manuscript of the *Chronicon sui temporis* of Adam de Murimuth, to which he was referred by Sir Edward Maunde Thompson, where Adam characterised the bishop in very harsh terms. Mr. Thomas published in "The Library" (vol. i. p. 335) an article entitled, "Was Richard de Bury an Impostor?" In this he expressed the opinion that Richard Aungerville—

(1) Was *not* an excellent bishop, *but* an ambitious self-seeker, who bought his way to preferment.

(2) Was *not* a scholar and patron of scholars, *but* merely a collector of books, that he might appear as a scholar.

(3) *Did not* bestow his collections on Durham College, Oxford, as he expressed his intention of doing; *but* that these collections were sold to pay debts incurred by his ostentatious extravagance.

(4) *Did not* write *Philobiblon*. The authorship was claimed for Robert Holkot, a Dominican, who for some time was a member of the bishop's household.

---

[1] A still more elaborate edition was published by the Grolier Club in 1889. This was edited by Professor A. F. West, and printed in three volumes small quarto. It was issued in a small edition, and a sight of it is therefore difficult to obtain.

It is certain that the evidence is such as to force
us to lower our estimate of the prelate's merits, but
these four charges are certainly not all proved. He
may not have been so learned and so unselfish a
lover of books as was supposed, but there is no
satisfactory reason for depriving him of the credit
of being the author of the *Philobiblon.*

Mr. Thomas shows that Richard de Bury was
born on 24th January 1287, and not 1281, as stated
in the "Dictionary of National Biography." He
completed the *Philobiblon,* and on the 14th April of
the same year *Dominus Ricardus de Bury migravit
ad Dominum.*

A singularly appropriate chapter from the earliest
" book about books " may here be quoted :—

"WHAT WE ARE TO THINK OF THE PRICE IN THE BUYING OF BOOKS.

(Chapter III. of the *Philobiblon* of Richard de Bury.[1])

" From what has been said we draw this corollary,
welcome to us, but (as we believe) acceptable to few ;
namely, that no dearness of price ought to hinder a man
from the buying of books, if he has the money that is
demanded for them, unless it be to withstand the malice
of the seller, or to await a more favourable opportunity of
buying. For if it is wisdom only that makes the price of
books, which is an infinite treasure to mankind, and if the
value of books is unspeakable, as the premises show, how
shall the bargain be shown to be dear where an infinite

---

[1] From Ernest C. Thomas's translation, 1888.

good is being bought? Wherefore that books are to be gladly bought and unwillingly sold, Solomon, the sun of men, exhorts in the *Proverbs*: *Buy the truth*, he says, *and sell not wisdom*. But what we are trying to show by rhetoric or logic, let us prove by examples from history. The arch-philosopher Aristotle, whom Averroes regards as the law of Nature, bought a few books of Speusippus straightway after his death for seventy - two thousand sesterces. Plato, before him in time, but after him in learning, bought the book of Philolaus the Pythagorean, from which he is said to have taken the *Timæus*, for ten thousand denaries, as Aulus Gellius relates in the *Noctes Atticæ*. Now Aulus Gellius relates this that the foolish may consider how wise men despise money in comparison with books. And on the other hand, that we may know that folly and pride go together, let us here relate the folly of Tarquin the Proud in despising books, as also related by Aulus Gellius. An old woman, utterly unknown, is said to have come to Tarquin the Proud, the seventh King of Rome, offering to sell nine books in which (as she declared) sacred oracles were contained; but she asked an immense sum for them, insomuch that the king said she was mad. In anger she flung three books into the fire, and still asked the same price for the rest. When the king refused it, again she flung three others into the fire, and still asked the same price for the three that were left. At last, astonished beyond measure, Tarquin was glad to pay for three books the same price for which he might have bought nine. The old woman straightway disappeared, and was never seen before or after. These were the Sibylline books. . . ."

The destruction of libraries, which was common in the Middle Ages, naturally caused an increase in the value of those which remained. How completely

these libraries passed away may be seen by the
instance of that which was once preserved in St.
Paul's Cathedral, and is noticed by the late Dr.
Sparrow Simpson in his "St. Paul's Cathedral
Library" (1893). Walter Shiryngton Clerk founded
the library, the catalogue of which (1458) fills eight
folio pages in the first edition of Dugdale's "History
of St. Paul's." Of all the manuscripts in this catalogue, only three are now known to exist : one is
still at St. Paul's, the second is at Aberdeen, and the
third at Lambeth.

The British Museum is fortunate in possessing
the beautiful library of the Kings and Queens of
England since Henry VII., which is full of the most
splendid specimens of artistic bindings. What the
market value of such literary gems as these may be
can scarcely be estimated, and fortunately they are
safe from the arising of any occasion which might
afford a test of their value. From this library we
are able to appreciate the good taste of James I.,
who, whatever his faults may have been, was certainly a true bibliophile, and to him we owe some
of the finest books in the collection.

It may be safely said that few collections of books
have been formed under such difficult and trying
circumstances as the invaluable Thomason Collection of Civil War Tracts, now happily preserved in
the British Museum. Mr. F. Madan has contributed to *Bibliographica* (vol. iii. p. 291) a most valuable article on the labours of the worthy Royalist
bookseller, George Thomason. Thomason commenced in November 1640, when the "Long or

Rebel Parliament" began, his great undertaking of collecting all the pamphlets published in England, and he continued it until May 1661. Many of these were printed surreptitiously, and were obtained with the greatest difficulty ; in fact, seventy-three of these were in manuscript, "which no man durst then venture to publish without endangering his ruine." The King and the Cavalier party knew of the existence of the collection, but every endeavour was made to keep the knowledge from the other party. If it were difficult to form the collection, it was still more difficult to preserve it. We are told that, "to prevent the discovery of them, when the army was Northwards, he packed them in several trunks, and, by one or two in a week, sent them to a trusty friend in Surrey, who safely preserved them, and when the army was Westward, and fearing their return that way, they were sent to London again ; but the collector durst not keep them, but sent them into Essex, and so according as they lay near danger, still by timely removing them at a great charge, secured them, but continued perfecting the work." Afterwards, for greater security, they were lodged in the Bodleian Library, and a pretended bargain was made, and a receipt for £1000 given to the University of Oxford, so that "if the Usurper had found them out the University should claim them, who had greater power to struggle for them than a private man."

On one occasion Charles I. wished to consult a particular pamphlet, and applied to Thomason for the loan of it. In small quarto vol. 100 is a manuscript note describing the particulars of this interesting loan :—

"Memorandum that Col. Will Legg and Mr. Arthur Treavors were employed by his Mātie K. Charles to gett for his present use, a pamphlet which his Mātie had then occasion to make use of, and not meeting with it, they both came to me, having heard that I did employ my selfe to take up all such things, from the beginning of that Parlement, and finding it with me, tould me it was for the King's owne use, I tould them all I had were at his Māties command and service, and withall tould them if I should part with it and loose it, presuming that when his Mātie had done with it, that little account would be made of it, and so I should loose by that losse a limbe of my collection, which I should be very loth to do, well knowing it would be impossible to supplie it if it should happen to be lost, with which answer they returned to his Mātie at Hampton Court (as I take it) and tould him they had found that peece he so much desired and withall how loath he that had it, was to part with, he much fearing its losse ; whereupon they were both sent to me againe by his Mātie to tell me that upon the worde of a Kinge (to use their own expressions) he would safely returne it, thereuppon immediately by them I sent it to his Mātie, who having done with it, and having it with him when he was going towards the Isle of Wight, let it fall in the durt, and then callinge for the two persons before mentioned (who attended him) delivered it to them, with a charge, as they would answer it another day, that they should both speedily and safely return it to him, from whom they had received it, and withall to desire the partie to goe on and continue what had begun, which book together with his Māties signification to me by these worthy and faithfull gentlemen I received both speedily and safely.   Which volume hath the marke of honor upon

it, which no other volume in my collection hath, and very
diligently and carefully I continued the same, until the most
hapie restoration and coronation of his most gratious mātie
Kinge Charles the second whom God long preserve.—
GEORGE THOMASON."

Here we have surely an interesting instance of the
poetry of bibliography.

According to Mr. Madan's calculation, there are
22,834 pamphlets in about 1983 volumes, and apparently some hundred or so pieces have been lost from
the original set. The collection of these pamphlets
was made at very considerable expense, and Thomason is said to have refused £4000 for them, "supposing
that sum not sufficient to reimburse him." On his
death in 1666 a special trust was appointed under his
will to take charge of the collection, and Dr. Thomas
Barlow (Bodley's librarian, 1652 to 1660) was one
of the trustees. In 1675 Barlow was appointed
Bishop of Lincoln, and in the following year requested the Rev. George Thomason (son of the
bookseller) to take over the charge. After many
vicissitudes the books were bought for the absurdly
small sum of £300 for George III., who presented
the collection to the British Museum. It is impossible to guess at the present price of what is
practically invaluable.

The famous antiquary Elias Ashmole, whose treasures are now preserved at Oxford in the Ashmolean
Museum, records in his Diary some of his purchases,
as, on May 1667, "I bought Mr. John Booker's study
of books, and gave £140 for them"; and again, on

June 12, 1681, " I bought Mr. Lilly's library of books of his widow for £50."[1] We can judge of the character of his library by these purchases of the collections of two of his famous astrological friends.

Even in the seventeenth century men began to be frightened at the increase of books, and Sir Thomas Browne in his *Religio Medici* suggested a system of destruction : " 'Tis not a melancholy *utinam* of my own, but the desires of better heads, that there were a general synod—not to unite the incompatible difference of religion, but—for the benefit of learning, to reduce it, as it lay at first, in a few and solid authors ; and to condemn to the fire those swarms and millions of rhapsodies, begotten only to distract and abuse the weaker judgments of scholars, and to maintain the trade and mystery of typographers." If there was reason for this complaint two centuries ago, how much more must there be now ! but the project is unworkable, and Time takes the matter in his own hand and destroys. Fortunately the destruction chiefly takes place among books not likely to be missed.

Three of the greatest book collectors of the eighteenth century were Bishop Moore, the Earl of Sunderland, and the Earl of Oxford. Bishop Moore's fine library, which consisted of about thirty thousand volumes, was offered in 1714 to Harley, Earl of Oxford, for £8000, but the latter did not accept the offer because the bishop insisted that the earl should pay the money at once, although he was not to receive the books till the

---

[1] Dibdin's *Bibliomania*, Part V.

collector's death. He would not really have had long to wait, for the bishop died on July 31st of the same year. The library, mainly through the influence of Lord Townshend, was purchased for £6000 by George I., who presented it to the University of Cambridge. This presentation gave rise to two well-known epigrams, which have been frequently misquoted. Dr. Trapp, the first Professor of Poetry at Oxford, expressed the disgust of his University in these lines—

> "Contrary methods justly George applies
> To govern his two Universities;
> To Oxford sent a troop of horse; for why?
> That learned body wanted Loyalty.
> To Cambridge he sent books, as well discerning
> How much that loyal body wanted learning."

Sir William Browne, the physician, put the Cambridge case in a form which extorted praise from the Oxonian Samuel Johnson—

> "Contrary methods justly George applies
> To govern his two Universities;
> And so to Oxford sent a troop of horse,
> For Tories hold no argument but force.
> To Cambridge Ely's learned troops are sent,
> For Whigs admit no force but argument." [1]

When Lord Treasurer Harley recommended Queen Anne to purchase Sir Symonds d'Ewes'

---

[1] The versions given in Noble's Continuation of Granger are inferior to the above, which were taken from an old MS. by the Rev. Cecil Moore, and are believed by him to be the originals. See "Bibliographer," vol. vi. p. 92.

manuscripts as the richest collection in England after Sir Robert Cotton's, and to present them to a public library, the Queen answered, "It was no virtue for her, a woman, to prefer, as she did, arts to arms; but while the blood and honour of a nation were at stake in her wars, she could not, till she had secured her *living* subjects an honourable peace, bestow their money upon *dead* letters." Thereupon the Lord Treasurer bought the collection himself for £6000.[1] The whole collection of the Harleian MSS. (one of the greatest treasures of the British Museum Library), which consists of 7639 volumes, exclusive of 14,236 original rolls, charters, deeds, and other legal instruments, was purchased by Government for £10,000, or only £4000 more than the Earl of Oxford gave for Sir Symonds d'Ewes' manuscripts alone.

The Earl of Sunderland's fine library was for several years housed in the mansion which formerly stood on the site of the Albany in Piccadilly. It was removed to Blenheim in 1749, where it remained till the great sale of 1881–83. Oldys reports that the King of Denmark offered Lord Sunderland's heirs £30,000 for the library,[2] and that the great Duchess Sarah of Marlborough was in favour of the offer being accepted, but it was not.

We learn from Hearne's "Remains" that £3000 was offered by the University of Oxford for the noble library of Isaac Vossius, the free-thinking

---

[1] William Oldys's "Choice Notes," 1862, p. 38.   [2] Ibid. p. 92.

Canon of Windsor, and refused. Hearne adds, "We should have purchased them, and not stood in such a case upon punctilio and niceties, when we are so lavish of our money upon trifles that bring dishonour on the University." The library was taken abroad, and soon afterwards sold to the University of Leyden for the same amount as that previously offered by Oxford (£3000).[1]

Thomas Osborne, the chief bookseller of his time, bought the great Harley library, consisting of about 50,000 volumes of printed books, 41,000 prints, and about 350,000 pamphlets, for £13,000. This seems a small amount for so matchless a collection, but it is not certain that Osborne made a very profitable investment by his purchase. We shall have more to say of the bookseller and the library in the next chapter.

As an instance of the low price of books at this time, the anecdote of Mr. David Papillon's agreement with Osborne may be mentioned here. The contract was that the bookseller should supply Mr. Papillon (who died in 1762) with one hundred pounds' worth of books at threepence apiece, the only conditions being that they should be perfect, and that there should be no duplicates. Osborne was at first pleased with his bargain, and sent in a large number of books; but he soon found that it would be impossible to carry out the agreement without great loss, as he was obliged to send in

[1] Bliss's *Reliquiæ Hearnianæ*, 1869, vol. i. pp. 206, 207.

books worth shillings instead of pence. Long
before he had supplied the eight thousand volumes
required, he begged to be let off the contract.

Things were worse in Russia, where Klostermann,
the bookseller to the Imperial Court, sold books by
the yard (fifty to one hundred roubles, according to
binding). Every courtier who had hopes of a visit
from the Empress Catharine was expected to have
a library, and as few of them had any literary taste,
they bought them at this rate. Sometimes waste-
paper books were lettered with the names of celebrated authors.

Authorship could hardly become a profession
until after the invention of printing, and even then
it was long before a living could be got out of
books. Dr. Edward Castell laboured for seventeen
years in the compilation of his immense undertaking — the *Lexicon Heptaglotton*, to accompany
Walton's Polyglot Bible. During this time he main-
tained at his own cost as writers seven Englishmen and as many foreigners. All of them died
before the work was completed. Besides expend-
ing £12,000 of his own money he was obliged to
borrow £2000 more, and this not being sufficient,
he petitioned Charles II. that a prison might not
be the reward of so much labour. Notwithstanding a circular letter from the king recommending
the purchase of this work the author ended his
days in poverty, and a great part of the impression
was thrown into garrets, where many of the copies
were destroyed by damp or rats.

A similar case was that of Thomas Madox, the

learned author of the " History of the Exchequer,"
who wrote to Dr. Charlett requesting him to get his
book into the College Libraries at Oxford, and explaining that the cost of the impression was £400
for paper and print, and as only 481 copies were
printed, "when all the books shall be sold I shall
be just able to pay the charges with a trifling over-
plus. . . . This affair," he adds, "has given me
much perplexity, and perfectly cured me of scrib-
bling."[1]

Thomas Hearne was more fortunate, and amassed
a small fortune by his publications. One thousand
guineas were found in gold in his rooms at St.
Edmund Hall after his death. His books were
soon out of print, and fetched large prices even in
his own lifetime.

Lord Spencer bought the whole of the library
of Count Revickzky, a catalogue of which had
been privately printed by the original owner at
Berlin in 1784. According to Dibdin, when the
Count was in England he offered his whole
collection to Lord Spencer for a certain round
sum to be paid to him immediately, and for a
yearly sum by way of annuity. The offer was
accepted, and as the Count died soon afterwards,
Lord Spencer obtained the library at a cheap rate.
The same noble collector offered the Duke di
Cassano Serra £500 for two books, viz., the *Juvenal*
of Ulric Han, and the *Horace* of Arnaldus de
Bruxella, Naples, 1474, but the offer was not

---

[1] " Letters from the Bodleian," vol. i. p. 214.

accepted.   In 1820 Lord Spencer bought the whole
collection.

The Duke of Devonshire purchased the valuable
library of Dr. Thomas Dampier, Bishop of Ely,
for nearly £10,000 after the bishop's death in
1812.   Dr. Dibdin has printed in his "Reminiscences" (vol. i. p. 363) a list of prices at which Dr.
Dampier valued the various classes of books in his
library.

Little idea of the prices of books can be obtained
from the amounts given for a whole library, but as
in future chapters particulars will be printed of
the great libraries that have been disposed of by
auction, it seemed well to mention here a few
instances of libraries that have been sold entire.
The greatest of these is the magnificent library of
Earl Spencer, which was sold in 1892 to Mrs.
Rylands, and has been transferred from Althorpe
to Manchester.   The exact amount paid for this
library has not been announced, but it is supposed
to have been about a quarter of a million pounds.

In respect to the history of prices of books, there
have been times of inflation and times of depression,
just as in the history of prices generally, but it will
be seen that in spite of these vicissitudes scarce
books have gradually increased in value.   The first
signs of the growth of *bibliomania* are seen in the
sales of Dr. Mead's and Dr. Askew's libraries in the
middle of the last century, which aroused a great
interest among book collectors.

During the great Napoleonic wars books became
very scarce, because Englishmen were prevented

from purchasing on the Continent, but upon the conclusion of the peace there was a steady flow of books into the country.

The Duke of Roxburghe's sale in 1812 was a great event, forming, as it did, an epoch in the history of book collecting, and the widespread fervour of biblio-maniacs may be dated from that period. Great sales followed, and then came the sale of the enormous Heber library, which let out too many books on the market at once. After this there followed a dull time, but a revival came with the Bright sale in 1846 and Stowe sale in 1849, and the Daniel and Corser sales between 1860 and 1870, and the Henry Perkins sale in 1873, were great events. The last few years have been marked by many great sales, those of the Sunderland, the Beckford, and Hamilton Libraries, and the Turner, Gaisford, Crawford, and Ashburnham collections being among the most remarkable. The greatly increased prices obtained for books have induced many proprietors to sell their literary treasures.

It is well to remember that the value of all books is not rising, but that whole classes have fallen in price. Greek and Roman Classics, and the Fathers and Theological Literature generally, have been most markedly depreciated in value.

Fashion guides alterations in the prices of books, just as she does in other less important matters. Thus we find at one time certain books quoted at high prices, which not many years afterwards have become drugs in the market. Still, a careful review of the subject will show that fashion is not nearly

B

so potent as in some other departments, say, for instance, in the case of pictures, which certainly vary in price more than books. In spite, therefore, of signs of variableness, it will be seen that there is a continuous increase of price among certain classes of books which are sure to retain their value, and even to be still more esteemed as time passes.

It may be well to inquire what are some of the causes which lead to an increase in the price, and to distinguish between those which are permanent and those which are ephemeral. The growth of book-collecting in the United States has had a most potent influence, and large purchases made for many years in England have drained off a large number of books, low priced as well as high priced, which will never return to this country. Another cause is the increase of public libraries in Great Britain, and when books are bought for these libraries they are permanently removed from the open market, as they are not when sold to an individual, because his library will most probably eventually come to the hammer. These two causes would be sufficient in themselves to permanently increase the price of scarce books, but there are still others to be mentioned. There has been of late years a greatly increased interest felt in the history of books—in printing, in binding—and increased knowledge has shown the great claims of a large number of books to a higher appreciation than hitherto. Then again, the class of the wealthy who can afford to collect choice libraries has largely

increased ; and lastly, the belief that the collecting
of books is by no means a bad investment has not
been without effect. This last point opens up a
very interesting question in ethics, Should a collector look upon his collections as an investment ?
The late Mr. J. Hill Burton argues very strongly
against this view in his " Book-Hunter." He
writes—

"'The mercenary spirit must not be admitted to a share
in the enjoyments of the book-hunter. . . . If [he] allows
money-making, even for those he is to leave behind, to be
combined with his pursuit, it loses its fresh relish, its
exhilarating influence, and becomes the source of wretched
cares and paltry anxieties.   When money is the object,
let a man speculate or become a miser." . . .

This is quite true, but we must remember that,
after all, increased price is only an outward mani-
festation of increased public estimation, and it is
always satisfactory to know that our opinion has
been accepted by the public.   The real point seems
to be that the collector should use his judgment
in respect to price, and not trouble himself whether
the market value of individual books goes up or
down, for he may be sure that if he buys wisely,
the ups and the downs will balance each other.
If a fair-sized library is purchased with judgment
and knowledge, it cannot fail to become a profitable investment,   because good books increase in
value by reason of their companionship.   All worthless books should therefore be ruthlessly weeded
out.   For instance, a library of 1000 choice books

would probably sell for less with 500 books of little
value added to them than if these were ruthlessly
eliminated.

Mr. Andrew Lang writes in his pretty little book,
"The Library"—

"When Osborne sold the Harley collection, the scarcest
old English books fetched but three or four shillings. If
the Wandering Jew had been a collector in the last century, he might have turned a pretty profit by selling his old
English books in this age."

But Mr. Lang did not think of a calculation, by
which Mr. A. W. Pollard, in an interesting article
on "English Booksales, 1676–86" (*Bibliographica*,
vol. ii. p. 126), overthrew this view of the possibility
of great gains. He writes—

"It is perhaps in accordance with precedent to remark
that, by the judicious expenditure of five-and-twenty
pounds during the ten years we have reviewed, a library
of about two hundred volumes might have been acquired, which would now be cheap at £10,000. But
as the £25, if invested at compound interest at five
per cent., would now have amounted to nearly a million,
it is well for bookmen not to make too much of such
mercenary considerations."

This question of price was formerly a delicate
one. Thus William Beloe was censured by some
collectors for drawing attention to the subject in
his "Anecdotes of Literature"; but that this objection is got over now may be seen from the great
success of such a valuable annual as the "Book-

Prices Current," notwithstanding the complaints of some second-hand booksellers of injury to their business from its revelation of the real value of their books !

Dibdin mentions a book-collector to whom he was pointed out at the Roxburghe sale, who exclaimed, " Hang him ! why did he not publish his book in 1810 ? My books would have brought double the prices." [1]

Dibdin doubtless influenced the market ; and in later times two men have exerted a very special influence in raising the prices of books : these are the late Mr. Henry Stevens and Mr. Bernard Quaritch. The former drew his countrymen's attention to early books printed in and relating to America, and he caused a considerable increase in the price of Americana. But neither of these great book-buyers could have permanently raised the price of books if they had not devoted their attention to books which were well worth these advanced prices. When we deal with books of great beauty and value, and of rare occurrence, which are wanted by several rich book-collectors, it is difficult to say what price is too great for such treasures.

It becomes, therefore, an important matter for the book-collector to consider what are the rules that guide the enhancement of price in books. It is not easy to codify these rules, for varying circumstances alter cases : thus new editions reduce the value of some high-priced books, but have no effect

---

[1] Dibdin's " Reminiscences," vol. i. p. 356 (note).

in the case of others; and time supersedes some
books, while it enhances the value of others.   There
are, however, one or two points which may be mentioned as regulating price, for those persons who
suppose prices to be altogether erratic are certainly
wrong.

What, then, are the chief characteristics of a
book which make it valuable ?   " Uniquity," to
use Horace Walpole's word, is one of these ; but
this is not always sufficient to keep up the price.

Good condition is the grand enhancer of value,
and dirty copies of even scarce works are seldom
worth much.   But nowadays much is done by the
artist to improve these books.   The leaves can be
washed, torn pages can be mended, imperfections
can be filled up by fac-similes, and then the whole
can be handsomely bound in morocco, so that the
owner scarcely knows his book again.   Still, however, one difficulty remains in the artistic make-up
—a short copy cannot be made into a tall one.

It is useless for the artist to spend his labour
upon other than the best books, such as the productions of the early presses, original editions of
masterpieces, and works of permanent value in
their best possible form, with the authors' final
corrections.   The only high-priced books which
can dispense with interesting contents are specimens of fine bindings ; while here again, if the
historical binding covers a really valuable book,
the two elements of value united will cause a
remarkable enhancement of price.

Little need be said as to those books which fetch

high prices for a time, and then when fashion alters sink to a much lower level, as it will usually be found that there was no intrinsic value attached to these books, and therefore they were not such as would be bought by the wise collector at a high price. The fictitious value has usually been attained by a system of limited editions and of judicious advertising. Success in these cases is attained among a class outside the experts in bibliography, and therefore there is no cause for wonder that mistakes are made. Sometimes the depression is caused by the unexpected appearance of several copies of a book, of which one or two copies only were believed to exist.

In considering the probability of high prices being sustained, it must always be borne in mind that the peaceful and prosperous condition of the country is taken for granted. In times of national calamity little money is available for luxuries. Two other important points must be remembered. (1) That it is of no use for a book to be scarce if nobody wants it. The money value of the phenomenally dull book mentioned by Sir Walter Scott is not recorded.

"We have heard of one work of fiction so unutterably stupid that the proprietor, diverted by the rarity of the incident, offered the book, which consisted of two volumes duodecimo, handsomely bound, to any person who would declare upon his honour that he had read the whole from beginning to end. But although this offer was made to the passengers on board an Indiaman during a tedious outward-bound voyage, the " Memoirs of Clegg the Clergyman "

(such was the title of this unhappy composition) completely baffled the most dull and determined student on
board, when the love of glory prevailed with the boatswain,
a man of strong and solid parts, to hazard the attempt, and
he actually conquered and carried off the prize."

(2) That good books are still very cheap, particularly those which it is necessary to possess. So
much is talked about the high prices which books
fetch, that many are led to believe that he must be a
rich man who commences to collect a library ; but
this is not so, for many good books in good condition can be bought for a few shillings ; in fact,
some of the best library books, well bound, do not
range at more than ten shillings per octavo volume,
and this cannot be called a high price. Ordinary
collectors must make up their minds to do without
Mazarin Bibles and first folios of Shakespeare, and
they will find that life can be lived without these
expensive luxuries.

In conclusion, it is necessary to strike a note of
warning respecting the bad paper which is used for
some books, and which render these books quite
worthless in a few years. Old books were made to
last ; the materials used—paper and ink—were of
the very best, but many books of the present day
are made of bad materials, and contain within them
the elements of decay. Lately a German Commission investigated this subject, and for their purpose
took out from the Berlin Library one hundred
volumes. They classified the paper upon which
these books were printed under the four headings

of (1) good ; (2) medium ; (3) bad ; (4) very bad. About five books came under the first two classes, and the remainder were about equally divided between the third and fourth classes. Can we with any confidence claim a better average for English books ? If not, the future of our modern books is a dark one.

CHAPTER II

IT has been frequently remarked that a history of
bookselling would be a valuable addition to our
literature, but such a book would require extensive
research. In place of this a history of some booksellers has been produced ;·but although the volumes
of Mr. Curwen and Mr. Roberts are interesting in
themselves, they do not go far to fill the vacant
space still open for a history of bookselling. Mr.
G. H. Putnam has gathered together much curious
information in his "Authors and their Public in
Ancient Times," and "Books and their Makers
during the Middle Ages," which, notwithstanding
some errors, form certainly a useful contribution
towards this history. The sellers of books have
greatly changed their habits with the altered conditions of their trade. Among the Greeks there were
public shops for the sale of manuscripts, and in them
the learned met together to hear the manuscripts
read. In Rome the general mart for books was to
be found in the district devoted to the bibliopole,
and in his shop advertisements of new works were
stuck up.

At the break up of the Roman Empire the
producers of books were mostly found in the

monasteries, and booksellers were sellers of Pater-
nosters, Aves, &c., as well as of books.

In the thirteenth century the *stationarii* not only
sold books, but accumulated much money by lend-
ing them at high rates. Bookstalls were sometimes
placed in the church porch, and one of the doors of
Rouen Cathedral is still called *le portail des libraires*.

When manuscripts were superseded by printed
books the business of selling books naturally became a more important concern, although the
London company established by printers and publishers was called the Company of Stationers. At first
one man often undertook all the varieties of book
production and bookselling, but gradually the four
broad divisions of printers, publishers, second-hand
booksellers, and auctioneers came into existence.

We know but little of the early publishers, although
much attention is now being paid to the lives and
works of the old book producers, and we may hope
to have in course of time much material for a history of them. The great houses founded in the
eighteenth and at the beginning of the present
century are still with us, and large additions have
been made of late years to the ever-increasing roll.
At all events, there is no sign of a failure of published books; whether they are all worthy to be
published is another matter.

Great changes have been made in the publishing
business, and one of the chief of these is the
frequent sale of remainders of new books. It is
worth a remark in passing that good books which
have been sold off often become scarce and more

valuable than those which have only been sold in the ordinary way. James Lackington was one of the first to make a great business out of the sale of re-mainders ; he was followed by Tegg, and these two men did much to cheapen and popularise literature.

Charles Knight will ever be remembered with honour as the great pioneer in the cheapening of good literature. The excellence of his shilling volumes was a marvel when they were first pub-lished, and even now it would be difficult to find their equal. Knight had a great belief in the adequacy of the penny as a price for a number of a book. He published large quantities of books at a penny a number—as one of the first cheap periodicals—the *Penny Magazine,* and the first of cheap encyclopædias—the *Penny Cyclopædia.* How much good has been done by the large issues of such excellent books as Knight's weekly and monthly volumes, the Libraries of Useful and Entertain-ing Knowledge, Constable's Miscellany, Murray's Family Library, Home and Colonial Library, and Bohn's Libraries !—books all of which are worthy of a place in the library, and not like too many of the cheap books of the present day, books to be read and then thrown aside.

In taking note of some of the old second-hand booksellers, special mention must be made of Joseph Kirton of St. Paul's Churchyard, whose sign was "The King's Arms," because he was Samuel Pepys's bookseller—"my poor Kirton," as the latter calls him when he was ruined by the Fire of London. Pepys tells us that " Kirton was utterly undone by the loss of all his stock, so that from being worth seven or eight thousand pounds, he was made two or three thousand pounds worse than nothing." (See "Diary," October 5, 1666.) The poor bookseller did not live long after his great loss, for he died in October 1667. Pepys records an interesting instance of the rise in price of one of the books burnt in the great fire. On March 20, 1666-67 he writes : "It is strange how Rycaut's 'Discourse of Turky,' which before the fire I was asked but 8s. for, there being all but twenty-two or thereabouts burned, I did now offer 20s., and he demands 50s., and I think I shall give it him, though it be only as a monument of the fire." On April 8, 1667, he gives us some fuller particulars, which are of interest : "So I away to the Temple, to my new bookseller's ; and there I did agree for Rycaut's late 'History of the Turkish Policy,' which costs me 55s. ; whereas it was sold plain before the late fire for 8s., and bound and coloured as this for 20s., for I have bought it finely bound and truly coloured, all the figures, of which there was but six books done so, whereof the King and Duke of York, and Duke of Monmouth and Lord Arlington had four. The fifth was sold, and I have bought the sixth." There is no copy of this edition in the British Museum.

John Dunton, the erratic bookseller and projector of the eighteenth century, has left us in his " Life and Errors" a most curious account of the book- sellers of his time, who are all, oddly enough, either handsome themselves or have beautiful wives.

Nearly all are also eminent Christians ; in fact, we are told that of three hundred booksellers trading in country towns the author knew not of one knave or blockhead amongst them all.

Thomas Osborne, the most celebrated bookseller of his day, is interesting to us as having had the honour of being knocked down by Dr. Samuel Johnson.   Whether or no he deserved such a summary punishment we cannot now tell, but although he appears to have been more of a business man than a literary character, what he did is sufficient to place him in an honourable position in the history of English bibliography.   He bought the finest library of the time, and sold it piecemeal at reasonable prices.   He employed two of the most capable men of his day—Johnson and Oldys— to make a Catalogue, which does credit to all concerned in its production, and he did not make much money by the transaction.   The amount he gave for the Harley library in 1742 (£13,000) was less by £5000 than the binding of a portion of the library had cost, but had he given more he would certainly have been a loser.   Osborne projected a Catalogue, in which it was proposed "that the books shall be distributed into distinct classes, and every class arranged with some regard to the age of the writers ; that every book shall be accurately described ; that the peculiarities of the editions shall be remarked, and observations from the authors of literary history occasionally interspersed, that by this Catalogue posterity may be informed of the excellence and value of this great collection, and thus promote the knowledge of scarce books and elegant editions." Maittaire drew up the scheme of arrangement, and wrote the Latin dedication to Lord Carteret, who was then Secretary of State. Dr. Johnson wrote the "Proposals" for printing the *Bibliotheca Harleiana*, which afterwards were prefixed to the first volume. But in spite of having such eminent helpers, Osborne had to give up his project of an annotated Catalogue, and he informed the public in the preface to the third volume of his failure—

"My original design was, as I have already explained, to publish a methodical and exact Catalogue of this library, upon the plan which has been laid down, as I am informed, by several men of the first rank among the learned. It was intended by those who undertook the work, to make a very exact disposition of all the subjects, and to give an account of the remarkable differences of the editions, and other peculiarities, which make any book eminently valuable; and it was imagined that some improvements might, by pursuing this scheme, be made in Literary History. With this view was the Catalogue begun, when the price [5s. per volume] was fixed upon it in public advertisements; and it cannot be denied that such a Catalogue would have been willingly purchased by those who understood its use. But when a few sheets had been printed, it was discovered that the scheme was impracticable without more hands than could be procured, or more time than the necessity of a speedy sale would allow. The Catalogue was therefore continued without notes, at least in the greatest part; and though it was still performed better than those which are daily offered to the public, fell much below the original intention."

The public were not very grateful for what they did receive, and resented Osborne's charge of five shillings a volume for the Catalogue, which seems reasonable enough now, but was then denounced as "an avaricious innovation." In answer to the clamour the bookseller announced that "those who have paid five shillings shall be allowed at any time within three months after the day of sale either to return them in exchange for books, or to send them back and receive their money." Another complaint was that the books were priced too high. As this was a serious charge, Osborne got Johnson to put his answer into sonorous language, that would at least make the complainers ashamed of themselves : " If, therefore, I have set a high value upon books, if I have vainly imagined literature to be more fashionable than it really is, or idly hoped to revive a taste well-nigh extinguished, I know not why I should be persecuted with clamour and invective, since I shall only suffer by my mistake, and be obliged to keep those books which I was in hopes of selling."

Dibdin proves that this charge of over-pricing is quite unjust. He writes : " Whoever inspects Osborne's Catalogue of 1748 (four years after the Harleian sale) will find in it many of the most valuable of Lord Oxford's books ; and among them a copy of the Aldine Plato of 1513 struck off upon vellum, marked at £21 only—for this identical copy Lord Oxford gave 100 guineas, as Dr. Mead informed Dr. Askew ; from the latter of whose collections it was purchased by Dr. Hunter, and is

now in the Hunter Museum.   There will be found
in Osborne's Catalogues of 1748 and 1753 some of
the scarcest books in English literature marked at
2 or 3 or 4s. for which three times the number of
pounds is now given."[1]   Dibdin has given a useful
analysis of the contents of the Harleian Library in
his *Bibliomania.*   Osborne published a large number
of catalogues full of literary curiosities, and with
interesting notes and prefaces.   In Mr. Thorpe's
Catalogue of 1851 there is a notice of a set of
Osborne's Catalogues from 1729 to 1768, in forty-
three volumes octavo.   This famous bookseller died
on 27th August 1767, and he is said to have left
behind him some forty thousand pounds.

No bookseller has ever been held in higher
esteem than Thomas Payne, who was honourably
known as "honest Tom Payne."   Payne's shop at
the Mews Gate, where the National Gallery now
stands, was for years the great afternoon resort of
the chief book collectors.   Here met such men as
Cracherode, George Steevens, Malone, Lord Spencer,
Grenville, Bishop Dampier, Towneley, and Colonel
Stanley.   Payne lived at the Mews Gate for forty
years, having commenced business as an assistant
to his elder brother, Oliver Payne.   Thomas's first
catalogue, when he set up for himself, is dated
1740.   He removed to Pall Mall, and retired from
business in 1790.   He died in 1799, at the age of
eighty-two.   He was succeeded by his son, who, in
partnership with Henry Foss, carried on a first-rate

---

[1] *Bibliomania,* Part V.

bookselling business in Pall Mall for many years. The catalogue of the Grenville Library was made and published by them.

George Nicol, styled by Beloe in his *Sexagenarian* " a superb bookseller," was a man of great influence in his day. He was largely instrumental in the purchase of much of two magnificent libraries —those of George III. and the Duke of Roxburghe— and he was highly esteemed by both his employers. He always spoke of the King as his beloved master. It was he who induced R. H. Evans, the bookseller, to adopt the business of an auctioneer by offering him the sale of the Roxburghe library.

Another bookseller who occupies a prominent position in the roll of learned and high-principled members of the calling was Thomas Rodd, of Great Newport Street. His catalogues were of great interest, and he numbered among his customers most of the book-collectors of his time. Lord Campbell referred to him in one of his books as " that very learned and worthy bookseller, my friend Thomas Rodd."

A rival of Rodd was Thomas Thorpe, who commenced business in Covent Garden, removed to Piccadilly, and in his later days returned to Covent Garden. Thorpe was a masterful man, who carried everything before him, and published a series of valuable catalogues, from which may be obtained a history of prices for many years. Dibdin, in his " Reminiscences" (1806), says, " I know of no such dogged, indomitable energy and perseverance as that of this renowned bibliopolist " ; and again, in

the preface to his " Library Companion," he writes,
" Mr. Thorpe is indeed a man of might. His
achievements at book-sales are occasionally described in the ensuing pages. It is his catalogues
I am here to treat. They are never-ceasing productions ; thronged with treasures which he has gal-
lantly borne off at the point of his lance, in many
a hard day's fight in the Pall Mall and Waterloo
Place arenas. But these conquests are no sooner
obtained than the public receives an account of
them ; and during the last year only, his catalogues
in three parts, now before me, comprise not fewer
than seventeen thousand nine hundred and fifty-
nine articles. What a scale of buying and selling
does this fact alone evince ! But in this present
year two parts have already appeared, containing
upwards of twelve thousand articles. Nor is this
all. On the 24th day of September, in the year of
our Lord 1823, there appeared the most marvellous
phenomenon ever witnessed in the annals of biblio-
polism. The *Times* newspaper had four of the five
columns of its last page occupied by an advertisement of Mr. Thorpe, containing the third part of his
catalogue for that year. On a moderate computa-
tion this advertisement comprised eleven hundred
and twenty lines." Greater things have been done
since.

The Bohns were mighty booksellers in their time
—John the father, and Henry and James the two
sons ; but Henry Bohn made the greatest name.
His famous Guinea Catalogue (" the guinea pig ")
was long a marvel, at least in respect to thickness,

till Mr. Quaritch decided to far outrival it, and make it appear slim by the side of his huge volumes. Henry Bohn was a remarkable man, and the cultivator of many tastes. In later life he neglected second-hand bookselling for publishing and the selling of remainders. He has already been mentioned as one of the chief of those who have supplied the public with sound cheap literature. Bohn was fond of exhibiting his importance, and when at a book-sale he would, catalogue in hand, inspect the lots far ahead, and occasionally look up and arrest the course of the sale by inquiring of the auctioneer what was the number of the lot then selling.

Mr. Quaritch has outdone all previous booksellers by the grandeur of his catalogues. They have grown in size and importance, until the last General Catalogue, in seven volumes and nine supplements, a large paper copy of which is in the Reading-room of the British Museum, throws all other catalogues into the shade. The volumes containing the various classes into which the catalogue is divided each form a most valuable bibliography and a grand record of the present prices of books.

This is not a history of booksellers, and therefore more need not be said of them here than that a body of men to whom book collectors are greatly indebted may well be proud of numbering in their ranks those already named, as well as the Pickerings, the Lillys, the Boones, the Ellises, and the Bains, upon whose exploits we have not space to enlarge.

AUCTIONEERS

William Cooper, a bookseller in a good way of business at the sign of the Pelican in Little Britain, was the first to introduce into England the practice of selling books by auction, when in 1676 he sold Dr. Seaman's library, and for some years he was the chief auctioneer in London. His first catalogue —the first sale catalogue in England—is exhibited in the Kings' Library at the British Museum.

In 1680 Edward Millington, a better known man and a bookseller of standing, took to auctioneering, and he and Cooper together divided the chief business in this department. Other booksellers, such as Moses Pitt, Zachary Bourne, Nathaniel Ranew, Richard Chiswell, and John Dunsmore, Robert Scott, &c., sold books by auction, and Oldys styles Marmaduke Foster, who made the catalogue of Thomason's Civil War Tracts in twelve folio manuscript volumes, an auctioneer. It is, however, of the two foremost men, Cooper and Millington, that we want to know more, and fortunately a wit of Christ Church, Oxford, George Smalridge, afterwards Dean of Christ Church and Bishop of Bristol, was struck by the humours connected with the sale in 1686 of the stock of a bankrupt Oxford bookseller—Richard Davis, the publisher of several of the Hon. Robert Boyle's works. Smalridge wrote a skit on the proceedings, under the title of "Auctio Davisiana Oxonii habita per Gulielmum Cooper, Edoar. Millingtonum, Bibliop. Lond. . . . Londini:

Prostant venales apud Jacobum Tonson, 1689."
This was reprinted in *Musarum Anglicanarum
Analecta*, vol. i. 1691.[1]

The sale, according to Anthony à Wood, took
place "in a large stone fabric opposite St. Michael's
Church, in Oxon., near the north gate of the city,
called Bocardo" (a prison in the Middle Ages),
and apparently it attracted a great deal of attention on account of the novelty of the mode of
sale. Smalridge fastened on the salient points,
and he has thus given us information respecting the conduct of a sale in the seventeenth
century which we should not otherwise have possessed. The persons of the little drama are six
Christ Church men—Arthur Kaye, Walter Bacon,
Ed. Stradling, George Dixon, Christopher Codrington, and William Woodward—and in the pride of
their learning they make sad fun of the pomposity
and ignorance of the poor auctioneers. We must,
however, remember that this is a satire and a carica-
ture. Cooper is described as "a man of wonderful
and notable gravity," with a monstrous paunch ;
and Millington as having a Stentor's lungs and con-
summate impudence, a very windbag, whose hollow
bellows blow lies.

Woodward took the part of Cooper, and Codrington that of Millington, but when these characters
were first pressed upon them, the latter urged that

---

[1] An annotated translation of *Auctio Davisiana* was published in
"Book-Lore," vol. iii. p. 166 ; vol. iv. p. 1. The translator possesses a
copy formerly belonging to Bishop Wordsworth of Lincoln, in which is
written, in a contemporary hand, *ex dono Bibliopolæ Ric Davis*.

"if a book is bad, I cannot pile encomiums on it, and prefer Wither to Virgil, or Merlin to the Sibyls." We are told that bids of one penny were taken, and that when the third blow of the hammer has been struck the sale was irrevocable. The auctioneers seem to have offended the ears of the Oxonians by saying "Nepŏtis" and "Stephāni." At the end of the day Woodward is made to say, " I have spoken, I the great Cooper, whose house is in Little Britain." Codrington recites a long rhodomontade ending thus : " I check myself and put a curb on the runaway muses. But this mallet, the badge of my profession, I affix as a dedicatory offering to this post — To Oxford and the Arts Millington con- secrates these arms." Dunton draws a favourable portrait of Millington in his " Life and Errors." He says he "commenced and continued auctions upon the authority of Herodotus, who commends that way of sale for the disposal of the most ex- quisite and finest beauties to their *amorosos ;* and further informs the world that the sum so raised was laid out for the portions of those to whom nature had been less kind : so that he'll never be forgotten while his name is Ned, or he, a man of remarkable elocution, wit, sense, and modesty— characters so eminently his, that he would be known by them among a thousand. Millington (from the time he sold Dr. Annesly's library) ex- pressed a particular friendship to me. He was originally a bookseller, which he left off, being better cut out for an auctioneer. He had a quick wit, and a wonderful fluency of speech. There was

usually as much comedy in his 'once, twice, thrice,'
as can be met with in a modern play. 'Where,'
said Millington, 'is your generous flame for learning ? Who but a sot or a blockhead would have
money in his pocket and starve his brains ?'
Though I suppose he had but a round of jests, Dr.
Cave once bidding too leisurely for a book, says
Millington, 'Is this your "Primitive Christianity ?"'
alluding to a book the honest doctor had published under that title. He died in Cambridge, and
I hear they bestowed an elegy on his memory, and
design to raise a monument to his ashes." Thomas
Hearne does not give him so good a character. He
writes under date 13th September 1723 : "Though
the late Mr. Millington of London, bookseller, was
certainly the best auctioneer in the world, being
a man of great wit and fluency of speech, and a
thorough master of his trade ; though, at the same
time, very impudent and saucy, yet he could not
at the end of the auction, be brought to give an
account to the persons who employed him, so that
by that means, he allowed what he pleased and no
more, and kept a great number of books that were
not sold to himself. Whence arose that vast stock
of books, though most of them but ordinary, that
he had when he dyed, and which, after his death,
were sold by auction." [1]

"An Elegy upon the Lamented Death of Mr. Edward Millington, the famous Auctioneer," alluded to
by Dunton, is printed in the "Works of Mr. Thomas
Brown," ed. 1744, iv. p. 320, but the Rev. C. H.

---

[1] *Reliquiæ Hearnianæ*, 1869, vol. ii. p. 172.

Hartshorne quotes it in his " Book Rarities of Cambridge," 1829, p. 450, from Bagford's Collection, British Museum, Harleian MSS., No. 5947.   It reads as follows :—

> " Mourn ! mourn ! you booksellers, for cruel death
> Has robb'd the famous auctioneer of breath :
> He's gone,—he's gone,—all the great loss deplore ;
> Great Millington—alas ! he is no more :
> No more will he now at your service stand
> Behind the desk, with mallet in his hand :
> No more the value of your books set forth,
> And sell 'em by his art for twice the worth.
> Methinks I see him still, with smiling look,
> Amidst the crowd, and in his hand a book :
> Then in a fine, facetious, pleasing way
> The author's genius and his wit display.
>
> O all you scribbling tribe, come, mourn his death,
> Whose wit hath given your dying fame new birth.
> When your neglected works did mouldering lie
> Upon the shelves, and none your books would buy,
> How oft has he, with strainèd eloquence,
> Affirm'd the leaves contained a world of sense,
> When all's insipid, dull impertinence ?
> ' Come, gentlemen,—come bid me what you please ;
> Upon my word it is a curious piece,
> Done by a learned hand—and neatly bound :
> One pound—once, twice, fifteen : who bids ?—a
>   crown !'
> Then shakes his head, with an affected frown,
> And says ' For shame ! consider, gentlemen,
> The book is sold in shops for more than ten.
> Good lack a day !—'tis strange!' then strikes the blow,
> And in a feignèd passion bids it go.

Then in his hand another piece he takes,
And in its praise a long harangue he makes;
And tells them that 'tis writ in lofty verse,
One that is out of print and very scarce:
Then with high language, and a stately look,
He sets a lofty price upon the book;
'Five pound, four pound, three pound,' he cries
        aloud,
And holds it up to expose it to the crowd,
With arm erect,—the bidders to provoke
To raise the price before the impending stroke;
This in the throng does emulation breed,
And makes 'em strive each other to outbid;
While he descants upon their learned heats,
And his facetious dialect repeats:
For none like him, for certain, knew so well
(By way of auction) any goods to sell.
'Tis endless to express the wayes he had
To sell their good, and to put off their bad.
But ah! in vain I strive his fame to spread;
The great, the wise, the knowing man is dead.

And you in painting skill'd, his loss bewail;
He's dead!—that did expose your works to sale.
Can you forget how he for you did bawl,
'Come, put it in?—a fine original,
Done by a curious hand:—What strokes are here,
Drawn to the life? How fine it does appear!
O lovely piece!—Ten pound,—five pound;—for
        shame,
You do not bid the value of the frame.'
How many pretty stories would he tell
To enhance the price, and make the picture sell!
But now he's gone!—ah! the sad loss deplore;
Great Millington!—alas! he is no more.

And you, the Muses' darlings, too, rehearse
Your sorrows for the loss of him in verse :
Mourn ! mourn ! together, for that tyrant death
Has robb'd the famous auctioneer of breath."

THE EPITAPH.

Underneath this marble stone
Lies the famous Millington ;
A man who through the world did steer
I' th' station of an auctioneer ;
A man with wondrous sense and wisdom blest,
Whose qualities are not to be exprest.

We have given so much space to Millington,
because it is interesting to see how similar were
the practices of auctioneers at the first institution
of the business to what they are at the present time,
and also because Millington seems to have been
considered the most famous of auctioneers, until
James Christie arose to take his place as chief representative of the profession. It may be added
to his honour that he was a friend of Milton, who
lodged in his house.

Richard Chiswell (1639–1711) was more of a
bookseller than an auctioneer, but his name must
be mentioned here. He was one of the four who
issued the fourth folio edition of Shakespeare's
Plays, and he was the official publisher of the
Votes of the House. Dunton describes him as
"the metropolitan bookseller of England, if not of
all the world," and says that he never printed a bad
book, or one on bad paper.

Jonathan Greenwood, bookseller and auctioneer,

is described by Dunton as a worthy but unfortunate man, " so that the chief thing he has left to boast of is a virtuous wife and several small children." He adds, " But he still deserves the love and esteem of all good men, for the worst that can be said of him is, ' There goes a poor honest man,' which is much better than ' There goes a rich knave.' "

How little is known of some of these early auctioneers may be seen from the fact that John Bullord, who sold books at the end of the seventeenth century, is said by the careful John Nichols to be a member of the well-known bookselling family of Ballard. I cannot find any information respecting Bullord, but it is very improbable that this name was merely a misspelling of Ballard.

The name of Samuel Paterson (1728–1802) will always be held in honour among English bibliographers, for he was one of the first to improve the art of cataloguing, and he gained great fame from his labours in this department. He had one great fault, however, for he was so insatiable a reader, that when in cataloguing he came upon a book he had not seen before, he must needs read the book then, and thus his work was much delayed, and often his catalogues could not be obtained until a few hours before the sale. He was the son of a woollen draper in St. Paul's, Covent Garden, but lost his father when he was only twelve years old; his guardian neglected him, and having involved his property in his own bankruptcy, sent him to France. Here he acquired a considerable knowledge of French literature, which served him in

good stead through life. When little more than
twenty years of age he opened a shop in the Strand,
opposite Durham Yard. This bookselling business
was unsuccessful, and he then commenced as a
general auctioneer at Essex House. It was during
this period of his life that he saved the collection
of valuable manuscripts formerly belonging to Sir
Julius Cæsar from being sold as waste-paper to a
cheesemonger. He classified the MSS., and made
an excellent catalogue of them, and when they
came to be sold by auction they realised £356.
Although Paterson made an excellent auctioneer,
he was no more successful financially than in his
other ventures. He therefore accepted the post of
librarian to the Earl of Shelburne (afterwards first
Marquis of Lansdowne); but after a few years there
was a quarrel, and he was obliged to return to the
business of cataloguing and selling of libraries.

The Rev. C. H. Hartshorne, in his "Book
Rarities," mentions a print by Nicholls in the
British Museum, called "The Complete Auctioneer," representing a man with spectacles on,
standing at a table covered with books, which are
lettered at the tops. Underneath are these lines—

"Come, sirs, and view this famous Library;
'Tis pity learning should discouraged be :
Here's bookes (that is, if they were but well sold)
I will maintain 't, are worth their weight in gold.
Then bid apace, and break me out of hand :
Ne'er cry you don't the subject understand.
For this I'll say—howe'er the case may hit,—
Whoever buys of me—I'll teach 'em wit."

Although the London booksellers went into the country to sell books, there were some local auctioneers, as, for instance, Michael Johnson (the father of Dr. Samuel Johnson), who kept a bookstall in Lichfield, and attended the neighbouring towns on market days. Johnson's address to his customers is taken from "A Catalogue of Choice Books, . . . to be sold by auction, or he who bids most, at the Talbot, in Sidbury, Worcester," and is quoted from Clarke's *Repertorium Bibliographicum* (1819)—

"To all Gentlemen, Ladies, and Others in or near Worcester,—I have had several auctions in your neighbourhood, as Gloucester, Tewkesbury, Evesham, &c., with success, and am now to address myself and try my fortune with you.—You must not wonder that I begin every Day's Sale with small and common books; the reason is a room is some time a filling, and persons of address and business, seldom coming first, they are entertainment till we are full; they are never the last books of the best kind of that sort for ordinary families and young persons, &c. But in the body of the Catalogue you will find Law, Mathematicks, History: and for the learned in Divinity there are Drs. Souter, Taylor, Tillotson, Beveridge, and Flavel, &c., the best of that kind : and to please the Ladies I have added store of fine pictures and paper hangings, and, by the way, I would desire them to take notice that the pictures shall always be put up by the noon of that day they are to be sold, that they may be view'd by day light. I have no more but to wish you pleas'd and myself a good sale, who am

Your Humble Servant,
M. Johnson."

The sale took place in the evening, commencing at six o'clock and continuing till all the lots were sold. The existing firms of literary auctioneers, Sotheby, Wilkinson & Hodge ; Puttick & Simpson ; Christie, Manson & Woods ; and Hodgsons, are all of considerable standing, but Sotheby's is of the greatest antiquity. Samuel Baker, the founder of the house, commenced business in 1744 with sale of Dr. Thomas Pellet's library (£859) in York Street, Covent Garden. He continued sole member of the firm till 1774, when he entered into partnership with George Leigh (who is styled by Beloe "the finical bookseller"). Baker died in 1778, in his sixty-sixth year, when he left his property to his nephew, John Sotheby, who in 1780 was in partnership with Leigh. In 1800 the style was Leigh, Sotheby & Son, John Sotheby's son Samuel being taken into partnership. In 1803 the business was removed from York Street to 145 Strand, opposite Catharine Street, and in 1818 to the present house in Wellington Street. The third and last Sotheby, Mr. Samuel Leigh Sotheby, became a partner in 1837, and in 1843 Mr. John Wilkinson entered the firm as a partner. The style was Sotheby and Wilkinson till 1864, when Mr. Edward Grose Hodge became a partner, and from that date the name of the firm has been Sotheby, Wilkinson, and Hodge.

The firm of Puttick & Simpson dates back to the establishment of the business by Mr. Stewart in 1794 at 191 Piccadilly. The business was bought by Wheatley & Adlard on the retirement of Mr. Stewart. For a short time it was carried on by Mr. Fletcher, who was succeeded in 1846 by Messrs. Puttick & Simpson. In 1858 the business was removed from Piccadilly to 47 Leicester Square. Mr. Puttick died in 1873.

The firm of Christie's was established soon after that of Sotheby's, and James Christie the elder's (1730–1803) first sale was on the 5th December 1766, at rooms in Pall Mall, formerly occupied by the print warehouse of Richard Dalton. Christie afterwards removed next door to Gainsborough, at Schomberg House, and died there, 8th November 1803. His son, James Christie the younger (1773–1831), was born in Pall Mall, and was educated at Eton. In 1824 he removed to the present premises in King Street, formerly Wilson's European Emporium. Mr. Christie died in King Street, 2nd February 1831, aged fifty-eight. Mr. George Christie succeeded his father. Mr. William Manson died in 1852, and was succeeded by his brother, Mr. Edward Manson. In 1859 Mr. James Christie, the great-grandson of the founder, and Mr. Thomas Woods, joined the firm.

CHAPTER III

IN a treatise devoted to an inquiry concerning the varying prices of books, it is necessary that at least one chapter should be devoted to manuscripts. There is no field of investigation which offers a more interesting subject for study, and few that are more difficult to master. Manuscripts are really more attractive than printed books, because they are so various, and have been produced over a much longer period of the world's history. It is therefore strange that so few authors care to trouble themselves about them ; that this is so may be seen from the large number of readers at the British Museum who are contented to quote over and over again from the much-used printed books, and the comparatively few who cultivate the virgin soil of the Manuscript Department, where there are endless stores of unused materials.

Manuscripts are usually somewhat miscellaneous in character, for they consist (1) of some of the finest examples of the pictorial art of many ages ; (2) of the originals of the great works of antiquity ; (3) of a large number of valuable works that have never been printed ; (4) of charters, documents, letters, memoranda, &c., which are of great value, but which are not books, and therefore do not come within the scope of our present inquiry. In respect to the prices of the manuscripts, it is very difficult to say anything of much value, because (1) many of the most important manuscripts have been transferred from library to library in bulk, and it is comparatively seldom that they come up for public sale ; (2) the buyers of manuscripts are fewer than those of printed books, and therefore it is more difficult to arrive at a real standard price for books which are practically unique, as there is no wide public opinion upon the subject. But for the present purpose, a still more important reason why this vast subject cannot be dealt with in a succinct manner is, that the materials for its history have not yet been thoroughly investigated by experts. The relative prices at different periods are hard to understand, even in England, where money has been better regulated than in most countries ; but when we have to deal with foreign countries and foreign coins, we are necessarily at a loss how to convert into their present value coins which may have been depreciated at the time we are dealing with, and have certainly been still more depreciated since : for instance, what idea is communicated to the mind of the modern reader when he is told that " Borso d'Este paid forty ducats for a *Josephus* and a *Quintus Curtius*, while his large two-volume Bible cost him 1375 sequins " ? [1]

In dealing with manuscripts, it is most important to distinguish between plain and illuminated

[1] Leader Scott's " Renaissance of Art in Italy," 1883, p. 193.

manuscripts. The neglect of this caution has led to an exaggerated idea of the cost of books before the invention of printing. Instances have been given of purchases at sums equal to a king's ransom. Hence it is supposed that books were so dear that they were quite out of the reach of any but the richest personages. But this view is erroneous, for we know that by means of the slave labour at Rome and the organised work in the monasteries, plainly written manuscripts could be obtained at a reasonable price. We know now that transcripts of MSS. can be had at a price which, if dear when compared with the price of a newly-published printed book, is by no means extravagant. What could be done at a centre of civilisation like Rome, where books were produced in large numbers and at low prices on account of the organisation of literary production, could be done at other places. There is evidence that at London, and at those seats of learning, Oxford and Cambridge, where caligraphy was a profession, books were not difficult to obtain. Every church and chapel must have had service-books. Probably during the Middle Ages, when travelling was arduous and expensive, persons living in out-of-the-way places had to pay special prices for their literary treasures.

The late Professor J. Henry Middleton referred to this matter of cost in his valuable work on " Illuminated Manuscripts " (1892). After quoting from Aulus Gellius, he wrote—

"But ordinary copies of newly-published works, even by popular authors, appear to have been but little more

expensive than books of this class are at the present day.
The publisher and bookseller Tryphon could sell Martial's
first book of *Epigrams* at a profit for two denarii—barely
two shillings in modern value (see Mart. xiii. 3). It may
seem strange that written manuscripts should not have been
much more costly than printed books, but when one con-
siders how they were produced, the reason is evident. Atticus,
the Sosii, and other chief publishers of Rome, owned a large
number of slaves, who were trained to be neat and rapid
scribes.   Fifty or a hundred of these slaves could write from
the dictation of one reader, and thus a small edition of a
new volume of Horace's *Odes* or Martial's *Epigrams* could
be produced with great rapidity, and at very small cost"
(p. 19).

In the fifteenth century, even, illustrated Books
of Hours were produced in France, Flanders, and
Holland at a cheap rate.   Mr. Middleton wrote—

" Education had gradually been extended among various
classes of laymen, and by the middle of the fifteenth century
it appears to have been usual not only for all men above the
rank of artizans to be able to read, but even women of the
wealthy bourgeois class could make use of prayer-books.
Hence arose a great demand for pictured *Books of Hours*,
which appear to have been produced in enormous quantities
by the trade scribes of towns, such as Bruges, Paris, and
many others.   These common manuscript Hours are mono-
tonous in form and detail ; they nearly always have the same
set of miniatures, which are coarse in detail and harsh in
colour" (p. 141).

Mr. Middleton gives some further information respecting the cost of production of certain service-
books taken from some church records in the
fourteenth and fifteenth centuries—

"From these accounts (1379–1385) we learn that six manuscripts were written, illuminated, and bound, one of them with gold or silver clasps or bosses, at a total cost of £14, 9s. 3d., more than £150 in modern value" (p. 222). "Three Processionals only cost £1, 17s. 4d., being on forty-six quaternions of cheap parchment made of sheepskin, which cost only 2½d. the quaternion " (p. 223).

There was thus great variety of cost in the production of the various kinds of books, but when we consider the matter, we shall find it impossible to do other than believe that a demand for service-books, the price of which was not prohibitive, must have existed.

The Rev. T. Hartwell Horne gave in his "Introduction to Bibliography" some instances of the prices of manuscripts in the Middle Ages, but as some of these were evidently exceptional cases, although they have been used by historians to draw conclusions which we must consider as erroneous, they need not be repeated here.

Dr. S. R. Maitland in his admirable work on the "Dark Ages" comments with much acuteness on some of these cases as quoted by Dr. Robertson, and shows that the historian has drawn a general conclusion from special instances, which in certain cases have not been correctly reported. Maitland adds that some writer a few centuries hence might—

"Tell his gaping readers . . . that in the year 1812 one of our nobility gave £2260 and another £1060 for a single volume, and that the next year a Johnson's Dictionary was sold by public auction to a plebeian purchaser for £200. A few such facts would quite set up some

future Robertson, whose readers would never dream that
we could get better reading, and plenty of it, much cheaper
at that very time.   The simple fact is, that there has always
been such a thing as bibliomania since there have been
books in the world, and no member of the Roxburghe Club
has yet equalled the Elector of Bavaria, who gave a town
for a single manuscript " (pp. 66-7).

Interesting particulars respecting the composition,
binding, and expenses of Petrarch's library will be
found in M. de Nolhac's monograph on the subject.
Petrarch kept copyists in his house, whose short-
comings occasioned him much vexation.   He bequeathed his library to Venice, and the Venetians
are accused of having suffered it to be dispersed,
but it would seem that it never reached them.

We may judge from the immense number of
manuscripts still existing, in spite of the wholesale
destruction that occurred at various times, how
large was the output in the Middle Ages.   It is
therefore preposterous to suppose that when books
were being produced in large numbers in hundreds
of monasteries in Europe they were only bought
by kings or great nobles.

During the troubled times of the Barons' Wars
there must have been great destruction of literary
treasures, and at the Reformation, when whole
libraries were destroyed and made waste-paper of,
the ignorant waste was appalling.   "The splendid and
magnificent abbey of Malmesbury, which possessed
some of the finest manuscripts in the kingdom, was
ransacked, and its treasures either sold, or burnt to
serve the commonest purposes of life.   An antiquary

who travelled through that town many years after
the dissolution, relates that he saw broken windows
patched up with remnants of the most valuable MSS.
on vellum, and that the bakers hadn't even then
consumed the stores they had accumulated in heat-
ing their ovens."[1] That so much is left after the
wholesale raid on the monasteries is largely due
to the sound antiquarian taste of John Leland, to
whom we of later ages are supremely indebted.

In all times of political convulsions the learning
of the world stands a bad chance of escaping great
loss, and we are told that twenty-five thousand
manuscripts were burnt during the horrors of the
French Revolution.

Carelessness and the contempt felt for old books
are still the great destructive forces in the East,
and the Hon. Robert Curzon, who travelled in
search of manuscripts, gives in his "Visits to the
Monasteries in the Levant" (1849) a lively account
of the irreparable losses that are constantly occur-
ring. (See also Archdeacon Tattam's and M. Pacho's
narratives of their negotiations with the monks of
the Nitrian Desert for Syrian MSS., and the subsequent experiences of Tischendorf and Mrs. Lewis.)
One of the most recent literary events is the re-
covery of a number of Jewish manuscripts from a
Genizah or storehouse of old papers and parch-
ments at Cairo, where they were preserved indeed,
but entirely neglected.

The late Mr. Thorold Rogers paid considerable
attention to the prices of books, and recorded many

[1] "Letters from the Bodleian," vol. i. p. 279 (note).

valuable facts respecting them in his important work, "History of Agriculture and Prices in England." After commenting on some prices in the thirteenth and fourteenth centuries, he adds, "such prices indicate that written literature was not wholly inaccessible to the general public" (vol. i. p. 646).

The particulars of the cost of church books give perhaps the best idea of prices, because these were needed by a large number of the population. Some of them were of small price, while others of a more elaborate character were of great price. In the year 1278 the bailiff of Farley spent six shillings and eightpence for books for the church, and in 1300 the monks of Ely paid six shillings for a *Decretal*, and two shillings for *Speculum Gregorianum*. In 1329 the precentor received six shillings and sevenpence, with an instruction to go to Balsham to purchase books.[1] In 1344 a Bible cost three pounds, and in 1357 a book was bought for Farley church for four shillings.

Mr. Blades printed in his Life of Caxton an inventory of the library of Jean, Duc de Berri, at the château of Mohun sur Yevre, 1416. At the death of the duke the library contained one hundred and sixty-two volumes, valued at 14,909 livres.

In 1443 twenty-seven volumes were purchased by the authorities of King's Hall, Cambridge, from the executors of John Paston (who had been their steward), at a cost of £8, 17s. 4d. In 1447 the same college bought a Psalter for three shillings and eightpence, and a Donatus for one shilling.

---

[1] Putnam's "Books and their Makers," 1897, vol. i. p. 159.

In 1449 twenty new Processionals cost All Souls College one hundred and thirteen shillings and fourpence, and in 1453 a book of Wycliffe's was bought for seven shillings and sixpence, and one written against him for three shillings and sixpence.[1] A manuscript of 157 leaves, containing some of the works of St. Gregory, was bought in 1455 for £3, 6s. 8d.

In 1459 Fastolfe's books were highly priced ; thus a fair Mass book was fixed at ten pounds, and a Holy Legend at the same sum, while two new great Antiphons were together £13, 6s. 8d.

One of St. Augustine's Epistles, containing 179 leaves, sold sometime after 1468 for £1, 13s. 4d., and about the same time one of St. Bernard's Treatises, written on 211 leaves, was bought by Richard Hopton from the executors of a former possessor for twenty shillings.

Perhaps a rather more accurate idea of the cost of manuscript books can be obtained from a consideration of the cost of materials and the pay of the scribes, and, fortunately, particulars have come down to us which allow of a comparison of the various expenses.

A pocket lectionary was made in 1265 for the use of Eleanor de Montfort, Countess of Leicester, and sister of Henry III. Twenty dozen of fine vellum were purchased for the work at the price of ten shillings, and the writing, which was executed at Oxford, cost fourteen shillings.

Richard du Marche, an illuminator, was paid

---

[1] Rogers's " Agriculture and Prices," vol. iv. pp. 509-604.

forty shillings for illuminating a Psalter and a pair of tablets for Queen Eleanor, consort of Edward I.

In the same accounts of this queen an entry is made of £6, 13s. 4d. to Adam the royal goldsmith for work done upon certain books.[1]

Professor Middleton printed in his "Illuminated Manuscripts" (pp. 220–23) extracts from the Manuscript Records of the Collegiate Church of St. George at Windsor, from which it appears that John Prust (Canon of Windsor from 1379 to 1385) was paid £14, 9s. 3d. for six manuscripts written, illuminated, and bound, one of them with gold or silver clasps or bosses. The six books were an *Evangeliarium*, a *Martyrologium*, an *Antiphonale*, and three *Processionals*. The items of each are as follows :—

Evangeliarium.

	£	s.	d.
19 quaternions (quires) of vellum at 8d. each	0	12	8
Black ink	0	1	2
Bottle to hold the ink	0	0	10
Vermilion	0	0	9
The scribe's "commons" (food) for eighteen weeks	0	15	0
Payment to the scribe	0	13	4
Corrections and adding coloured initials .	0	3	0
Illumination	0	3	4
Binding	0	3	4
Goldsmith's work (on the binding) . .	1	0	0
	£3	13	5

Two journeys to London and some smaller items made a total of £3, 15s. 8d.

---

[1] "Manners and Household Expenses" (Roxburghe Club).

Martyrologium.

	£	s.	d.
7 quaternions of vellum at 8d. . . .	0	4	8
Payment to the scribe	0	15	0
Illumination	0	5	10
Binding	0	2	2
Coloured initials	0	0	8
	£1	8	4

Antiphonale.

	£	s.	d.
34 quaternions of larger and more expensive sheets of vellum at 15d. . . .	2	2	6
Payments to the scribe	3	3	0
Adding to the musical notation . . .	1	0	6
Coloured initials	0	1	0
Illumination	0	15	11
Binding	0	5	0
	£7	7	11

(Twelve quires of vellum which were in stock were also used for this *Antiphonale*.)

The three *Processionals* only cost £1, 17s. 4d., being written on forty-six quaternions of cheap parchment made of sheepskin, which cost only 2½d. the quaternion.

Mr. Falconer Madan tells us that "in 1453 John Reynbold agreed at Oxford to write out the last three books of Duns Scotus's *Commentary on the Sentences of Peter Lombard*, in quarto, for 2s. 2d. each book," and that "a transcript in folio by this Reynbold of part of Duns Scotus on the *Sentences* is in both Merton and Balliol College Libraries at Oxford, one dated 1451."[1]

[1] "Books in Manuscript," 1893, p. 43.

Sir John Fenn quotes in illustration of one of
the *Paston Letters* the account of Thomas, a limner
or illuminator of manuscripts residing at Bury St.
Edmunds, against Sir John Howard of Stoke by
Neyland in Suffolk (afterwards Duke of Norfolk),
dated July 1467.

For viij hole vynets [miniatures], prise the vynett, xijd	viijs		
Item, for xxj demi vynets, prise the demi vynett, iiijd	vijs		
Item, for Psalmes lettres xvᶜ and di', the prise of C. iiijd		vs	ijd
Item, for p'ms letters lxiijᵉ, prise of a C. jd.		vs	iiijd
Item, for wrytynge of a quare and demi, prise the quayr, xxd		ijs	vjd
Item, for wrytenge of a calendar			xijd
Item, for iij quayres of velym, prise the quayr, xxd.		vs	
Item, for notynge of v quayres and ij leves, prise of the quayr, viijd		iijs	vijd
Item, for capital drawynge iijᶜ and di', the prise			iijd
Item, for floryshynge of capytallis, vᶜ.			vd
Item, for byndynge of the boke		xijs	
		cs	ijd [1]

This list of charges is of great interest and of
much value in illustrating the cost of illumination
in the fifteenth century. The price of the binding
seems to be very considerable as compared with
the work of the illuminator, unless it included the

[1] *Paston Letters*, ed. Gairdner, 1874, vol. ii. p. 336.

cost of gold or other expensive decoration. Mr. Middleton gives also particulars of the cost of writing, illuminating, and binding a manuscript *Lectionary*, 1469–71, the total expense of which was £3, 4s. 1d. These are taken from the Parish Accounts of the Church of St. Ewen, in Bristol—

1468–69.

Item, for j dossen and v quayers of vellom
    to perform the legend [*i.e.* to write the
    lectionary on] . . . . . xs vjd
Item, for wrytyng of the same . . . xxvs
Item, for ix skynnys and j quayer of velom
    to the same legend . . . . vs vjd
Item, for wrytyng of the forseyd legend . iiijs ijd

1470–71.

Item, for a red Skynne to kever the legent . vd
Also for the binding and correcting of the
    seid Boke . . . . . . vs
Also for the lumining of the seid legent . xiijs vjd[1]

Among the *Paston Letters* is a letter from William Ebesham to his "moost worshupfull maister, Sir John Paston," 1469(?), asking for payment for his labours in writing, the charge for which was a penny per leaf for verse, and twopence a leaf for prose. Appended to this letter is the following interesting account :—

---

[1] "Transactions of the Bristol and Gloucester Archæological Society," vol. xv., 1891, pp. 257 and 260, *quoted* "Illuminated Manuscripts," p. 223.

Folowyng apperith, parcelly, dyvers and soondry maner
of writynge, which I, William Ebesham, have wreetyn for
my gode and woorshupfull maistir, Sir John Paston, and
what money I have resceyvid and what is unpaide.

First, I did write to his maistership a little
  booke of Pheesyk, for which I had
  paide by Sir Thomas Leevys in Westminster   .   .   .   .   .   .   xxd
Item, I had for the wrytyng of half the Prevy
  seale of Pampyng   .   .   .   .   viijd
Item, for the wrytynge of the seid hole prevy
  seale of Sir Thomas   .   .   .   . ijs
Item, I wrote viij of the Witnessis in parche-
  ment, but aftir xiiijd a peece, for which
  I was paide of Sir Thomas .   .   . xs
Item, while my seide maister over the see in
  Midsomertime.   Calle sett me a warke
  to wryte two tymes the prevy seale in
  papir, and then after cleerely in parche-
  ment .   .   .   . iiijs   viijd
And also wrote the same tyme oon mo of
  the largest witnessis, and other dyvers
  and necessary wrytyngs, for which he
  promisid me xs, whereof I had of Calle
  but iiijs viijd. car. vs iiij   .   .   . vs   iiijd
I resceyvid of Sir Thomas at Westminster
  penultimo die Oct. anno viiij   .   . iijs   iiijd
Item, I did write to quairs of papir of witnessis, every quair conteyning xiiij leves
  after ijd a leff   .   .   .   .   . iiijs   viijd
Item, as to the Grete Booke—First, for
  wrytyng of the Coronacion, and other
  tretys of Knyghthode, in that quaire
  which conteyneth a xiij levis and more
  ijd a lef   .   .   .   .   .   . ijs   ijd

Item, for the tretys of Werre in iiij books,.
which conteyneth lx levis aftir ijd a
leaff . . . . xs
Item, for *Othea* pistill, which conteyneth
xliij leves . . . . . . vijs iid
Item, for the Chalengs and the acts of
Armes which is xxviij^{ti} less . . iiijs viijd
Item, for *De Regimine Principum*, which
conteyneth xlv^{ti} leves, aftir a peny a
leef, which is right wele worth . . iijs ixd
Item, for Rubrissheyng of all the booke . iijs iiijd[1]

The "Grete Booke," described above, is now
among the Lansdowne Manuscripts (No. 285) in
the British Museum, and is fully described in the
Catalogue of that Collection, 1812 (Part II., pp.
99–102).

In quoting the foregoing particulars of the early
sale of MSS. and of the cost of production, no
attempt has been made to calculate the present
value of the amounts set down, because the data
for such a calculation are not available. It will,
however, be well if the reader remembers that the
various amounts mentioned must have been equal
at the very least to ten times these sums in the
present day. Professor Middleton multiplies by
ten, but when we find an expert scribe charging
one penny and twopence for one leaf, and the
"commons" of another is set down at tenpence
per week, we may safely reckon the multiplier at
considerably more than ten in the fourteenth and
fifteenth centuries.

[1] *Paston Letters*, ed, Gairdner, 1874, vol. ii. pp. 334–35.

The scribes and illuminators already mentioned
were the individual workers, who were employed
by corporations and men of wealth to produce
books for their libraries ; but the wholesale producers of books, who employed armies of scribes,
must not be overlooked in this place. ˙Vespasiano
di Bisticci of Florence (*b.* 1421) was the chief of
these booksellers, and he assisted to form the three
most famous libraries in Italy—the Laurentian in
Florence, that of the Vatican, and the library of
Federigo, Duke of Urbino, which was afterwards
bought by Pope Alexander VII. and incorporated
into the Vatican Library. Vespasiano was an author
as well as a bookseller, and has recorded some of his
doings in his *Vite degli Uomini Illustri.* He gives a
detailed list of the works he obtained for the Duke
of Urbino, which comprised all the known classics,
the Fathers, books on astrology, science, medicine,
art, music, and all the Italian authors and poets.
Vespasiano claimed that in this magnificent library,
which cost 30,000 ducats, every author was found
complete, and not a page of his writings was missing. Every book was written on vellum, and there
was not a single one of which he was ashamed.
Vespasiano was ever ready to form a library, as the
following anecdote will prove.

Niccolo Niccoli having spent a long life and all
his patrimony in collecting, left his books to Cosimo
to found a public library. Cosimo built the fine
pillared hall in the Convent of San Marco, and then
proposed to form a worthy public library, of which
the legacy of Niccoli should be the nucleus. He sent

for Vespasiano for his advice, who said, "You could not *buy* books enough." "Then what would you do?" asked Cosimo. "Have them written," replied the bookseller. On which Cosimo gave the commission, and Vespasiano set forty-five scribes and illuminators to work, and furnished two hundred volumes in twenty-two months. Cosimo was so pleased with the books, that he employed the successful purveyor to supply the illuminated Psalters and Missals for the Church of the new Convent of San Marco.[1] No wonder, perhaps, that Vespasiano expresses his great dislike for the new-fangled art of printing. Every century has its own social convulsion, and thinks it the most important of all time. We talk of the revolutionary change made by the introduction of machinery in the nineteenth century, but we seldom realise how great a change in the occupations of the people took place in the fifteenth century, at the period of the invention of printing. Large numbers of men entirely dependent on their labours as scribes were thrown out of work. Many of these men were members of influential bodies, who were not inclined to sit down idly under their misfortunes, so they petitioned against the use of printing; but fate was too powerful for them, and their endeavours to boycott the printing-press were not successful, even though Vespasiano di Bisticci said that Duke Federigo would have been ashamed to have a printed book in his library.

---

[1] Leader Scott's "Renaissance of Art in Italy," 1883, p. 194.

John of Trittenheim, Abbot of Spanheim, who is known in literature as Trithemius, said some hard things against printing in an essay, *De Laude Scriptorum Manualium*, thus—

"A work written on parchment could be preserved for a thousand years, while it is probable that no volume printed on paper will last for more than two centuries. Many important works have not been printed, and the copies required of these must be prepared by scribes. The scribe who ceases to perform his work because of the invention of printing can be no true lover of books, in that, regarding only the present, he gives no due thought to the intellectual cultivation of his successors. The printer has no care for the beauty and the artistic form of books, while with the scribe this is a labour of love."

When, however, Trithemius found it necessary to exhort his own monks, he was not able to speak very favourably of their love of books—

"There is, in my opinion, no manual labour more becoming a monk than the writing of ecclesiastical books, and preparing what is needful for others who write them, for this holy labour will generally admit of being interrupted by prayer and of watching for the food of the soul no less than of the body. Need, also, urges us to labour diligently in writing books, if we desire to have at hand the means of usefully employing ourselves in spiritual studies. For you see that all the library of this monastery, which formerly was fine and large, has been so dissipated, sold, and made away with by the disorderly monks before us, that when I came I found but fourteen volumes."[1]

---

[1] Maitland's "Dark Ages," 1844, p. 272.

Others were wiser than to oppose the new art, and many scribes, recognising the inevitable destruction of their trade, became printers. Caxton's master, Colard Mansion, was an extensive writer of manuscripts before he took to the business of printing at Bruges. Much has been written upon famous collections of manuscripts, and upon the individual works which compose them, but it is not often that these come to public auction, so that the particulars of prices are comparatively meagre. The grand collections of the British Museum and the Bodleian [1] are preserved in safety for the use of the learned, and we only know that they are of the greatest value. What they would fetch if sold now can only be guessed, and it would be merely frivolous to inquire. Three of the grandest collections in the Museum—the old Royal Library, the Cotton, which was only saved from slow destruction by the establishment of the British Museum, to which it was transferred, and the Harley, which the nation obtained for £10,000—must now be of untold value.

The purchase by the British Museum of the library of Dr. Charles Burney greatly added to the completeness of the collections of Greek Classics.

[1] Mr. Madan has given in Appendix A to his most useful and interesting work on "Books in Manuscript," 1893, a list of public libraries which contain more than 4000 MSS. The largest collections are as follows :—British Museum, 52,000, and 162,000 charters; Bodleian Library, 31,000 ; Royal Library, Vienna, 20,000 ; Brussels, 30,000 ; Bibliothèque Nationale, Paris, 80,000 ; Royal Library, Berlin, 16,000 ; Munich, 26,000 ; the Vatican, Rome, 23,600 ; Biblioteca Nazionale, Florence, 15,000 ; Biblioteca Nacional, Madrid, 25,000.

Among the manuscripts is the wonderful Iliad of Homer on vellum, formerly belonging to Mr. Towneley, which, although it cannot be dated further back than the beginning of the fourteenth century, is supposed to be of the earliest date of the MSS. of the Iliad known to scholars. A committee appointed to consider the purchase of the library stated in their report: "With respect to the value of the manuscripts, the Homer is rated by the different witnesses at from £600 to £800, and one of them supposed it might even reach so high a price as £1000;[1] the Greek rhetoricians are estimated at from £340 to £500 ; the larger copy of the Greek Gospels at £200; the geography of Ptolemy at £65 ; and the copy of Plautus at £50. One witness estimates the whole of the ancient manuscripts at upwards of £2500, and an eminent bookseller at £3000." "The books with manuscript notes, together with Dr. Burney's *Variorum Compilation*, including the *Fragmenta Scenica Græca*, are estimated by one at £1000, and by another as high as £1340." It must be remembered that this was written in 1818, and these prices may be multiplied considerably at the present day.

Even those large private collections which have been in the market of late years have mostly been sold in bulk, so that little light has been thrown upon the current value of fine manuscripts.

One of the best sources of information respecting present prices is to be found in Mr. Quaritch's

---

[1] Dr. Burney gave £620 for it at Towneley's sale, 1815.

admirable catalogues of his collections of literary treasures.

When the treasures of Hamilton Palace were dispersed by public auction, the priceless collection of manuscripts was sold by private contract to the German Government. The amount paid has never been officially announced, but it is believed to have reached the sum of £75,000. Some of these manuscripts were not required at Berlin, and they were sold in May 1889 by Messrs. Sotheby for £15,189.

The gem of the collection was the fifteenth-century manuscript of Dante's *Divina Commedia*, illustrated with upwards of eighty drawings, attributed to Sandro Botticelli. Of it a writer in the *Times* said, "This priceless volume may, without exaggeration, be described as the most valuable manuscript in existence, from its artistic interest, for it stands alone as an example of a literary work of the first order illustrated by an artist of the highest rank."

It is impossible here even to register some of the many beautiful works that made the manuscripts of the Duke of Hamilton so famous. Great dissatisfaction was felt by the British public when it was found that these treasures were to be transported to Berlin. Before the final decision was made, Mr. Ruskin, in a "General statement explaining the nature and purposes of St. George's Guild," wrote—

"I hear that the library of Hamilton Palace is to be sold some time this spring. That library contains a collection of manuscripts which the late Duke permitted me to examine at leisure, now some thirty years ago. It contains many manuscripts for which I have no hope of contending successfully, even if I wished to do so, against the British Museum or the libraries of Paris and Vienna. But it contains also a very large number of manuscripts, among which I could assuredly choose some for which the partly exhausted general demand might be not extravagantly outbid, and I think the English public ought to have confidence enough in my knowledge of art and history to trust me with a considerable sum for this purpose."

Mr. Quaritch, who entered into Mr. Ruskin's plans, circulated this pamphlet, and asked for contributions to be sent to him, which he would forward to Mr. Ruskin. Had the Government of this country been of the same mind with Mr. Ruskin, these manuscripts would not have been lost to the country.

The sale of the Hamilton manuscripts to a foreign Government naturally caused those who were interested in these matters to feel great anxiety lest the Earl of Ashburnham's manuscripts, which it was known the owner wished to sell, should also be sent abroad. This collection consisted of upwards of three thousand manuscripts in about four thousand volumes, and were made up of purchases from the Duke of Buckingham (Stowe) and M. Libri; and of an Appendix consisting of separate manuscripts purchased from time to time by the late Lord Ashburnham.

(1) The Stowe collection grew out of the library of MSS. formed by Thomas Astle, the palæographer, and Keeper of the Records in the Tower. Astle

directed by his will that his collection should be
offered to the Marquis of Buckingham on certain
specified terms, one of which was the payment of the
sum of £500. This amount was not of course any
measure of their value, and the bequest was made in
gratitude to the Grenville family for favours which
Astle had received from them. A room was built
at Stowe by Mr. (afterwards Sir John) Soane to
receive the collection, in which were charters, registers, wardrobe accounts, inventories, correspondence, and many items of the greatest historical
value. O'Conor's Irish MSS. and the State Papers
of Arthur Capel, Earl of Essex, Lord-Lieutenant of
Ireland in the reign of Charles II., afterwards found
a home at Stowe. In April 1849 the Marquis of
Chandos wrote to Sir Robert Peel, stating that he
had recently had offers from private parties for the
Stowe manuscripts, and offering them to the British
Museum. Sir Frederick Madden valued the collection at £8300, but he was only authorised to
treat with Lord Chandos for the Irish manuscripts
separately, and to seek for further information
respecting other portions of the collection. In the
meantime, however, the whole number were sold
to Lord Ashburnham for £8000.

(2) Libri collection. In June 1846 the Trustees of
the British Museum applied for Treasury sanction
to the expenditure of £9000 in the purchase of the
Libri manuscripts, but this was refused. In September following renewed application was made
for £6600 for the collection, less the Napoleon
papers valued at £1000. The Treasury allowed

£6000 with commission to agents, but the negotia-
tion failed, and Lord Ashburnham obtained the
MSS. for £8000.

(3) Barrois collection, chiefly consisting of French
romances and poems, was offered to the British
Museum in 1848 for £6000. It was examined by
the Keeper of the Manuscripts, who recommended
the purchase, but apparently no application was
made to the Treasury, and the collection was soon
afterwards sold to Lord Ashburnham for the same
amount.

(4) Appendix of MSS. collected separately by
Bertram, fourth Earl of Ashburnham, among which
were some splendid illuminated manuscripts.

With respect to some of these manuscripts a
difficulty had arisen, owing to M. Léopold Delisle's
claim that a large number of the manuscripts in
the Libri collection had been stolen from libraries
in France by Libri while holding the office of
Inspector-General of Libraries. M. Delisle also
alleged that at least sixty of the Barrois manuscripts
were stolen from the Paris National Library. In
November 1879 Lord Ashburnham offered to treat
for the sale of his library of printed books and
manuscripts with the Museum alone, or jointly with
the French Government, naming £160,000 as the
price for the whole, and stated that he had received
an offer to that amount "from another quarter."
The Trustees then asked whether Lord Ashburnham
would treat for the manuscripts alone, and his
answer in January 1880 was that he had ascertained
that the offer he had received of £160,000 for the

whole library from a private individual was intended for private speculation, and that the collection was worth a great deal more. This amount, which comes to about £500 for each manuscript, seems to be very large, but competent authorities have agreed to the valuation. At any rate, the Treasury was not prepared to buy the whole at such a price, and the Principal Librarian treated for the Stowe collection alone, the price of which Lord Ashburnham fixed at £30,000.[1]   In the end these were purchased for the nation.

For many years the late Sir Thomas Phillipps was an omnivorous collector of manuscripts, and his collections were vast.   They are gradually being sold by auction.   Several portions have passed under the hammer of Messrs. Sotheby, and others are still to follow.

A very fine collection of illuminated manuscripts was gathered in a very short period by William Morris.   It is fortunate that a collection made by one who knew so well what to buy is not to be dispersed or taken out of the kingdom.   As long as it remains intact it will be a worthy monument of an enthusiastic lover of art who, while teaching the present age, was not forgetful of the history of the earlier workers in the same spirit.

We cannot register prices of such priceless manuscripts as the Gospels of St. Cuthbert, for two centuries at Lindisfarne, and now among the Cottonian MSS. in the British Museum, or the Book of Kells at Trinity College, Dublin—both of the seventh

---

[1] These particulars are obtained from the official reports.

century; but some few books of great interest which
have been sold by auction may be mentioned here.
The chief of these is the splendid manuscript of the
Bible in the British Museum, said to have been presented by Alcuin to Charlemagne. The vicissitudes
of this book are very remarkable. It was confiscated during the French Revolution, and eventually
came into the possession of M. Speyr Passavant of
Basle, who unavailingly offered it for a large sum to
the chief libraries of Europe. It was offered to the
Trustees of the British Museum, first for £12,000,
then for £8000, and lastly for £6500. The un-
founded claims of the proprietor, who appears to
have been very much of a charlatan, appear to have
damaged the repute of the MS., and it remained on
his hands. On 27th April 1836 the volume was put
up to auction at Evans's rooms, and was described
in six pages of a catalogue in which it was the chief
lot. It was catalogued as the Emperor Charlemagne's Bible—a manuscript on vellum by Alcuin,
completed A.D. 800, presented to Charlemagne A.D.
801 at the ceremony of his coronation, and mentioned in his will. The date is not undisputed, and
it is supposed by some to be of about forty years
later. The statement that this Bible is mentioned
in the Emperor's will is absolutely denied. The
price registered in Evans's sale catalogue is £1500,
and the purchaser is given as Scordet, but the book
was really bought in, and it is said that few of the
biddings for it were genuine. After this failure
fresh overtures were made to the British Museum,
and in the end it was bought for that library for

£750, which must be considered a small price for so splendid and interesting a book. There was some correspondence on this Bible in the *Gentleman's Magazine*, in which Sir Frederick Madden took part. These letters are reprinted in Gomme's *Gentleman's Magazine Library* ("Literary Curiosities," 1888, pp. 234–64). Another historical manuscript of particular beauty which has been several times sold by auction, and now safely reposes at the British Museum, is the famous so-called Bedford Missal (really Book of Hours), written and illuminated for John, Duke of Bedford, Regent of France under Henry VI., to whom he presented the book in the year 1430. It passed into the hands of Henry II. of France, and long subsequently into those of Lady Worsley (widow of Sir Robert Worsley), from whom it was purchased by the Earl of Oxford, who bequeathed it to his daughter, the Duchess of Portland. At the latter's sale in 1786 it was bought by James Edwards the bookseller for £213, 3s. At Edwards's sale in 1815 it was bought for £687, 15s. by the Marquis of Blandford, who afterwards sold it to Mr. Broadley. At Broadley's sale in 1833 Sir John Tobin bought it for £1100. Sir John's son sold it to the bookseller from whom the British Museum purchased it in 1852.

Two instances of most interesting manuscripts sold at very inadequate prices may here be recorded. One of the most distinguished among the Ashburnham manuscripts was one known as the Albani Missal. It is a manuscript of offices, and was executed apparently for Alemanno Salviati, gonfalonier

of Florence and brother - in - law of Lorenzo de'
Medici, and given by him to one of his relatives
of the house of Baroncelli. This beautiful volume
contains five full-page miniatures, each the work of
a master. The first is by the hand of Amico Asper-
tini, of Bologna, the pupil of Francia ; the next is
attributed to Lorenzo di Credi ; the third and fourth
of high excellence, though unassigned; and the fifth
by Perugino, signed " Petrus Perusinus pinxit."
For this artistic treasure Mr. James Dennistoun
gave £20 in Rome in the year 1838. When he had
purchased it he found that opposition to its leaving
Italy would be made on the part of the Roman
authorities, so he had it unbound and divided, and
got it sent to England privately a few pages at a
time. He afterwards sold it to Lord Ashburnham
for £700. These facts were printed in the *Times* in
1883 by a cousin of Mr. Dennistoun.

Mr. Madan gives in his " Books in Manuscript,"
1893, a very interesting account of a bargain obtained
by the Bodleian Library, which account is here re-
produced in a somewhat condensed form. " Six
years ago [1887] a little octavo volume, in worn
brown binding, stood on the shelves of a small parish
library in Suffolk, but was turned out and offered
at the end of a sale at Sotheby's, presumably as
being unreadable to country folk." It was described in the catalogue as "Latin Gospels of the
Fourteenth Century, with English Illuminations."
For the sum of £6 it passed into the Bodleian
Library, and came to be catalogued as an ordinary
accession. It was noticed that the writing was of

the eleventh century, and that the illuminations were valuable specimens of old English work of the same century, comprising figures of the four evangelists, of the Byzantine type, which was common in the west of Europe; the drapery, however, colouring, and accessories were purely English. The book itself was seen to be not the complete Gospels, but such portions as were used in the service of the Mass at different times of the year. On a fly-leaf was found a Latin poem, describing how the book had dropped in the water and was brought up by a soldier, who plunged in after it. Surprise was expressed that the book was uninjured, save a slight contraction of two of the leaves, and to this expression was added, " May the king and pious queen be saved for ever, whose book was but now saved from the waves !" Curiosity was felt as to the identity of this king and queen, when the difficulty was solved by a reference to Forbes-Leith's "Life of St. Margaret of Scotland," where this passage occurs : " She had a book of the Gospels beautifully adorned with gold and precious stones, and ornamented with the figures of the four evangelists painted and gilt. . . . She had always felt a particular attachment for this book, more so than for any of the others which she usually read." Then follows a story almost identical with the one given above, which proves that the identical book is now preserved in the Bodleian Library.

It is not often that bargains such as these can be obtained, but in spite of a great rise in price large numbers of manuscripts are still purchaseable on reasonable terms. The late Mr. J. H. Middleton was particularly urgent in pointing this out, and his words may appropriately close this chapter—

"On the whole, a fine manuscript may be regarded as about the cheapest work of art of bygone days that can now be purchased by an appreciative collector. Many of the finest and most perfectly preserved manuscripts which now come into the market are actually sold for smaller sums than they would have cost when they were new, in spite of the great additional value and interest which they have gained from their antiquity and comparative rarity. For example, a beautiful and perfectly preserved historical Anglo-Norman Vulgate of the thirteenth century, with its full number of eighty-two pictured initials, written on between six and seven hundred leaves of finest uterine vellum, can now commonly be purchased for from £30 to £40. This hardly represents the original value of the vellum on which the manuscript is written.

" Manuscripts of a simpler character, however beautifully written, if they are merely decorated with blue and red initials, commonly sell for considerably less than the original cost of their vellum.

" A collector with some real knowledge and appreciation of what is artistically fine can perhaps lay out his money to greater advantage in the purchase of manuscripts than by buying works of art of any other class, either mediæval or modern." [1]

---

[1] J. H. Middleton, "Illuminated MSS.," 1892, pp. 263–64.

CHAPTER IV

PUBLISHED PRICES

IT was impossible for the scribe (however low his pay might be reduced) to compete with the printing-press, and we have good authority for saying that printed books could be obtained in the fifteenth century for one-fifth of what would have been the cost of the same books in manuscript. Mr. Putnam, in his interesting work on the history of bookselling, quotes from Bishop John of Aleria, who, writing to Pope Paul II. in 1467, said that it was possible to purchase in Rome for 20 gulden in gold works which a few years earlier would have cost not less than 100 gulden. Other books selling for 4 gulden would previously have cost 20. Mr. Putnam also quotes Madden, to the effect that in 1470 a copy of the forty-eight line Bible, printed on parchment, could be bought in Paris for 2000 francs, while the cost of the same text a few years earlier in manuscript would have been 10,000 francs.

It is rather curious to find that the present custom of fixing a published price is comparatively modern, and that the system for which some of our present retail booksellers yearn—that is, of buying from the publishers in bulk and retailing at their own price—

was formerly in common use. In the old catalogues of English books no prices are affixed to the various entries, and the custom of printing the prices of books was not general until the end of the seventeenth century. But after all the booksellers' latitude was not very great, for the law stepped in to limit the price of books.

We might naturally have supposed that the invention of printing would have made a complete break in the mode of selling books, but this was not so. Continuity was preserved, and the company to which the London trade belongs is not called after the printers, but after the older order of stationers. In a "Note of the State of the Company of Printers, Bookesellers, and Bookebynders comprehended under the name of Stacioners," dated 1582, we are told that "in the tyme of King Henry the Eighte, there were but fewe Printers, and those of good credit and competent wealth, at whiche tyme and before there was an other sort of men that were writers, lymners of Bookes and diverse thinges for the Church and other uses, called Stacioners, which have, and partly to this daye do use to buy their bookes in grosse of the saide Printers, bynde them up, and sell them in their shops, whereby they well mayntayned their families."[1]

It seems probable that the English booksellers before the introduction of printing experienced little interference in their business from foreign

---

[1] *Archæologia*, xxv. 104.

scribes, and therefore the bringing in of printed books from abroad was distasteful to them. What they particularly objected to was the importation of these books bound instead of in sheets.

By "an Act touching the Marchauntes of Italy" (1 Ric. III. cap. 9) aliens were prohibited from importing certain goods into this country, but this Act was not to "extend to Importers of Books, or to any writer, limner, binder, or printer."

In Henry VIII.'s reign this importation was found intolerable, and "an Act for Printers and Binders of Bokes" was passed (25 Hen. VIII. cap. 15). It is stated in the preamble when the provision in the Act of Richard III. was made there were few books and few printers in England, but that at this time large numbers of printed books were brought into the country—

Whereas, a great number of the King's subjects within this realm having "given themselves diligently to learn and exercise the said craft of Printing, that at this day there be within this realm a great number cunning and expert in the said science or craft of printing, as able to exercise the said craft in all points as any stranger, in any other realm or country, and furthermore where there be a great number of the King's subjects within this realm which [live] by the craft and mystery of binding of books, . . . well expert in the same," yet "all this notwithstanding, there are divers persons that bring from [beyond] the sea great plenty of printed books—not only in the Latin tongue, but also in our maternal English tongue—some bound in boards, some in leather, and some in parchment, and them sell by retail, whereby many of the King's subjects, being binders of books, and having none other faculty wherewith to get

F

their living, be destitute of work, and like to be undone, except some reformation herein be had."

Then follow some provisions respecting the sale of books at too high a price—

"And after the same enhancing and increasing of the said prices of the said books and binding shall be so found by the said twelve men or otherwise by the examination of the said lord chancellor, lord treasurer, and justices, or two of them; that then the same lord chancellor, lord treasurer, and justices, or two of them at the least from time to time shall have a power and authority to reform and redress such enhancing of the prices of printed books by their discretions, and to limit prices as well of the books as for the binding of them; and over that the offender or offenders thereof being convict by the examination of the same lord chancellor, lord treasurer, and justices, or two of them or otherwise, shall lose and forfeit for every book by them sold whereof the price shall be enhanced for the book or binding thereof, three shillings four pence."

By the first Copyright Act (8 Anne, cap. 21) any person thinking the published price of a book unreasonable was to complain to the Archbishop of Canterbury or other great dignitaries.

It would have been enlightening if our lawmakers had told us what was in their opinion a reasonable price for a book, but they are silent on this point.

We have unfortunately no information as to the price for which Caxton sold his various books, but he bequeathed fifteen copies of his "Golden Legend" to the churchwardens of St. Margaret, Westminster, who succeeded in selling twelve of them between the years 1496 and 1500. For the

first three copies they obtained six shillings and
eightpence each, but then they had to reduce the
price to five shillings and eightpence, at which price
they sold the next seven copies. The last two
copies only brought five shillings and sixpence and
five shillings respectively, so that evidently there
was a falling market.

Mr. ·Blades makes the following remarks on this
point—

"The commercial results of Caxton's trade as a printer
are unknown; but as the fees paid at his burial were far
above the average, and as he evidently held a respectable
position in his parish, we must conclude that his business
was profitable. The preservation of the *Cost Book* of the
Ripoli Press has already been noticed, and some extracts
of interest translated therefrom. We may presume that
Caxton also kept exact accounts of his trade receipts and
expenditure, and if such were extant, the many doubts
which now surround the operations of his printing-office
would be definitely solved. We should then know the
price at which he sold his books—how many pence he
asked for his small quarto 'quayers' of poetry, or his pocket
editions of the 'Horæ' and 'Psalter'—how many shillings
were required to purchase the thick folio volumes, such
as 'Canterbury Tales,' 'King Arthur,' &c. That the price
was not much dearer than that paid for good editions now
we may infer from the rate at which fifteen copies of the
'Golden Legend' sold between 1496 and 1500. These
realised an average price of 6s. 8d. each, or about
£2, 13s. 4d. of modern money, a sum by no means too
great for a large illustrated work. This, however, would
depend on the number of copies considered necessary for
an edition, which probably varied according to the nature
of the work. . . . Some foreign printers issued as many as

275 or 300 copies of editions of the Classics, but it is not probable that Caxton ventured upon so large an impression, as the demand for his publications must have been much more restricted."[1]

It will be noticed that Mr. Blades is wrong in saying that the copies of the "Golden Legend" were sold at an *average* price of 6s. 8d., and it would probably be more correct to give the equivalent amount in modern money as £4, rather than £2, 13s. 4d., but this is perhaps more a matter of opinion.

Several old priced lists of books have come down to us, and the most interesting of these are the two printed and edited by Mr. F. Madan in the first series of the *Collectanea* of the Oxford Historical Society, and further annotated by the late Mr. Henry Bradshaw. The first of these is an inventory, with prices of books received in 1483 for sale by John Hunt, stationer of the University of Oxford, from Magister Peter Actor and Johannes de Aquisgrano, to whom he promises to restore the books or pay the price affixed in the list ; and the second is the Day-Book of John Dorne, bookseller in Oxford A.D. 1520. Mr. Bradshaw's valuable annotations ("A Half-Century of Notes") were printed in fac-simile of his handwriting in 1886, and afterwards included in his "Collected Papers" (1889).

Dorne's list is of great value, as showing what was the literature sold at a great university city at the beginning of the sixteenth century, and with the much-needed explanations of Messrs. Madan

---

[1] "Life and Typography of William Caxton," vol. ii. p. lix.

and Bradshaw, it forms an important addition to our knowledge, but there is not much in it that can be quoted here with advantage. Latin theology forms the bulk of the more important books sold, and next to that Latin classics. English books are few ; among the cheapest items, service-books and ballads, Christmas carols, and almanacs are common. A large proportion of the entries are marked in pence from one penny upwards, but some are in shillings, and the largest amount for one sale of several books was forty-eight shillings.

Bibliographica (vol. i. p. 252) contains "Two References to the English Book-Trade *circa* 1525." The first, which is from the " Interlude of the Four Elements," suggests that a large amount of the output of the English presses at the beginning of the sixteenth century was made up of ephemeral publications—

> " Now so it is in our Englyshe tonge,
>   Many one there is that can but rede and wryte,
> For his pleasure wyll oft presume amonge
>   New bokys to compyle and balades to indyte,
>   Some of lore or other matter, not worth a myte."

The next is from the prologue to Robert Copland's "Seven Sorrows that Women have when theyr husbandes be deade," which consists of a conversation between Copland and a customer, "Quidam"—

> " *Quidam.* Hast thou a boke of the wydowe Edith,
> That hath begyled so many with her wordes,
> Or els suche a geest that is ful of bourdes?
> Let me se, I wyll yet waste a peny
> Upon suche thynges and if thou have eny.

Copland. How say ye by these, wyll ye bestowe a grote?
Quidam. Ye syr so muche? nay, that I shorowe my cote,
A peny I trow is ynough on bokes,
It is not so soone goten, as this worlde lokes."

Much information respecting the prices of books
is found in the churchwardens' accounts of the
various parishes of the kingdom, and extracts from
some of these have been printed in the *Gentleman's
Magazine* and other places. Mr. Thorold Rogers also
has given several instances in the various volumes
of his great work on "Agriculture and Prices."

Archbishop Cranmer, in his "Articles to be in-
quired of . . . within the Diocese of Canterbury,"
A.D. 1548, asks "whether in every case they have
provided one book of the whole Bible of the largest
volume in English, and the Paraphrases of Erasmus, also in English, upon the Gospels, and set up
the same in some convenient place in the church."
In 1548 we find that the churchwardens of St.
Margaret's, Westminster, paid five shillings for the
half part of the Paraphrases of Erasmus, and in
1549 the churchwardens of Wigtoft, Lincolnshire,
paid seven shillings for the same book. Archbishop
Parker required Jewel's "Defence of the Apology"
to be placed in parish churches, and in 1570 the
churchwardens of Leverton, Lincolnshire, paid four
shillings for "half Mr. Juylle's booke, called the
'Appologie of Ingland,'" and fourpence for the
carriage of the same.

From the churchwardens' accounts of the parish
of Stratton, county Cornwall, we learn that in 1565

two shillings were "paid for newe songes for the church," and twopence "for a nother lyttell boke." In 1570 twelvepence was "paid to Nicholas Oliver of sent tives for a song of te deum," fourpence was paid "for mendyng of John Judes bybell which he lonyd to the churche when the other was to bynd," and six shillings "for a newe communion book and a psalter in the same." On the other side twelvepence was received "for two peces of old bookes sold." [1]

The churchwardens of Canterbury parish gave forty-one shillings for a church Bible in 1586, four shillings for a prayer-book in 1598, and three shillings and fourpence for a book of statutes in 1599.

Sir John Evans communicated to the *Archæologia* [2] some most interesting extracts from the Private Account Book of Sir William More of Loseley, in Surrey, in the time of Queen Mary and Queen Elizabeth, which contains an inventory of a collection of about one hundred and twenty volumes. This inventory gives us a vivid idea of the contents of a country gentleman's library in the sixteenth century. There are the best chronicles of the time, as Fabyan, Harding, &c., translations of the classics, and some in their original languages, statutes, new books of justices and other legal works, books of physic, dictionaries, &c., and each of the books is marked with a price. The most expensive books :—
Cronica Cronicarum, xxs ; Munster's *Cosmografye*, xvjs ; un byble, xs ; a calapyne, xs [Calepino's Vocabulary of the Latin Tongue] ; Fabyan's *Cronicle*,

---

[1] *Archæologia*, xlvi. 228, 229.   [2] xxxvi. 284-310.

vs; Statuts of Henry theight, xijs; all the Statuts
of Kyng Edward the VI., ijs; all the Statuts of
the Quene, ijs; Chausore, vs. There were four
New Testaments, "one in ffrench," xxd, two "in
Italion," respectively xxjd and ijs vjd, and one "in
lattyn," xijd. The *Legenda Aurea* was priced
iijs iiijd; Tullye's *Officys* translated, viijd; ij bokes
conteyning Tully's *Philosophy*, ijs vjd; Cezar's *Commentary*, xvjd; ij bokes of Machevale's works in
Italion, iijs iiijd; Hardyng's *Cronycle*, ijs vjd; *Utopea*,
viijd. Of low-priced books we find—A lyttle cronicle, id; Lydgates' *Proverbs*, id; Alexander Barkley's
Eclogs, id; Skelton's Work, iiijd; and *Triumph of
Petrark*, vjd.

Sir Egerton Brydges also quoted from a Household Book an interesting list of about the same
date as the above—

Anno 1564.

Iteme, for booke of the dysease of horses .	iiijd
Iteme, for printing the xxv orders of honest men	xxd
Iteme, pd for a Lytlton in English . .	xijd
Iteme, for a diologge betwine the cap and the heade	ijd
Iteme, pd for the booke of the ij Englishe lovers	vjd
Iteme, for a French booke called the his- torye de noster ternes	xvjd
Iteme, pd for iij French bokes, the on called Pawlus Jovius	xxs [1]

[1] *Censura Literaria*, iii. 370.

In the days before copyright acts authors and publishers often tried to safeguard their property by obtaining patents. These were sometimes for a particular book, as, for instance, Richard Field, printer, in February 1592 was granted the sole licence to print " Orlando Furioso translated into English verse by John Harrington." More often, however, patents were granted to printers allowing them the sole privilege of printing certain classes of books. A licence " to imprint all manner of books concerning the common laws of this realm" was granted to Richard Tottell ; one for primers and books of private prayers to William Seres ; one to print all manner of songs of musick to Thomas Tallis and William Bird ; one for dictionaries generally to H. Binneman ; and one for almanacks and prognostications to James Roberts and Richard Watkins.[1] Gradually by purchase or inheritance nearly all the monopolies came into the possession of the Stationers' Company. Certain printers, however, made a practice of pirating some of the most popular English privileged books. The Company resisted, and memorialised Lord Burghley in October 1582, with a complaint of the opposition met with in making their search in the printing-house of one " who printed all kinds of books at his pleasure."[2]

The chief leader of these invaders of privilege was John Wolf, a freeman of the Fishmongers'

---

[1] The late Mr. Cornelius Walford contributed to the *Bibliographer* some articles on Book Patents and Printing Patents. See vol. v. pp. 125, 156 : vol. vi. pp. 129, 171.

[2] *Archæologia*, vol. xxv. pp. 100–112.

Company. In 1583 the Stationers' Company drew up thirteen heads of the "insolent and contemptuous behaviour of John Wolf, printer, and his confederates," which they presented to the Privy Council. From this indictment it appears that when Wolf was "frendly persuaded to live in order and not print men's privileged copies," he answered that "he would print all their bokes if he lacked work," and added that "it was lawfull for all men to print all lawfull bookes, what commandement soever her Majestie gave to yᵉ contrary." Wolf was no respecter of persons, and his motto was, "I will live." Being admonished that he "being but one so meane a man should not presume to contrarie her Highnesse Governmente," "Tush," said he, "Luther was but one man, and reformed all the world for religion, and I am that man that must and will reforme the government in this trade!" The Queen appointed a Commission to inquire into the matter, but the Commissioners could make nothing of Wolf and his party. In the end the opposition was bought off ; and on 1st July 1583 Wolf was admitted a freeman of the Stationers' Company by redemption, paying the usual fees of 3s. 4d.[1]

Andrew Maunsell, a bookseller living in Lothbury, was the first to publish (1595) a catalogue of English books, and this book is a very satisfactory bit of bibliographical work. The compiler only published two parts, the first on theological books, and the second on scientific books. Maunsell proposed

---

[1] Arber's "Transcript of the Registers of the Company of Stationers."

the publication of others on more popular branches
of literature, but unfortunately he left his work incomplete. In his dedication to Queen Elizabeth
he says—

"What great account (most gracious Soueraigne) hath
beene made of godly bookes, may euidently appeare by
the value set uppon the bookes of curious actes brought to
the Apostles feete to be burnt. For if those bookes were
valued to two thousand markes, of what estimation shall
wee account the bookes whose author is God himselfe . . .
all the goods upon the earth cannot value them."

It is remarkable how difficult it must have been
in the sixteenth and seventeenth centuries to obtain
information respecting new books. There were no
public libraries, and the booksellers, according to
Maunsell, were not well acquainted with the titles
of the books published, and he constantly refers to
the scarceness of books issued only a few years
before. He writes—

"And seeing also many singular Bookes, not only of
Diuinitie, but of other excellent Arts, after the first impression, so spent and gone, that they lie euen as it were buried
in some few Studies. That men desirous of such kind of
Bookes, cannot aske for that they neuer heard of, and the
Bookeseller cannot shew that he hath not: I have thought
good in my poor estate to undertake this most tiresome
business, hoping the Lord will send a blessing on my
labours taken in my vocation. Thinking it as necessarie
for the Bookeseller (considering the number and nature of
them) to haue a Catalogue of our English Bookes as the
Apothecaire his Dispensatorium or the Schoolmaster his
Dictionarie. By means of which my poore trauailes I will

draw to your memories Bookes that you could not remember and shew to the learind such Bookes as they
would not thinke were in our owne tongues. . . ."

Besides dedicating his book to Queen Elizabeth,
he addresses "the Companie of Stationers, and all
other printers and booksellers," to whom he says—

"I have in my vocation laboured to do somwhat : my
purpose is to shew (in such sort as I can) what we have in
print, in our own tongue, a thinge not regarded but of a
few. For some soare so hie that they looke not so low, as
on their owne countrie writers, and some regard not old
Bookes, but aske what newes? or new writers?"

To the reverend divines he says—

"The consideration whereof hath moved me (most un-
worthie and unable of many others) to undertake this trife-
ling yet most toylesome & troublesome busines, wherby the
reader shall haue this help, and he may see at home in his
Studie what Bookes are written and how many translated.
And though it be imperfect as I know not what first Booke
either of Dictionarie or Herball or such like was perfect at
the first or second edition, yet he that helpeth me to put in
one Booke that I have not seene, I hope I shall shew him
ten that he never heard of either new or old."

The second part of Maunsell's catalogue was
dedicated to Robert, Earl of Essex, and the scarceness of books not twenty or forty years old is again
referred to in it—

"Seeing still many excellent Bookes written and printed
in our owne tongue, and that many of them after twenty
or fortie yeares Printing are so dispersed out of Bookesellers

hands, that they are not onely scarce to be found but almost quite forgotten, I have thought it worth my poore labour, to take some paynes heerin though that the more learnd sort would not willingly imploy their labour in the same) to gather a Cathalogue in suche sort as I can of the Bookes printed in our tongue which I doe hope will be delight-some to all English men that be learnt or desirous of learning."

The next bibliography of new English books was William London's "Catalogue of the most vendible Books," 1658, to which two small supplements were published, bringing the list of publications down to 1660.

R. Clavel was the next to publish a catalogue of new books, and the period covered by him was from 1666 to 1695. To none of these books are prices attached, but some of the books in Clavel's supplement are priced ; and in the monthly cata-logue commenced by Bernard Lintott in May 1714, all the books are priced.

Bent's General Catalogue of Books, issued in 1786, contained the titles of books published since 1700, and this was succeeded by the London Cata-logue, which appeared for several years. The British and English catalogues followed, and the latter is published annually.

In order to obtain some idea of the varying prices at which books have been published, it will be well to enumerate a few at different periods, arranged under the different sizes of books.

FOLIOS

Corpus Christi College, Oxford, gave seven shillings in 1621 for Bacon's work on Henry VII., and in 1624 £3, 6s. 8d. for four volumes of "Purchas's Pilgrims." The published price of the first edition of Shakespeare's Plays is said to have been £1.

John Ogilby, who was one of the first projectors of grand illustrated books in large folio, found himself burthened with a heavy stock of expensive books which did not sell, so he hit upon the expedient of getting rid of them by means of a lottery, licensed by the Duke of York and the Assistants of the Corporation of the Royal Fishery. These books were an illustrated Bible, printed by John Field at Cambridge in 1660, two volumes folio ; the "Works of Virgil," translated by Ogilby, 1654; Homer's "Iliads," translated by Ogilby, 1660 ; Homer's "Odysseys," 1665. Pope frequently spoke in later life of the great pleasure Ogilby's "Homer" gave him when a boy at school. "Æsop's Fables paraphrased by Ogilby," 1665; and Ogilby's "Entertainment of Charles II. in his Passage through the City of London to his Coronation," 1662—a splendid book, which is said to have proved of great service in succeeding coronations.

It is worthy of note that Samuel Pepys was a subscriber to the lottery, and obtained the "Æsop" and the "Coronation," which cost him £4 (Feb. 19, 1665–66).

Ogilby issued a Proposal for a second lottery,

which was reprinted in the *Gentleman's Magazine* (1814, part 1, pp. 646-48).[1] This is valuable as containing the prices at which the books are valued, viz.—

	£
An imperial Bible, with chorographical and an hundred historical sculps	25
"Virgil," translated, with sculps and annotations	5
Homer's "Iliads," adorned with sculps . .	5
Homer's "Odysseys," adorned with sculps .	4
"Æsop's Fables," paraphrased and sculped .	3
"His Majestie's Entertainment " . . .	2

In 1689 St. John's College, Cambridge, gave £10, 15s. for David Loggan's *Cantabrigia illustrata*, 1688, but this probably included a present to the author; for in 1690 Eton College paid £4 for *Cantabrigia illustrata* and *Oxonia illustrata*, 1675, two volumes together, so that we may suppose the published price of each to be £2.

The Rev. John Flavel's Works, in two volumes folio, was published in 1700 for forty shillings, which shows that the price of an illustrated volume in folio was still about £1.

Colin Campbell's *Vitruvius Britannicus*, a handsome work containing a large number of fine architectural plates, was published at a very reasonable price. The first and second volumes, published in 1715 and 1717 respectively, were sold for four guineas on imperial paper, and three guineas on royal paper.

---

[1] Gomme's *Gentleman's Magazine Library*, "Literary Curiosities," 1888, p. 79.

The price of Johnson's Dictionary of the English Language, two volumes folio, was in 1755 four guineas in sheets, and £4, 15s. in boards.

Folios are so completely out of fashion now, except for gorgeously illustrated books, or for fac-similes of books and documents, that it is scarcely worth while to carry the inquiry to a later period.

QUARTOS

The small quarto volumes of the seventeenth century were by no means high priced, and we learn that three shillings bought Milton's " Paradise Lost" when first published. The price of the early editions of the separate plays of the Elizabethan dramatists, which now are so much sought after, was sixpence. This we learn from the address prefixed to the early issue of " Troilus and Cressida," 1609, published before that play was acted—

"Amongst all these is none more witty than this; and had I time, I would comment upon it, though I know it needs not—for so much as will make you think your *testern* well bestowed,—but for so much worth as even poor I know to be stuffed in it."

The poets had a profitable time when their poems, handsomely printed in quarto volumes, were priced so high as two guineas. Sir Walter Scott made great sums by these editions which sold in large numbers, but no other poet was so fortunate as he was. Moore did well with his poems, and in his

Diary (Dec. 23, 1818) he records an amusing instance of the practical appreciation of an admirer. He writes—

"The young Bristol lady who enclosed me £3 after reading 'Lalla Rookh' had very laudable ideas on the subject; and if every reader of 'Lalla Rookh' had done the same, I need never have written again."

Wordsworth's "Excursion" was published in 1814, in a two guinea quarto volume, but it took six years to exhaust an edition of five hundred copies. Such are the inequalities in the rate of the remuneration of authors.

Rees's "Cyclopædia," which was published between 1802 and 1820 (in forty-five volumes and six volumes of plates), cost in all £85. The "Encyclopædia Britannica," which has superseded it, is published at the small price of twenty-eight shillings per volume.

In the early part of this century, when it was the fashion to print standard works in quarto, they were very high priced, thus the first edition of "Pepys's Diary" was published in two volumes for six guineas. Now the quarto is almost as much out of date as the folio, and is confined to illustrated books.

OCTAVOS

The ordinary octavo volume was published at the beginning of the eighteenth century for five or six shillings. Thus Boyer's translation of "The ingenious and entertaining Memoirs of Count

G

Gramont, who lived in the court of King Charles II., and was afterwards Ambassador from the King of France to King James II.," 1714, was published at five shillings, and George Psalmanazar's " Historical and Geographical Description of Formosa " at six shillings. Since then the price for an octavo has gradually increased to seven shillings and sixpence, then to ten shillings and sixpence. In the latter half of the present century there has been a considerable advance to twelve shillings, to sixteen and eighteen shillings, and now fully illustrated books are often priced as high as one guinea a volume. Plays, trials, and pamphlets generally have averaged about one shilling apiece.

DUODECIMOS

Walton's "Complete Angler," first published in 1653, was issued at one shilling and sixpence, as appears from the following contemporary advertisement, quoted by Hone in his " Every-Day Book " : " There is published a Booke of Eighteen-pence price, called 'The Compleat Angler ; or, The Contemplative Man's Recreation,' being a Discourse of Fish and Fishing. Not unworthy the perusall. Sold by Richard Marriot at S. Dunstan's Churchyard, Fleet Street."

In 1663 Pepys bought the first part of Butler's " Hudibras" for two shillings and sixpence, and sold it again for one shilling and sixpence. The Master of Corpus Christi College, Oxford, gave at the same time one shilling for the first part and the same sum for the second part, but later on he gave half-a-crown for the latter.

"The Works of the celebrated Mons. de Molière, translated from the last edition printed at Paris, containing his life, all his comedies, interludes, &c., with a large account of his life and remarkable death, who, as he was acting the part of Death in one of his own plays, was taken ill and died a few hours after. . . ." This was printed in six volumes 12mo, "on a fine paper and Elzevir letter," and published by B. Lintott for fifteen shillings (or two shillings and sixpence a volume) in May 1714.

Tom D'Urfey sold his "Wit and Mirth ; or, Pills to purge Melancholy," at two shillings and sixpence a volume.

Duodecimos have now gone out of fashion, at least in name, as small books are mostly known as post octavos, foolscap octavos, &c. The price of these small handy volumes remains much the same, as the half-crown of the last century is the equivalent of our five or six shillings.

The greatest change in price has been made in poetry and novels, and six shillings has become a favourite price for both. The two guineas for the poem, and the guinea and a half for the three-volume novel, are become things of the past.

Although in the last century many books were published and sold which could not be sold at the present time, it is probable that some of these books paid the publisher but badly, and it was therefore found to be a wise precaution to publish certain books by subscription, and this plan was therefore frequently adopted.

Dr. Brian Walton's Polyglot Bible (six vols. folio, 1657, £10) is often said to be the first book printed by subscription in England ; but Minsheu's Dictionary, in eleven languages, 1617, was certainly sold by the author to subscribers. The number of these subscribers was 174, among whom are six—viz., Sir John Laurence, Dr. Aileworth, Mr. Paul Peart, Mr. Brigges, Sir Henry Spelman, and Mr. Booth—who largely assisted the author with money to complete his great undertaking.

"The Monthly Catalogue" of new books commenced by Bernard Lintott in May 1714 frequently contained lists of the books printed by subscription. In the number for January 1714–15 the terms of subscription to the worst edition of Chaucer's works ever published are announced—

"Whereas John Urry, Student of Christ-Church, Oxon, has obtained from her late Majesty, Queen Anne, a Licence for Printing the Works of the celebrated Jeffrey Chaucer, corrected from all the printed editions, and from several rare and ancient MSS. not hitherto consulted : from the collating of which he has restored many single lines and added several Tales never yet printed, by which alterations, amendments, and additions, the work is in a manner become new. Thirty copper plates by the best gravers will be printed before each tale ; a more compleat Glossary and Table will be added at the end. A small number will be printed on Royal Paper at 50s. per book, and those on the finest demy at 30s. Half to be paid in hand. Subscriptions are taken in by the Undertaker, Bernard Lintott between the Temple Gates, and by most Booksellers in London and the country. *N.B.*—A new Black Letter, accented, has been cast on purpose for this work, for the ease of the Reader."

Dryden made very good terms with Tonson for the publication of his translation of Virgil, but Pope was still more successful with the subscription to his translation of Homer's "Iliad." The subscription for six quarto volumes was fixed at six guineas, and 575 persons subscribed for 654 copies. The booksellers eagerly made their offers of publication, and the highest bidder was B. Lintott, who agreed to supply all the subscription copies at his own expense, and to pay £200 for every volume. Pope therefore received altogether £5320 without any deduction.

Lintott engaged not to print any quartos except for Pope, but he printed the quarto pages on small folio, and sold each volume for half-a-guinea. These being cut down by some dishonest traders, were sold as subscription copies.

Lintott was defrauded of his profit by the sale of a duodecimo edition, printed in Holland, which obliged him to print an edition in a similar form. Of Lintott's first duodecimo edition 2500 copies were quickly sold off. Five thousand further copies were at once printed.

Some of Hearne's antiquarian works were subscribed at ten shillings and sixpence per volume for small paper, and one guinea for large paper.

It seems to have been the practice for the

subscriber to a book to pay down half the purchase-money on sending in his name, and the other half on publication.

Another expedient for the rapid sale of books was their issue in numbers. Smollett's "History of England" was published in sixpenny numbers, and had an immediate sale of 20,000 copies. This immense success is said to have been due to an artifice practised by the publisher. He sent down a packet of prospectuses carriage free (with half-a-crown enclosed) to every parish clerk in the kingdom, to be distributed by him through the pews of the church. This being generally carried out, a valuable advertisement was obtained, which resulted in an extensive demand for the work.

Books are published at an equal price, according to size, whether they are good or bad, but they find their level in the catalogues of the second-hand booksellers. The bad soon become waste-paper, or are marked down to very low prices, while the good books increase in price till they come in some cases to be marked more than the original published price.

Sometimes when books are printed in limited numbers the public will give more than the published price even before publication ; thus the large paper edition of the "Life of the Queen," by Mr. R. R. Holmes, was subscribed at £8, and the right of receiving a copy when ready is said to have been sold for from £20 to £25.

Publishers occasionally reduce the price of a book after publication, but this is seldom a successful operation. The selling-off of remainders has been the means of distributing books to the public at a low rate, and it will often be found that some of the scarcest and highest priced books in the present day are those which have been sold-off. These were good books, which sold too slowly, but which went off quickly when the price was low. When the stock is exhausted, and more are required, the price naturally goes up.

A most remarkable instance of this increase in price of a sold-off book is that of Edward Fitzgerald's wonderful version of the *Rubáiyát* of Omar Khayyam, the first edition of which was published by Quaritch in 1859. Though the number printed was few, nobody bought, and eight years afterwards the publisher, in disgust, threw the whole remainder into a box outside his door, and marked all these one penny each. It is said that Dante Rossetti found them there, and soon the remainder was exhausted. Now this penny book is worth six guineas.[1]

---

[1] This was quite true when written a few months ago, but on the 10th February 1898 a copy with the original wrappers was sold at Sotheby's salerooms for £21. It was bought by Mr. Quaritch, the original publisher.

CHAPTER V

THE exact date of the first introduction into England of the convenient plan of selling books by auction is known to us through the amiable weakness of the auctioneers for writing prefaces to the sale catalogues ; and this history, therefore, is singularly unlike that of most other inventions and customs, the origin of which is usually open to doubt, because the originators have not thought it worth while to explain that they were doing some new thing. The auctioneers, on the other hand, tell us which was the first sale, and which were the second, the third, and the fourth. After this the freshness may be said to be exhausted, and we are contented with less exact particulars.

The custom was prevalent in Holland in the middle of the seventeenth century, and the honour of introducing it into England is due to William Cooper, the bookseller of Little Britain, about whom some notice has been given in a former chapter. He was largely interested in alchemy, and three years before he sold his first sale he published a " Catalogue of Chemical Books."

We must not, however, suppose that this was the

introduction of auctions into England, for sale by inch of candle had long been practised here, a plan adopted by the Navy Office for the sale of their old stores. The earliest use of the word auction, quoted by Dr. Murray in the "New English Dictionary," is from Warner's translation of Plautus, 1595 : "The auction of Menæchmus, . . . when will be sold slaves, household goods," &c. ; and the next quotation is from the Appendix to Phillip's Dictionary, 1678 : "*Auction*, a making a publick sale and selling of goods by an outcry." We shall see that the word was far from familiar to the general public, as the auctioneers considered it wise to explain the word, thus : "Sale of books by way of auction, or who will give most for them." The more usual words in old English were outcry, outrope (still familiar in Scotland as *roup*, *cf.* German *ruf*) and port sale.

The first sale by auction was that of the library of Lazarus Seaman, a member of the Assembly of Divines, and chaplain to the Earl of Northumberland. He was also minister of All Hallows, Bread Street, and Master of Peterhouse, Cambridge. In the latter college a Diary written by him between 1645 and 1657 is preserved. He seems to have been an active man on his own side in politics, and we find that he was a member of the Committee for ejecting Scandalous Ministers for London and the Counties of Cambridge and Huntingdon. It is therefore not surprising to find that at the Restoration he was ejected both from his living and from the Mastership of Peterhouse. He died at his house in Warwick Court, London, in September 1675, and in the following year his library was sold in his house by Cooper, who makes the following interesting remarks in his preface—

"Reader, it hath not been usual here in England to make sale of Books by way of auction, or who will give most for them : But it having been practised in other countreys to the advantage both of buyers and sellers, it was therefore conceived (for the encouragement of Learning) to publish the sale of these Books this manner of way, and it is hoped that this will not be unacceptable to Schollers. . . . "

Mr. Alfred W. Pollard, in a very valuable article on English Book Sales, 1676–80 (*Bibliographica*, vol. i. p. 373), quotes an interesting letter from David Millington to Joseph Hill, an English Nonconformist minister in Holland, dated June 1697, and now preserved in the British Museum (Stowe MS., 709), in which the writer tenders to the divine his thanks for the "great service done to learning and learned men in your first advising and effectually setting on foot that admirable and universally approved way of selling librarys amongst us ; " and distinctly states that it was Hill who "happily introduced the practice into England." Mr. Pollard goes on to say that "Hill, who from 1673 to 1678, owing to his publication of a pamphlet which gave offence to the Dutch Government, was resident in England, must have advised the executors of Dr. Seaman, a theologian of principles not widely different from his own, to adopt this method of selling his friend's library to the best advantage."

Seaman was the author of "A Vindication of the Judgement of the Reformed Churches, &c., concerning Ordination, &c.," 1647, and the chief class of books in his library was what we might expect to find, viz., theological works that he required in his vocation. Some few books (such as the Eliot Bible of 1661–63, nineteen shillings) fetched small prices as compared with their present value, but Mr. Pollard says that "nine-tenths of the books sold for more than they would at the present day."

The library was a large one, and the lots numbered between five and six thousand, and the amount realised by the sale was a little over £700, which may be roughly estimated at about £3500 of our present money.

The second auction sale (February 1676–67) was also carried out by Cooper, and consisted of the library of Thomas Kidner, Rector of Hitchin, in Hertfordshire, who died 31st August 1676. The library, like that of Dr. Seaman, consisted largely of theological works. It is evident from Cooper's preface to this catalogue that Seaman's sale had given considerable satisfaction, although the reference to an attempt to stifle this manner of sale shows that there were some opponents of the system. Cooper writes—

"Reader, the first attempt in this kind (by the Sale of Dr. Seaman's library) having given great content and satisfaction to the gentlemen who were buyers, and no great discouragement to the Sellers, hath encouraged the making this second trial, by the exposing (to auction or sale) the Library of Mr. Tho. Kidner, in hopes of receiving such encouragement from the Learned as may prevent the stifling of this manner of sale, the benefit (if rightly considered) being equally balanced between buyer and seller."

The third sale (February 1677–78) was of the library of Thomas Greenhill, a Nonconformist minister of some repute, who died in 1671, seven years before his books were sold. This sale is worthy of note, for the auctioneer was Zachariah Bourne, and not Cooper, as in the two former cases. It took place at the Turk's Head Coffee-House in Bread Street (in ædibus Ferdinandi Stable, Coffipolæ, ad insigne Capitis Turcæ). Bourne states in his preface that—

"The attempts in this kind having given great content and satisfaction to the gentlemen who were the buyers, and no discouragement to the sellers, hath encouraged the making this trial by exposing (to auction or sale) the library of Mr. William Greenhill."

The fourth sale (25th May 1678) was occupied with the library of Thomas Manton (1620–77), one of the ministers appointed to wait upon Charles II. at Breda. It took place at the house of the late possessor, in King Street, Covent Garden. More English literature was included in this library than in the former three. The auctioneer was Cooper, and his preface is worth quoting. It will be seen that the plan of allowing an inspection of the books before the sale had now been adopted—

"Reader, we question not but that this manner of sale by way of auction is pretty well known to the Learned, nor can we doubt their encouragement for the advantage which they (as well as we) may in time reap thereby. Wherefore we are resolved (*Deo volente*) to make a fourth triall with the Library of Dr. Tho. Manton, which is not contemptible either for the Value, Condition, or Number, as will appear upon a sight thereof, which is free for any Gentleman that shall please to take that pains."

Cooper was not satisfied with the catalogue, which had been made by one considered by him to be incompetent, and of whom he writes thus—

"This Catalogue was taken by Phil Briggs, and not by W. Cooper, but afterwards in parts methodized by him. Wherefore he craves your excuse for the mistakes that have hapned; and desires that the Saddle may be laid upon the right horse."

The sale of Benjamin Worsley's library (May 1678) is interesting, as being the first auction in which a fair representation of old English literature occurs, in addition to the ordinary theological works. Chaucer (1602) fetched £1, 3s. 6d.; Ben Jonson's Works (1640), £1, 13s. 6d.; Shakespeare, second folio, 16s., and third folio, £1, 8s. 6d. The auctioneers were John Dunsmore and Richard Chiswell, and the sale took place over against the Hen and Chickens, in Paternoster Row. The sixth sale consisted of the libraries of John Godolphin and Owen Philips, and took place in November 1678, when a Caxton—"Geffrey Chaucer's translation of Boethius' *De Consolatione Philosophiæ* in English" —fetched five shillings. We thus see that in two years there were only six sales. After this time they became more frequent, and in this same

month of November 1678 an attempt was made at
rigging a sale; the booksellers were so well satisfied with the prices obtained, that they thought it
would be a good stroke of business to lift some of
their old stock under the cover of a good name.
Moses Pitt adopted this expedient, and issued a
catalogue of books described as including "the
library of a worthy and learned person deceased,
with a considerable number of the choice books of
most sciences, some of which have been bought
out of the best libraries abroad, particularly out of
the late famous and learned Gilbert Voetius's."

This fraud was greatly resented by the book-
buyers, and it was felt by the other auctioneers
that a blow had been dealt to the newly-established
system of sale; so when in December of this same
year the libraries of Lord Warwick and Gabriel
Sangar came to be sold at the Harrow, over
against the College of Physicians, in Warwick
Lane, Nathaniel Ranew, the auctioneer, thought it
expedient to make a statement in the preface to
the catalogue, where he informed his patrons that
this is "no collection made by any private hand
(which hath been imputed to some auctions as a
reflection), but the works were really belonging to
their proprietors deceased mentioned on the title-
page, and by the direction of their respective executors exposed to sale."

Moses Pitt made up another sale in February
1678-79, chiefly of books printed at the Sheldonian
Theatre, Oxford, which took place in Petty Canons
Hall, near St. Paul's Churchyard. In June 1679

William Cooper sold the libraries of Stephen Watkins and Dr. Thomas Shirley (the catalogue of which contained an appendix of Richard Chiswell's books) at the Golden Lion, over against the Queen's Head Tavern, in Paternoster Row. John Dunsmore sold in November 1679 the library of Sir Edward Bysshe, Clarenceux King at Arms, at his house, near the sign of the Woolpack, in Ivy Lane. This library was more varied in its character than many of those that were sold before it, and it contained a considerable amount of French, Italian, and Spanish literature, including some early editions of Molière. This catalogue is deserving of particular attention, because the books are described as "curiously bound and richly gilt." Hitherto no mention had been made of bindings in the various catalogues. This attention to binding was to grow, and Thomas Hearne protested against it some years after. In his memoranda under date 15th February 1725-26 he wrote respecting the sale of John Bridges' library : " I hear they go very high, being fair books in good condition, and most of them finely bound. This afternoon I was told of a gentleman of All Souls' College (I suppose Dr. Clarke) that gave a commission of eight shillings for a Homer in two vols., a small 8vo, if not 12mo. But it went for six guineas. People are in love with good binding more than good reading." [1]

The British Museum Library contains a valuable collection of early sale catalogues, and one of the

volumes, containing the first eleven sales from Seaman to Bysshe, is of considerable interest from
having the following note in Richard Heber's handwriting—

"This volume, which formerly belonged to Narcissus
Luttrell, and since to Mr. Gough, is remarkable for containing the eleven first Catalogues of Books ever sold by
auction in England. What renders it still more curious, is
that the prices of nearly all the articles are added in MS.
When it came into my possession it had suffered so much
from damp, and the leaves were so tender and rotten, that
every time the volume was opened, it was liable to injury. This has been remedied by giving the whole a strong
coat of size. At Willett's sale, Booth, the bookseller of
Duke Street, Portland Place, bought a volume of old
catalogues for £2, 3s. (see Merly Catalogue, 531), and
charged the same in his own shop catalogue for 1815, £21
(6823). It contained merely the eight which stand first
in the present collection, of which Greenhill's and Godolphin's were not priced at all; and Voet's and Sangar's only
partially. However, it enabled me to fill up a few omissions in the prices of my copy of Sangar's.—*N.B.* The
prices of Willett's and the present copy did not always
tally exactly."

Heber paid six shillings for this volume at Gough's
sale in 1810, and Charles Lewis's labours in sizing
and binding in 1824 cost £2, 15s. At Heber's sale
the volume sold for £3.

In April 1680 was sold "the Library of the Right
Hon. George, late Earl of Bristol, a great part of
which were the curiosities collected by the learned
Sir Kenelm Digby, together with the Library of

another Learned person." It is impossible from the catalogue to tell which lots belonged to Sir Kenelm ; and there seems to be little doubt that few of the books which he left in Paris when he came to London, and which were confiscated by the French Government on his death in 1665, were included in this catalogue. According to M. Léopold Delisle,[1] Sir Kenelm's books eventually reached the French national library. The proceeds of the sale of 3878 lots was only £908, and this does not look as if there were many of Digby's books, nobly bound by Le Gascon, in this sale.

In 1681 Edward Millington's name came into notice as the seller, in May of that year, of the libraries of Lawson, Fawkes, Stockden, and Brooks.

Richard Chiswell sold in 1682 the *Bibliotheca Smithiana*, or library of Richard Smith, Secondary of the Poultry Compter, who is better known to us as the author of the useful "Obituary" published by the Camden Society in 1849. This was probably the finest library brought to the hammer up to this date. Oldys wrote of the possessor, that "for many years together [he] suffered nothing to escape him that was rare and remarkable"; and he added, that his "extraordinary library makes perhaps the richest catalogue of any private library we have to show in print, making above four hundred pages in a very broad-leaved and close-printed quarto." Richard Chiswell sold the library in May

---

[1] "Sir Kenelm Digby et les anciens rapports des Bibliothèques françaises avec la Bretagne." Quoted by Mr. Pollard, *Bibliographica*, vol. i. p. 383.

H

"at the auction house known by the name of the
Swan, in Great St. Bartholomew's Close."

The auctioneer made the following remarks in
his Address to the Reader—

"Though it be needless to recommend what to all in-
telligent persons sufficiently commends itself, yet perhaps
it may not be unacceptable to the ingenious to have some
short account concerning this so much celebrated, so often
desired, so long expected library, now exposed to sale.
The gentleman that collected it was a person infinitely
curious and inquisitive after books; and who suffered
nothing considerable to escape him that fell within the
compass of his learning, for he had not the vanity of
desiring to be master of more than he knew how to use.
He lived to a very great age, and spent a good part of it
almost entirely in the search of books. Being as constantly
known every day to walk his rounds through the shops as
he sat down to meals, where his great skill and experience
enabled him to make choice of what was not obvious to
every vulgar eye. He lived in times which ministered
peculiar opportunities of meeting with books that are not
every day brought into publick light; and few eminent
libraries were bought where he had not the liberty to pick
and choose. And while others were forming arms, and
new-modelling kingdoms, his great ambition was to become
master of a good book. Hence arose, as that vast number
of his books, so the choiceness and rarity of the greatest
part of them; and that of all kinds, and in all sorts of
learning. . . . Nor was the owner of them a meer idle
possessor of so great a treasure; for as he generally collated
his books upon the buying them (upon which account the
buyer may rest pretty secure of their being perfect) so he
did not barely turn over the leaves, but observed the defects
of impression, and the ill acts used by many; compared

the differences of editions; concerning which and the like cases, he has entered memorable and very useful remarks upon very many of the books under his own hand : observations wherein, certainly never man was more diligent and industrious. Thus much was thought fit to be communicated to public notice, by a gentleman who was intimately acquainted both with Mr. Smith and his books."

Dibdin condemns the compiler of the catalogue severely, and adds—

"A number of the most curious, rare, and intrinsically valuable books—the very insertion of which in a bookseller's catalogue would probably now make a hundred bibliomaniacs start from their homes by starlight, in order to come in for the first picking—a number of volumes of this description are huddled together in one lot, and all these classed under the provoking running title of 'Bundles of Books,' 'Bundles of stitcht Books.'"[1]

Smith was one of the earliest collectors of Caxtons, and eleven books produced by our first printer sold for £3, 4s. 2d. at his sale. But one of the greatest points of interest connected with Smith's library is that it included the books of Humphrey Dyson, collected at a much earlier date. Hearne notes in his "Collections"—

"That Mr. Rich. Smith's rare and curious collection of books was began first by Mr. Humphrey Dyson, a publick notary, living in the Poultry. They came to Mr. Smith by

---

[1] *Bibliomania* (The Drawing Room).

marriage. This is the same Humphrey Dyson that assisted Howes in his continuation of Stow's 'Survey of London,' ed. folio."

Under date 4th September 1715 Hearne says—

"Mr. Richard Smith's Catalogue that is printed contains a very noble and very extraordinary collection of books. It was begun first in the time of King Hen. VIII., and comeing to Mr. Smith, he was so very diligent and exact in continueing and improving, that hardly anything curious escaped him. He had made the best collection that possibly he could of Erasmus's works."[1]

In another place Hearne describes Dyson as—

"A person of a very strange, prying, and inquisitive genius in the matter of books, as may appear from many libraries; there being books chiefly in old English, almost in every library, that have belonged to him, with his name upon them."[2]

The following interesting entry from Smith's catalogue corroborates Hearne's statement as to Smith's acquisition of Dyson's books—

"115. Six several catalogues of all such books, touching the state ecclesiastical as temporal of the realm of England, which were published upon several occasions, in the reigns of K. Henry the VIIth and VIIIth, Philip and Mary, Q. Elizabeth, K. James and Charles I., collected by Mr. H. Dyson: out of whose library was gathered by Mr. Smith a great part of the rarities of this catalogue."

This lot only fetched seven shillings and six-pence.

[1] *Reliquiæ Hearnianæ*, 1869, vol. i. p. 310.
[2] Peter Langtoft's "Chronicle," vol. i. p. 13.

The number of sales seem now to have increased annually, but it was some years before a library that could rank with Richard Smith's was sold. In April 1683 the books of Brian Walton, Bishop of Chester, were sold (twenty-two years after his death) " by Samuel Carr, at his house of the King's Head in St. Paul's Churchyard." About this time auction sales took place in various parts of the country, and Edward Millington was largely employed as a peripatetic auctioneer. In September 1684 he sold books at Stourbridge Fair (*Bibliotheca Sturbitchiana*). In 1686 two sales occurred at Trumpington (Obadiah Sedgwick in March, and William Whitwood in May) and two at Cambridge (Dr. Edmond Castell in June, and Rev. J. Chamberlaine, of St. John's College, at Stourbridge Fair, in September). When we forget the change that has taken place in the value of money, and express our surprise that rare books should only realise a few shillings, we should note that the cost of the hire of thirteen carts for conveying Dr. Castell's books from Emmanuel College to the sign of the Eagle and Child, where they were sold, was only three shillings.[1] In 1685 and 1686 occurred the famous sales of the stock of Richard Davis, the Oxford bookseller, which was satirised in the *Auctio Davisiana*, noticed in an earlier chapter.

In 1682 William Cooper published a list of booksales up to that date, and again a fuller list in 1687, which contained a note of seventy-four sales in the

---

[1] *Bibliographica*, vol. ii. p. 126.

ten years 1676–86. The following note is printed
on the back of page 33 of *Catalogus Librorum Biblio-
thecæ viri cujusdam Literati*, 14th February 1686–87—

"To gratifie those Gentlemen whose curiosities may lead
them to make perfect their Collection, I have caused to be
printed the names of those persons whose libraries have
been sold by auction, and the series of the time when"
[1676–1686].

This list is reprinted by Hartshorne in his "Book
Rarities of the University of Cambridge," 1829 (pp.
454–57), and it forms the text for two excellent
articles by Mr. A. W. Pollard in *Bibliographica*.

In 1687 Millington sold the valuable library of
Dr. Thomas Jacomb, a Nonconformist minister
(*Bibliotheca Jacombiana*), which realised £1300 ; and
in February of the following year the library of a
counsellor of the Parliaments of Montpelier, which
had been brought from France to be sold in England (*Bibliotheca Mascoviana*).

T. Bentley and B. Walford sold in November 1687
an interesting library of an anonymous but distinguished defunct—*Bibliotheca Illustrissima*, which
is described as follows in the Address to the
Reader—

"If the catalogue here presented were only of common
books and such as were easie to be had, it would not have
been very necessary to have prefaced anything to the reader ;
but since it appears in the world with circumstances which
no auction in England (perhaps) ever had before, nor is it
probable that the like should frequently happen again, it

would seem an oversight if we should neglect to advertise the reader of them. The first is, that it comprises the main part of the library of that famous secretary, William Cecil, Lord Burleigh : which considered, must put it out of doubt that these books are excellent in their several kinds and well chosen. The second is, that it contains a greater number of rare manuscripts than ever yet were offered together in this way, many of which are rendered the more valuable by being remarked upon by the hand of the said great man."

A considerable number of sales took place between this date and the end of the century, but few were of any particular mark until the fine library of Dr. Francis Bernard came to the hammer in 1698.

Millington continued his travels in the country, and sold, among others, the library of Mrs. Elizabeth Oliver at Norwich in 1689, and some modern English books at Abingdon in 1692 ; and John Howell sold the Rev. George Ashwell's library at Oxford in 1696.

Dr. Francis Bernard, physician to St. Bartholomew's Hospital, was also physician to James II. He was a good judge of books, and collected a very fine library, which was sold by auction in October 1698 at his late dwelling in Little Britain. Dibdin says he was "a stoic in bibliography. Neither beautiful binding nor amplitude of margin ever delighted his eye or rejoiced his heart ; for he was a stiff and straightforward reader, and learned in literary history beyond all his contemporaries. His collection was copious and excellent."

The account given of the doctor in the Address

to the Reader prefixed to the catalogue is of considerable interest—

"The character of the person whose collection this was
is so well known, that there is no occasion to say much of
him, nor, to any man of judgment that inspects the Catalogue, of the collection itself. Something, however, it
becomes us to say of both; and this, I think, may with
truth and modesty enough be said, that as few men knew
books, and that part of learning which is called *Historia
Literaria*, better than himself, so there never appeared in
England so choice and valuable a Catalogue to be thus
disposed of as this before us. Certain it is, this library
contains not a few which never appeared in any auction
here before, nor indeed, as I have heard him say, for aught
he knew—and he knew as well as any man living—in any
printed Catalogue in the world. It was very seldom that
he bought any book without some very particular reason.
For if any man died, he certainly knew what we call the
secret history of learning so well, that if there were but
one single passage in an author for which only it was to
be valued, it never escaped him. Being a person who collected his books, and not for ostentation or ornament, he
seemed no more solicitous about their dress than his own;
and therefore you'll find that a gilt back or a large margin
was very seldom any inducement to him to buy. 'Twas
sufficient to him that he had the book. . . . He himself
was not a mere nomenclator, and versed only in title-pages,
but had made that just and laudable use of his books which
would become all those that set up for collectors. . . .
Give me leave to say this of him upon my own knowledge,
that he never grudged his money in procuring, nor his time
or labour in perusing any book which he thought could be
any ways instructive to him; and having the felicity of a
memory always faithful, always officious, which never forsook

him, though attacked by frequent and severe sickness, and by the worst of all diseases, old age, his desire for knowledge attended him to the last, and he pursued his studies with equal vigour and application to the very extremity of his life."

He had thirteen Caxtons, which sold altogether for less than two guineas, less than these books fetched at Richard Smith's sale. A curious volume of Tracts, consisting of "The Bellman's Night Walks" (1632), "The Bellman of London" (1608), "Life of Ned Browne," "Cut Purse," &c., sold for 2s. 8d.; Stubbe's "Anatomie of Abuses" (1585), for 8d.; and Tusser's "Five Hundred Points of Good Husbandry" (1590) for 4d. In spite of these low prices, the total amount of the sale was £1600, the expenses of the sale—4s. in the pound = £320—being deducted.

The catalogue was charged 2s. 6d.

The last sale in the seventeenth century to be recorded is that of John Lloyd, Bishop of St. Davids, sold in 1699 by John Bullord at Tom's Coffee-House.

When auctions were first started conditions of sale were formulated, and with the exception of a little elaboration, they remain pretty much what they were at first; but there were certain peculiarities which are worthy of mention.

The catalogues were not at first divided into day's sales, but as many lots as possible were sold in the time fixed for the sale. The hours were usually from nine to twelve, and from two to six.

Sometimes the sales only took place in the evening. In 1681 we learn that an average sale of 544 lots in a day was considered satisfactory. In the Conditions of Sale printed in the Catalogue of Seaman's library we read—

"That the Auction will begin the 31st of October at the Deceased D^{rs} house in Warwick Court in Warwick Lane punctually at nine Of the Clock in the morning and two in the afternoon, and this to continue daily until all the books be sold."

The early hour was found a disadvantage, and books often sold for low prices at the beginning of sales, so that Cooper was forced to make a rule that the sale should not be commenced unless there were twenty present. At this time biddings of a penny were common.

Two great evils came to light on the first institution of auctions; one was due to the buyers, and the other to the auctioneers. It was found that in cases where the buyer thought he had given more for a book than was wise, he often forgot to pay and fetch away the books. Millington refers specially to this in 1681—

"I question not but the well disposed, and the Learned will give us such incouragement in the Sale by Bidding in some measure to the value of the Books so exposed, as may further incourage and keep on foot such a commendable and serviceable a way of sale (as this of Auction is) to the great purposes of promoting Learning and Knowledge. Which, when I consider, I cannot but wonder that so many persons have appeared at our auctions, and buy with a great freedom to the injury of others (that are truly conscientious to pay for, and fetch away the Books so bought); yet in most auctions have hitherto neglected to fetch away and pay for their own. To the end therefore that they may know, we will not be damaged after so great expences, as inevitably attends the management of an auction; we do intend to prosecute them according to the law if forthwith they do not send for their books, or give us some reasonable satisfaction. To prevent any abuses for the future that may happen to other gentlemen who suffer by this unhandsome practice (of having Books bought out of their hands by persons that never will, or perhaps never designed to fetch them away), we shall, at a convenient time, for the further satisfaction of gentlemen, give an account of their names, and desire their absence if any of them happen to be present." [1]

The other evil was the attempt of the booksellers to get rid of some of their old stock by introducing it into the sales of collectors' libraries. This trick has already been alluded to.

The frequenters of auctions seem to have been very jealous of being bid against by any one interested in the sale. This jealousy found voice in the complaints of Wanley and others at Bridges' sale in 1726.

The lots were not numbered throughout in the catalogues, but the octavos, quartos, and folios were each numbered separately, the number of each section running on from the previous day's sale. This is very confusing, as when you look at the end for the purpose of finding the total number

---

[1] Millington's preface to catalogue of libraries of Lawson, Fawkes, Stockden, and Brooks, 30th May 1681.

of the lots, you only find the number of folios in the sale. Millington found that it was not advisable to bid for books, in case it might be supposed that he was running them up in price, and Mr. Pollard believes that he adopted a plan of getting men to bid for him.

In corroboration of this view Mr. Pollard refers to a copy of the catalogue of the libraries of Button, Owen, and Hoel, 7th November 1681, in the British Museum which belonged to Millington. It has two receipts by persons whose names are among the bidders for money received from Millington for various books. "At first sight this seems a reversal of what we should expect, but after the first few sales the auctioneers had renounced the right of making bids themselves, lest they should be accused of running up prices, and Millington had obviously employed these friends to bid for him." [1]

Another evil connected with auctions comes from *knocks out*, which are thoroughly dishonest, and in fact, criminal, being, as they are, a form of conspiracy, but the agreements of two persons not to bid against one another are not necessarily to be condemned. Mr. Henry Stevens was very urgent against any kind of agreement, and in his reminiscences amusingly describes his frustration of a knock-out ; and it has been said that when the Duke of Roxburghe and Lord Spencer made an agreement, they were parties to a knock-out ; but this view is founded on a fallacy,

----

[1] *Bibliographica*, vol. ii. p. 115.

viz., that whatever price a book fetches at public auction is the proper price. We know, however, that this is not correct; for instance, the Valdarfer *Boccaccio* fetched its huge price at the Roxburghe sale because two great book-buyers with long purses bid against one another. When one of these buyers died and the book was again in the market, seven years after the first sale, the survivor obtained the book at a smaller price. Hence who is to say whether £2260 or £918 is the actual value of the book!

CHAPTER VI

THE sales of the last quarter of the seventeenth century are of the greatest interest in the history of the subject, but they are not of any great value as guides to present prices, for circumstances and tastes have greatly changed. The sales were largely those of the working libraries of theologians, and the books which their owners found of use in their studies sold well, while books in other classes which have now taken their place in public esteem fetched prices which seem to us very small. Among the number of sales noticed in the last chapter, two only stand out as the libraries of true collectors in the modern acceptation of the term, that is, of those who collect for love of the books rather than from an appreciation of their utility. Much the same conditions ruled during the first quarter of the eighteenth century, although the library of Charles Bernard, serjeant-surgeon to Queen Anne and brother of Dr. Francis Bernard, previously referred to, was sold in March 1711 at the Black Boy Coffee-House in Ave Maria Lane, and the sale of the vast collection of Thomas Rawlinson commenced in 1721. Then followed the sale of John Bridges' library in February 1726, but the middle of the century was passed when the great sale of Dr. Richard Mead occurred. This (1754–55), when compared with Askew's sale in 1775, may be said to mark an era in bibliography. These two great physicians were friends with similar tastes. We are, therefore, able to gauge the considerable growth of the taste for book-collecting during the few years that parted these two sales. Askew bought many books at Mead's sale, and when the same volumes came to be sold at his own sale they realised twice and thrice the prices he had given. We shall see in the register of the sales after Askew's day how the prices gradually advanced, until we arrive at the culmination of the bibliomaniacal spirit in the Roxburghe sale of 1812.

We will now enumerate some of the principal sales which took place during the eighteenth century, which led up to the long list of sales which have formed so marked a feature of the nineteenth century.

Charles Bernard's library, sold in 1711, was said by Oldys to contain "the fairest and best editions of the classics." Swift, in his "Journal to Stella" (19th March) wrote, "I went to-day to see poor Charles Bernard's books, and I itch to lay out nine or ten pounds for some fine editions of fine authors"; and on the 29th he adds, "I walked to-day into the city and went to see the auction of poor Charles Bernard's books. They were in the middle of the Physic books, so I bought none; and they are so dear, I believe I shall buy none."

The sale of the library of Thomas Britton, the well-known small-coal man of Clerkenwell, in January 1715, deserves mention on account of the worthiness of its owner. The books were sold by auction at St. Paul's Coffee-House by Thomas Ballard, and the sale catalogue consists of forty closely-printed pages in quarto. There were 664 lots in octavo, 274 in quarto, and 102 in folio, besides 50 pamphlets and 23 manuscripts. This was the second library Britton had collected, for some years before his death he sold the first one by auction.

Thomas Rawlinson (1681–1725) was one of the most insatiable of book collectors, and he left the largest library that had been collected up to his time. His chambers were so filled that his bed had to be moved into a passage, and he took London House, in Aldersgate Street, to accommodate his ever-increasing library. Oldys says of him—

"If his purse had been much wider he had a passion beyond it, and would have been driven to part with what he was so fond of, such a pitch of curiosity or dotage he was arrived at upon a different edition, a fairer copy, a larger paper than twenty of the same sort he might be already possessed of. In short, his covetousness after those books he had not increased with the multiplication of those he had, and as he lived so he died in his bundles, piles, and bulwarks of paper, in dust and cobwebs, at London House." [1]

He did, in fact, commence the sale of his library before his death, and the first part was sold in

---

[1] "Memoir of William Oldys," 1862, p. 101.

December 1721. The catalogue of the whole library occupied sixteen parts, the last being sold in 1734. A complete set of these catalogues is very rare, and the lists of them in the various bibliographical works are mostly incomplete. There is, however, a set in the Bodleian Library. The books in the first five parts sold for £2409, and the manuscripts alone took sixteen days of March 1734 to sell, and went cheap. Hearne writes in his Diary (9th November 1734)—

"The MSS. in Dr. Rawlinson's last auction of his brother Thomas's books went extraordinary cheap, and those that bought had great penny worths. The Doctor purchas'd many himself, at which here and there one were disgusted, tho' all the company supported the Doctor in it, that as a creditor he had a right equal to any other. My friend Mr. Tom Brome, that honest gentleman of Ewithington in Herefordshire in a letter to the Doctor, says that he cannot but wonder at the low rates of most of the MSS., and adds 'had I been in place I should have been tempted to have laid out a pretty deal of money, without thinking myself at all touched with bibliomania.'" [1]

On 10th November Hearne further writes—

"Dr. Rawlinson by the sale of his brother's books hath not rais'd near the money expected. For it seems they have ill answer'd, however good books; the MSS. worse, and what the prints will do is as yet undetermin'd." [2]

It is worthy of mention here that Dr. Rawlinson purchased Hearne's Diaries for a hundred guineas

---

[1] *Reliquiæ Hearnianæ*, 1869, vol. iii. p. 159.
[2] *Ibid.*, p. 160.

from the widow and executrix of Dr. William
Bedford, to whom they had been given by Hearne,[1]
and he bequeathed them with other property to the
University of Oxford. The auctioneers who dis-
persed Thomas Rawlinson's large collections were
Charles Davis and Thomas Ballard.

The sale of the valuable library of John Bridges
at his chambers in Lincoln's Inn by Mr. Cock, in
February 1726, was an event of much literary
interest. The number of lots was 4313, occupying
twenty-seven days, and the total proceeds of the
sale were £4001. This is therefore worthy of note
as the first sale at which the prices averaged nearly
one pound per lot.

There was much dissatisfaction among the buyers
at the high prices, and a conspiracy to "bull" the
market was suspected.

Humphry Wanley expressed his opinion strongly
on this point—

"*Feb.* 9, 1725-6.—Went to Mr. Bridges's chambers, but
could not see the three fine MSS. again, the Doctor his
brother having locked them up. He openly bid for his
own books, merely to enhance their price, and the auction
proves to be, what I thought it would become, very
knavish."

"*Feb.* 11, 1725-6.—Yesterday at five I met Mr. Noel
and tarried long with him; we settled then the whole
affair touching his bidding for my Lord [Oxford] at the
roguish auction of Mr. Bridges's books. The Reverend
Doctor one of the brothers hath already displayed himself

---

[1] Nichols's "Literary Anecdotes," vol. v. p. 490.

so remarkably as to be both hated and despised, and a combination among the booksellers will soon be against him and his brother-in-law, a lawyer. These are men of the keenest avarice, and their very looks (according to what I am told) dart out harping-irons. I have ordered Mr. Noel to drop every article in my Lord's commissions when they shall be hoisted up to too high a price. Yet I desired that my Lord may have the Russian Bible, which I know full well to be a very rare and a very good book." [1]

The frontispiece to the sale catalogue exhibited an oak felled, and persons bearing away the branches, signifying that when the oak is cut down every man gets wood. Nichols, referring to the motto, $\Delta\rho\nu\grave{o}s$ $\pi\epsilon\sigma o\acute{\nu}\sigma\eta s$ $\pi\hat{a}s$ $\grave{a}\nu\eta\rho$ $\xi\nu\lambda\epsilon\acute{\nu}\epsilon\tau a\iota$, speaks of it as "an affecting memento to the collectors of great libraries, who cannot or do not leave them to some public accessible repository." [2]

Besides the sale catalogue, there was a *catalogue raisonné* of Bridges's library, a large paper of which, bound in old blue morocco, and ruled with red lines, Dr. Gosset bought for Dibdin for four shillings, and the latter styles it a happy day when he received it.

In 1731 was sold, at St. Paul's Coffee-House, the extensive library of Anthony Collins, the famous freethinker and author, and a friend of Locke. His books were sold in two divisions. Part 1 of the catalogue contained 3451 lots, and part 2, 3442.

The sale of Dr. Thomas Pellet's library in 1744 is

[1] Wanley's " Diary,'' Lansdowne MS., 808, *quoted* Nichols's " Literary Anecdotes," vol. i. pp. 91–92.
[2] Ibid., vol. ii. p. 106.

of especial interest as the first undertaken by Samuel
Baker, the founder of the house of Sotheby.

In 1746 two sales of note took place, those of
Sir Christopher Wren and Michael Maittaire, the
scholar and bibliographer. The following advertisement of the former is from the *Daily Advertiser*
of 26th October 1748—

"To be sold by auction, by Messrs. Cock and Langford,
in yᵉ Great Piazza, Covent Garden, this and yᵉ following
evening, the curious and entire libraries of yᵉ ingenious
architect Sir Christopher Wren, Knt., and Christopher
Wren, Esq., his son, late of Hampton Court; both deceased. Consisting of great variety of Books of Architecture, Antiquities, Histories, etc., in Greek, Latin, French,
and English; together with some few lots of Prints. The
said books may be viewed at Mr. Cock's in yᵉ Great Piazza
aforesaid, till yᵉ time of sale, which will begin each evening
at 5 o'clock precisely. Catalogues of which may be had
gratis at yᵉ place of sale aforesaid."

Maittaire's library was sold in two parts, in
November 1748 and January 1749, by Mr. Cock,
and occupied· forty-five evenings in the selling.
For some reason or other the books appear to
have been sacrificed, and they realised little more
than £700. One reason was, that they were not
very presentable in appearance. The auctioneer
writes in the "advertisement" to the catalogue—

"Tho' the books in their present condition make not
the most ostentatious appearance, yet like the late worthy
possessor of them, however plain their outside may be,
they contain within an invaluable treasure of ingenuity and
learning. In fine, this is (after fifty years' diligent search

and labour in collecting) the entire library of Mr. Maittaire, whose judgement in the choice of books as it ever was confessed, so are they undoubtedly far beyond whatever I can attempt to say in their praise. In exhibiting them thus to the public, I comply with the will of my deceased friend, and in printing the catalogue from his own copy, just as he left it (tho' by so doing it is more voluminous), I had an opportunity not only of doing the justice I owe to his memory, but also of gratifying the curious."

According to a very interesting account of the sale in Beloe's "Anecdotes" (vol. v. pp. 389–452), it appears that if "the curious" attended the sale, they did not do much to raise the prices. Beloe writes, "The library of Michael Maittaire was of incalculable value, from its great variety, from the number of early printed books which it contained, from the extraordinary collection of Greek and Latin tracts by the famous French printers of the sixteenth century, from the most uncommon books in criticism which it exhibited, and lastly, from the high reputation of its possessor." And, in conclusion, he says, "Such a collection was never before exhibited for public sale, and perhaps never will again."

A striking instance of the absurdly low prices obtained for the books is that of *Homeri Batracho-myomachia* (Venet. per Leonicum Cretensem, 1486, 4to), which sold for sixteen shillings. In this copy a subsequent possessor wrote the following note—

"This book is so extremely rare that I never saw any other copy of it except that of Mons. de Boze, who told me he gave 650 livres for it. Mr. Smith, our consul at

Venice, wrote me word that he had purchased a copy, but
that it was imperfect. Lord Oxford offered Mr. Maittaire
fifty guineas for this identical copy."

Askew's copy, supposed to be the same as this,
fetched at his sale fourteen guineas.

Martialis, apud Vindelinum Spirensem—*sine anno*—
which is described as " one of the rarest of rare
books," only brought four shillings and sixpence.
The *editio princeps* of Plautus (*Venet. per Joh. de
Colonia et Vindelinum Spirensem*, 1472, folio) was
sold for sixteen shillings, while the Pinelli copy
fetched £36. These are no exceptions to the rule,
for Beloe mentions a large number of rare books
which only fetched a shilling or two shillings each.

The great library of Richard Mead, M.D., was
dispersed by Samuel Baker in November and
December 1754 and in April and May 1755. In the
first sale there were 3280 lots in 28 days, which
realised £2475, 18s. 6d. The second sale consisted
of 6741 lots in 29 days, realising £3033, 1s. 6d.,
making the totals for the two sales, 57 days, 10,021
lots, amount of sale £5509. It is usually stated
that Mead's library consisted of 10,000 volumes,
but there must have been at least 30,000 volumes.
The numbering of lots in Mead's sale followed the
confusing rule adopted at the first printing of auction catalogues, viz., the leaving three separate
numberings of octavos, quartos, and folios. As
already said, this was the first really renowned
sale that took place in England, and there can
be little doubt that the owner spent considerably

more money in the collection of his books than they realised after his death. Johnson said of Mead, that he lived more in the broad sunshine of life than almost any man. The dispersion of his library was a loss to the world, for every scholar had been allowed access to it during the owner's life.

The novelist Fielding's library was sold by Baker in 1755. The sale consisted of 653 lots, occupied four nights, and realised £364.

Richard Rawlinson, D.D., younger brother of Thomas Rawlinson, died on the 6th of April 1755, and his large and valuable library was sold by Baker in March of the following year. The sale of the books lasted fifty days, and there was a second sale of pamphlets, books of prints, &c., which occupied ten days. The prices realised for old English literature were very small, and the total of the whole sale was under £1200.

The year 1756 was remarkable for the sale of the library of Martin Folkes by Samuel Baker. It consisted of 5126 lots, and realised £3091. Martin Folkes occupied a prominent position in the literary and scientific worlds as President of the Royal Society and of the Society of Antiquaries. He was more a generally accomplished man than a man of science, and it has been the fashion to laugh at his pretensions to the chair of the Royal Society, but his contemporaries thought well of him. Dr. Jurin, secretary of the Royal Society, said that "The greatest man that ever lived (Sir Isaac Newton) singled him out to fill the chair, and to preside in the Society when he himself was so frequently prevented by indisposition ; and that it was sufficient to say of him that he was Sir Isaac's friend."

Edwards, the ornithologist, said of Folkes—

"He seemed to have attained to universal knowledge, for in the many opportunities I have had of being in his company, almost every part of science has happened to be the subject of discourse, all of which he handled as an adept. He was a man of great politeness in his manners, free from all pedantry and pride, and in every respect the real, unaffected, fine gentleman."

The earliest sale recorded of Samuel Paterson was that of the library of "Orator" Henley, which took place in June 1769, and contained some curious books.

Joseph Smith, British Consul at Venice, was a cultivated book collector. He printed a catalogue of his library in 1755, *Bibliotheca Smitheana, seu Catalogus Librorum D. Josephi Smithii, Angli . . . Venetiis, typis Jo. Baptistæ Pasquali*, MDCCLV. This is of value as containing an appendix to "the prefaces and epistles prefixed to those works in the library which were printed in the fifteenth century." George III. bought the whole library, and added it to his own matchless collection. On the sale of his library Consul Smith set to work to collect another, and in 1773, a year after his death, this second library was sold by auction by Baker & Leigh, occupying thirteen days in the selling. The books were described as being "in the finest preservation, and consisting of the very best and scarcest editions of the Latin, Italian, and French authors, from the Invention of Printing, with manuscripts and missals upon vellum, finely illuminated." The last day's sale contained all the English books in black letter. This fine library realised £2245, not so large an amount as might have been expected. In fact, Dibdin says in his *Bibliomania* that Mr. Cuthell exclaimed in his hearing that "they were given away."

In this same year, 1773, was sold the splendid library of James West, President of the Royal Society, the catalogue of which was digested by Samuel Paterson. The preface informs the reader that "the following catalogue exhibits a very curious and uncommon collection of printed books and travels, of British history and antiquities, and of rare old English literature, the most copious of any which has appeared for several years past; formed with great taste and a thorough knowledge of authors and characters." There were 4633 lots, and they occupied twenty-four days in the selling, the auctioneer being Langford. West's large collection of manuscripts was sold to the Earl of Shelburne, and is now in the British Museum.

Although this sale attracted much attention, and was well attended, the prices did not rule high according to our present ideas, but doubtless it was not thought then that the following Caxtons realised less than their value : Chaucer's Works, first edition by Caxton, £47, 15s. 6d. ; "Troylus and Cresseyde," £10, 10s. ; "Book of Fame," £4, 5s. ; "Gower de Confessione Amantis," 1483, £9, 9s.

Dibdin has given a very full analysis of this fine library in his *Bibliomania*. In contrast to this sale may be mentioned, on account of the distinction of the owner, the library of Oliver Goldsmith, which was sold on 12th July 1774 by Mr. Good of Fleet Street. There were 162 lots, and Mr. Forster has reprinted the catalogue in his "Life of Goldsmith" (vol ii. p. 453).

A very curious library was sold in this same year (1774) by Paterson. The title of the catalogue describes it as follows—

"A Catalogue of rare books and tracts in various languages and faculties, including the Ancient Conventual Library of Missenden Abbey in Buckinghamshire, together with some choice remains of that of the late eminent Sergeant at Law, William Fletewode, Esq., Recorder of London in the reign of Queen Elizabeth ; among which are several specimens of the earliest typography, foreign and English, including Caxton, Wynkyn de Worde, Pynson, and others; a fine collection of English history, some scarce old law books, a great number of old English plays, several choice MSS. upon vellum, and other subjects of literary curiosity. . . ."

It will be seen from this that works of our early printers were beginning to come into vogue, but they did not fetch very high prices, varying from five pounds to eight guineas. Two copies of the first edition of Bacon's "Essays," 1597, went for sixpence.

In 1775 one of the finest sales of the century took place at the auction rooms of Baker & Leigh, that of Anthony Askew, M.D. (1722-1772), whose ambition it was to have every edition of a Greek author. His library largely consisted of classics, and most of the books were in good condition. There were 3570 lots sold in twenty-two days, which realised £3993, or about £1 per lot. Mead's library consisted of 10,021 lots, which realised £5509, or a little over half the average amount per lot obtained at Askew's sale. As the character of Mead's and Askew's libraries was somewhat similar, the difference may be partly accounted for by the increased price of good books in the interval between the two sales.

Mr. Christie sold in March 1776 the valuable library of a very remarkable book-collector, John Ratcliffe, who kept a chandler's shop in the Borough. It is said that he bought some of his treasures by weight in the way of his business. His skill as a collector was recognised by his brother collectors, and on Thursday mornings he was in the habit of giving breakfasts at his house in East Lane, Rotherhithe, and to them Askew, Croft, Topham Beauclerk, James West, and others, were constant visitors. At these breakfasts he displayed his latest purchases. He was a very corpulent man, and a few years before his death, when a fire happened in his neighbourhood, and his furniture and books were removed for safety, he was unable to help those who were engaged in the task. He stood lamenting the loss of his Caxtons, when a sailor, who heard him, attempted to console him, and cried, "Bless you, sir, I have got them perfectly safe." While Ratcliffe was expressing his thanks, the sailor produced two of his fine curled periwigs which he had saved. He had no idea that a man could make such a fuss over a few books.[1]

There were nine days' sale of 1675 lots. The Caxtons numbered thirty, and realised an average of £9 each.

Topham Beauclerk, the fashionable friend of Dr. Johnson, collected a very large library, which was distributed by Paterson in 1781. There were thirty thousand volumes, which took fifty days to sell. The library was rich in English plays, English history, travels, and antiquities, but there were not many high-priced books.

The sale of the library of the Rev. Thomas Crofts in 1783, also by Paterson, was a much more important event. It consisted of 8360 lots, distributed over forty-three days, and realised £3453. We are told in the preface to the sale catalogue that—

"The great reputation which the late Rev. and learned Mr. Crofts had acquired, with respect to bibliographical knowledge, cannot be better established than by the following digest of his excellent library, in which no pains have been spared to render it worthy the character of the collector, and such as he himself, it is presumed, would not have disapproved. The collection on the 'Origin of Letters,' and of Grammars and Dictionaries, is admirable, and much fuller of curious books than is to be found in many libraries of the first description. The theological divisions comprehend many curious and valuable articles. . . . The classical part of the library is indeed a treasure of

---

[1] Dibdin's " Reminiscences," vol. i. p. 327 (note).

Greek and Roman learning, comprising many of the early editions, almost all the Aldine editions, and those of the best modern commentators."

Other classes well represented in the library were Italian poetry, novels and plays, Spanish and Portuguese poetry, &c., history, topography, antiquities, and voyages and travels. There is a portrait of Mr. Crofts in Clarke's *Repertorium Bibliographicum*.

In this same year, 1783, was sold by Mr. Compton the elegant and curious library of an eminent collector (Joseph Gulston), which contained a considerable number of books printed on large paper, and well bound. The library is described in the catalogue as "undoubtedly the most select ever offered to the public for beauty, scarcity, and condition." There were eleven days' sale of 2007 lots, which realised £1750. In 1784 the remaining portion of Mr. Gulston's library was sold by the same auctioneer. This consisted chiefly of a fine collection of English typography, and the 784 lots occupied four days in the selling.

Dr. Samuel Johnson's library, which was sold in 1785, was not a very valuable one. It consisted of 650 lots, which sold for £100. Among them was the second Shakespeare folio, now in the possession of Sir Henry Irving.

In 1785 Dr. Askew's collection of manuscripts were sold, ten years after the printed books, when they realised £1827. When Askew died in 1774 they were offered to a collector for two thousand guineas, but the price was considered too large.

The library of Major Thomas Pearson (1740–1781) was sold by T. & J. Egerton in 1788. The sale extended over twenty-three days, and consisted of 5525 lots. This library was very rich in old English literature, and contained two volumes of original ballads, which were bought by the Duke of Roxburghe for £36, 4s. 6d., and with the Duke's additions are now safely preserved in the British Museum.

The famous Pinelli library, founded by John Vincent Pinelli in the sixteenth century, and augmented by his descendants (the last possessor was Maffeo Pinelli, a learned printer at Venice, who died in 1785), was bought in 1788 by Messrs. Robson & Edwards, booksellers, for about £7000; and on being brought to London was sold by auction in Conduit Street in two divisions—the first, in March and April 1789, consisted of sixty days' sale, and the second, in February and March 1790, of thirty-one days. The total number of lots was 14,778, and they realised £9356, which did not allow much profit to the purchasers after payment of duties, carriage, and costs of the sale. The library was very rich in Greek and Latin classics, and Italian literature generally. The chief lot was the *Complutensian Polyglot* (6 vols. folio, 1514–17), printed on vellum, which fetched £483.

The sale of the choice library of M. Paris de Meyzieux (Bibliotheca Parisina), which took place in March 1791, is worthy of special record in that the prices realised averaged considerably more than in any previous sale, and has seldom been equalled even in our own day. The title of the English catalogue is as follows—

"A Catalogue of a Collection of Books formed by a Gentleman in France, not less conspicuous for his taste in distinguishing than his zeal in acquiring whatever of this kind was most perfect, curious, or scarce : it includes many first editions of the classics : books magnificently printed on vellum with illuminated paintings ; manuscripts on vellum, embellished with rich miniatures ; books of natural history, with the subjects coloured in the best manner or with the original drawings and books of the greatest splendour and rareness in the different classes of literature. To these are added from another grand collection, selected articles of high value. The whole are in the finest condition, and in bindings superlatively rich."

The library was bought from the executors of Mons. Paris by M. Laurent of Paris and Mr. James Edwards, and brought to London to be sold. There were six days' sale, and the 636 lots realised £7095, 17s. 9d., or a little over eleven pounds per lot. One of the most beautiful books in the sale was the *Opere* of Petrarch, 1514, printed on vellum, with charming miniatures attributed to Giulio Clovio. Six of these were the Triumphs of Love, Chastity, Death, Fame, Time, and the Deity. The borders of the pages were ornamented with 174 exquisite miniatures of birds, beasts, fishes, monsters, fabulous histories, and various compositions of the greatest ingenuity. This splendid folio volume fetched £116, 11s. A similar book, but apparently much less elaborate, a vellum Aristotle, recently fetched £800 at the Ashburnham sale.

The library of Michael Lort, D.D., F.R.S., was
sold by Leigh & Sotheby in this same year, 1791;
it contained a large number of interesting books,
particularly those on English history and antiquities,
many of which were enriched with MS. notes by
the Rev. George North. There were 6665 lots,
which occupied twenty-five days in the selling, but
the amount realised (£1269) was not large for so
considerable a collection.

In 1792 a great sale occurred at Dublin ; it was of
the library of the Right Hon. Denis Daly, and was
dispersed under the hammer of James Vallance.
There is a good description of the library in the
Gentleman's Magazine (1792, Part I., pp. 326–28),
but although Dibdin gives in his *Bibliomania* a
notice of some of the books, he does not record the
prices of several of the most interesting items mentioned in the *Gentleman's Magazine*. The number
of lots was 1441, which realised £3700. The library
was purchased entire from the executors of Mr.
Daly by John Archer and William Jones, two
Dublin booksellers, and the former told Dibdin
that Lord Clare offered £4000 for it before the
auction sale, but this offer was refused.

The Earl of Bute's botanical library was sold by
Leigh & Sotheby in 1794 for £3470. It was a ten
days' sale.

The first part of Thomas Allen's library was dispersed in June 1795, and the second part in 1799,
both parts coming under the hammer of Leigh and
Sotheby. There were in all 3460 lots sold during
nineteen days, which realised £5737.

The sale of the library of George Mason commenced in January 1798, and continued till 1807, when the fifth part was sold. The first part contained 497 lots (three days), which realised £620 ; the second part 480 lots (three days), £784 ; the third part 547 lots (three days), £670 ; the fourth part, sold in 1799, 338 lots (two days), £586. All were sold by Leigh & Sotheby. The four parts contained 1862 lots, and the total amount of the sale was £2663. The fifth part, sold in 1807, contained few lots of any importance.

The library of Richard Farmer, D.D., sold by Mr. King in May 1798, was a peculiarly interesting one, as containing a rich collection of early English poetry, of which he was one of the earliest purchasers. Although he employed agents to purchase for him, he was not very liberal, and is said to have made a rule not to exceed three shillings for any book. The number of lots in the sale was 8199, and thirty-six days were occupied in selling them. The total amount of the sale was £2210, and the library is supposed to have cost Dr. Farmer in collecting about £500.

Dr. Farmer (1735-1797), author of the famous " Essay on the Learning of Shakspeare," and for two-and-twenty years Master of Emanuel College, Cambridge, was a curious character, who was said to have loved three things—old port, old clothes, and old books. It was further said that there were three things which nobody could persuade him to do, viz., to rise in the morning, to go to bed at night, and to settle an account. He is said to have

K

imbibed his passion for collecting books from Dr.
Askew. Dr. Parr, who composed his Latin epitaph,
wrote of him—

"How shall I talk of thee, and of thy wonderful collection, O rare Richard Farmer?—of thy scholarship, acuteness, pleasantry, singularities, varied learning, and colloquial
powers! Thy name will live long among scholars in general,
and in the bosoms of virtuous and learned bibliomaniacs
thy memory shall ever be enshrined! The walls of Emanuel
College now cease to convey the sounds of thy festive
wit; thy volumes are no longer seen, like Richard Smith's
'bundles of stitcht books,' strewn upon the floor; and thou
has ceased in the cause of thy beloved Shakespeare to delve
into the fruitful ore of black letter literature. Peace to thy
honest spirit; for thou wert wise without vanity, learned
without pedantry, and joyous without vulgarity."

Dr. Farmer at one time proposed to have had a
catalogue taken of his library, to which he intended
to have prefixed the following advertisement—

"This Collection of Books is by no means to be considered as an essay towards a perfect Library; the circumstances and the situation of the Collector made such an
attempt both unnecessary and impracticable. Here are
few publications of great price which were already to be
found in the excellent Library of Emanuel College; but
it is believed that not many private collections contain a
greater number of really curious and scarce books; and
perhaps no one is so rich in the antient philological
English literature.—R. FARMER."

CHAPTER VII

THE sales of the nineteenth century are so numerous, that they must be treated in a more summary manner than those of the two previous centuries. The Roxburghe sale in 1812 marks an era in bibliography, and after it a series of valuable sales occurred until about the middle of the century, when there was a certain period of dulness, although great sales like those of the libraries of the Duke of Sussex and the Duke of Buckingham (Stowe) took place. In 1864 the fine library of George Daniel was dispersed, when many editions of Shakespeare's plays, and much valuable dramatic literature, were sold at high prices. In 1873 was the great sale of Henry Perkins's library, in 1881-83 the Sunderland sale, and in 1882-84 the Beckford and Hamilton sales. These three sales deserve an historian, such as the Roxburghe sale had in Dibdin; but although they created a great sensation, they have not been written about as the Roxburghe sale was. The effect of the high prices realised at these sales has been to cause a great number of fine libraries to be brought to the hammer. The century opened with the sale by Mr. King of the valuable library of

George Steevens, the Shakespearian commentator, which commenced on 13th May 1800, and continued during the ten following days. There were 1943 lots, which realised £2740. Useful lists of some of the most interesting books in the sale are given in Dibdin's *Bibliomania* and Clarke's *Repertorium Bibliographicum*. The whole of the library was sold, with the exception of an illustrated copy of Shakespeare, bequeathed to Earl Spencer, the corrected copy of Steevens's edition of Shakespeare to Mr. Reed, and a fine set of Hogarth's prints, in three volumes, to the Right Hon. William Windham.

The sale of the library of Greffier Fagel of the Hague was announced for sale in 1802, but instead of coming to auction it was sold entire to Trinity College, Dublin, for £7000. A catalogue, digested by Samuel Paterson, in two parts, was printed in 1806.

The very valuable library of Robert Heathcote was sold by Leigh, Sotheby & Son in 1802 and 1808. The first sale, on 8th April 1802 and five following days, was described as "an elegant collection of books, comprising a very extraordinary assemblage of the Greek and Roman classics, and other books in the English, French, and Italian languages; the greater part upon large paper, and the whole in fine condition, in morocco and other splendid bindings." The number of lots was 958, which realised £3361.

The second part was described as "a portion of the singularly elegant library, late the property of a very distinguished amateur [R. H.], likewise a few duplicates belonging to the present possessor [John Dent]. . . . The books are almost universally bound in different coloured morocco, by Roger Payne and other eminent binders." This sale took place on 4th April 1808 and five following days, and consisted of 858 lots, which fetched £2469.

The third sale took place on 2nd May 1808 and following day, when 222 lots were sold for £1246. The books are described as bound by "the most eminent English and French binders." The totals of the three sales were 2038 lots, which realised £7076.

The sale of the library of John Woodhouse, which was carried out by Leigh, Sotheby & Son, on 12th December 1803 and four following days, was one of great interest. The books were in fine condition, and besides works on English history, topography, &c., there was a good collection of old English poetry and romances. There were 862 lots, and the amount realised was £3135.

James Edwards, who commenced bookselling in Pall Mall about the year 1784, was in 1788 the joint purchaser with James Robson, bookseller, of New Bond Street, of the Pinelli library. He retired to the Manor House, Harrow, some years before his death, and gathered around him a very choice collection of books. He is mentioned in the index to Nichols's "Literary Anecdotes" (1813) as the possessor, "with numberless other literary treasures," of the famous Bedford Missal. On 25th April 1804 and three following days Mr. Christie sold a selection from his library, which was described as "a most splendid and valuable collection of books, superb missals, original drawings, &c., the genuine property of a gentleman of distinguished taste, retiring into the country." There were only 339 lots, which fetched £4640, or nearly £14 per lot, a very considerable average, but then the books were highly distinguished. Dibdin gives, in part 5 of his *Bibliomania*, a list of some of the more important items, and in part 6 a notice of the large number of books printed on vellum, in the collection. Dibdin does not, however, mention that it belonged to James Edwards.

On 5th April 1815 and five following days Mr. Evans sold "the valuable library of James Edwards, Esq., containing a splendid assemblage of early printed books, chiefly on vellum, highly curious and important manuscripts, magnificent books of prints," &c. In this sale was the Bedford Missal, which was bought by the Marquis of Blandford for £687. There were 830 lots, which sold for £8421, or rather more than £10 per lot. Edwards died on 2nd January 1816, aged fifty-nine years.

The library of the first Marquis of Lansdowne (previously Earl of Shelburne) was sold by Leigh & Sotheby in January and February 1806. The sale occupied thirty-one days, and contained 6530 lots, which realised £6701. Amongst the books was a very rare collection of tracts, documents, and pamphlets relating to the French Revolution, in more than 280 volumes, which sold for £168. In 1807 the Marquis's collection of manuscripts were catalogued for sale, but they never came to auction, as they were purchased by Parliament for the British Museum for £6000.

The Rev. Jonathan Boucher (1738–1804) possessed a large library, which was sold by Leigh & Sotheby in three parts for a total of £4510. Part 1, 24th February 1806 and twenty-six following days, 6646 lots sold for £2990. Part 2, 14th April 1806 and eight following days, 1940 lots sold for £815. Part 3, 29th May 1809 and three following days, 857 lots sold for £704. The library was full of valuable and useful books in divinity, history, voyages and travels, poetry, classics, &c., but there were few books of extreme rarity. Dibdin says in his *Bibliomania*—

"I attended many days during this sale, but such was the warm fire, directed especially towards divinity, kept up during nearly the whole of it, that it required a heavier weight of metal than I was able to bring into the field of battle to ensure any success in the contest."

The extensive library of the Rev. John Brand was sold by Mr. Stewart in two parts. Part 1, in May and June 1807, 8611 lots and MSS. 294 lots, in thirty-seven days, sold for £4300. Part 2, February 1808, 4064 lots sold for £1851. The last lot in the first part of the sale was Brand's own work on "Popular Antiquities," with additions prepared for republication, which, with copyright, sold for £630. The books were in poor condition, and had been mostly bought for small sums; in addition, no money was expended by the proprietor on the binding of his books.

On the twenty-fourth day's sale Dr. Gosset found in one of the volumes of Menage's French Dictionary sixty-five pounds in bank-notes, and a rare portrait of Margaret Smith, engraved by W. Marshall, which was subsequently sold for twenty-seven guineas. Previous to the removal of the library from Somerset House, where Brand lived as secretary of the Society of Antiquaries, Stewart, the auctioneer, found by accident in an old waste-paper volume seventy guineas wrapped up in paper and placed in various parts of the book. The money was handed to Mr. Brand's executor.

Isaac Reed's interesting library of old English literature was sold by King & Lochée in November and December 1807. The sale occupied thirty-nine days, and consisted of 8957 lots, which realised £4386.

A five days' sale of Lord Penrhyn's library at Leigh & Sotheby's in March 1809 brought £2000.

In June 1809 Leigh & Sotheby sold the library of Richard Porson, which consisted of 1931 lots, and realised £1254. A list of the prices given for the principal classics in this sale is printed in the *Classical Journal* (i. 385-90).

The eminent antiquary Richard Gough bequeathed his collection of British topography to the Bodleian Library, but the rest of his library was sold by Leigh & Sotheby in April 1810 during twenty days. There were 4373 lots, which sold for £3552.

The Rev. Benjamin Heath, D.D., sold his very fine library during his lifetime to Joseph Johnson, bookseller, of St. Paul's Churchyard, who consigned it to Mr. Jeffery in 1810 to be sold by auction. The sale consisted of 4786 lots, and realised £8899. Dibdin describes this sale in enthusiastic terms in his *Bibliomania*. He writes—

"Never did the bibliomaniac's eye alight upon 'sweeter copies,' as the phrase is, and never did the bibliomaniacal barometer rise higher than at this sale! The most marked phrensy characterised it. A copy of the *editio princeps* of Homer (by no means a first-rate one) brought £92, and all the Aldine classics produced such an electricity of sensation, that buyers stuck at nothing to embrace them! Do not let it hence be said that black letter lore is the only fashionable pursuit of the present age of book collectors. This sale may be hailed as the omen of better and brighter prospects in literature in general; and many a useful philological work, although printed in the Latin or Italian language—and which had been sleeping unmolested upon a bookseller's shelf these dozen years — will now start up from its slumber, and walk abroad in a new atmosphere, and be noticed and 'made much of.'"

We now arrive at the year 1812, which will ever be memorable in bibliographical annals on account of the sale of the grand library of the Duke of Roxburghe during forty-six days. The catalogue was arranged by Messrs. G. & W. Nicol, and in the preface we read—

"When literature was deprived of one of its warmest admirers by the death of the Duke of Roxburghe, his grace was in full pursuit of collecting our dramatic authors. But when his collection of English plays is examined, and the reader is informed that he had only turned his mind to this class of literature for a few years, his indefatigable industry will be readily admitted."

Mr. Robert H. Evans, the bookseller of Pall Mall, was induced to commence the business of auctioneer with his sale, and he continued to sell by auction for over thirty years.

The Roxburghe library consisted of 10,120 lots, which sold for £23,397. Although one of the finest libraries ever brought to the hammer, the glory of the majority of the books was eclipsed by the Valdarfer *Boccaccio*, 1471, which fetched £2260, the largest sum ever paid for a book up to that time. It has been said that the amount of the *Boccaccio* day's sale equalled what had been given by the Duke for the entire collection.[1]

Leigh & Sotheby sold in May 1812 the library of the Marquis Townshend, during sixteen days, for £5745.

The splendid library of Colonel Stanley was sold by Evans in April and May 1813, during eight days. There were 1136 lots (or above 3000 volumes), which sold for £8236. A unique copy of De Bry's Voyages, with duplicates of parts x. and xi. and a large number of duplicate plates, bound in blue morocco, sold for £546. Brunet wrote that at this sale the thermometer of the bibliomania reached its highest point.

The library of Stanesby Alchorne, of the Mint, was bought entire by Earl Spencer, who sold at Evans's, in 1813, the portion which he did not

---

[1] Dibdin's "Reminiscences," vol. i. p. 369 (note).

require, and added to the sale some of his own duplicates. There were only 187 lots in this sale, and they sold for £1769.

Leigh & Sotheby sold the library of the Rev. Isaac Gosset, a constant attendant on book-sales, in 1813 (the year after his death), during twenty-three days. There were 5740 lots, which sold for £3141. Gosset (the Lepidus of Dibdin) was much attached to Richard Heber, whom he regarded as his pupil.

In this same year (1813) the famous Merly library (Ralph Willett) was sold by Leigh & Sotheby. There were seventeen days, and 2906 lots, which sold for £13,508. It was said at the time that if ever there was a unique collection this was one.

A choice and small library of a well-known collector (John Hunter) was sold in this same year by Leigh & Sotheby, in a three days' sale, with 405 lots, which realised £1344.

Messrs. King & Lochée sold the library of John Horne Tooke, 1813. There were four days, and 1813 lots, which fetched £1250.

In 1814 and 1815 the library of John Towneley was sold by Evans. Part 1 in June 1814, seven days, 904 lots, amount of sale £5890. Part 2, June 1815, ten days, 1703 lots, amount of sale £2707, or a total for the two parts of £8597. The Towneley Mysteries sold for £147. A small remaining portion of the Towneley library was sold by Evans in 1817.

Mr. Towneley's collection of drawings, prints, books of prints, &c., was sold by Mr. King in 1816 for £1414, and a collection of the works of Hollar, also by Mr. King, in May 1818 for £2108.

In 1816 there were several fine sales. Evans sold Edward Astle's library, which occupied two days' sale, and consisted of 265 lots, realising £2366 ; Dr. Vincent's, Dean of Westminster, library, in six days' sale, 1176 lots, which sold for £1390 ; and the library of Marshal Junot, which consisted chiefly of books printed on vellum—the 139 lots sold for £1397; but this fact by itself is misleading, insomuch that the books of more than half that value were bought in, viz., £779, making those sold amount only to £618.

Messrs. Leigh & Sotheby sold in 1816 the library of Prince Talleyrand, which was described as *Bibliotheca splendissima.* There were eighteen days' sale, and the amount realised was £8399.

In this same year (1816) Mr. J. G. Cochrane sold the Gordonstoun library of Sir Robert Gordon. It contained 2421 lots, occupying twelve days in the selling, and realising £1539. This sale is specially alluded to by Mr. Hill Burton in his " Book-Hunter" as a remarkable exception to the rule that great book-sales seldom " embrace ancestral libraries accumulated in old houses from generation to generation." This library " was begun by Sir Robert Gordon, a Morayshire laird of the time of the great civil wars of the seventeenth century. He was the author of the ' History of the Earldom of Sutherland,' and a man of great political as well as literary account. He laid by heaps of the pamphlets, placards, and other documents of his stormy period, and thus many a valuable morsel, which had otherwise disappeared from the world, left a representative in the Gordonstoun collection. It was increased by a later Sir Robert, who had the reputation of being a wizard. He belonged to one of those terrible clubs from which Satan is entitled to take a victim annually ; but when Gordon's turn came, he managed to get off with merely the loss of his shadow."

William Roscoe's fine library was also sold in 1816 by Winstanley of Liverpool. There were 1918 lots, and fourteen days' sale, the amount realised being £5150.

It is worthy of mention that in 1817 Evans sold the library of Count Borromeo of Padua, and that the books were very fully described in the catalogue. In one instance a book which only sold for half-a-crown was described in fourteen lines. The catalogue of 324 lots occupied seventy-seven octavo pages. The total proceeds of the sale were £726.

The cataloguing of the time was not affected by this example, and it was many years before full descriptions were given in sale catalogues. M. Libri's annotated catalogues of 1859–62 set the new fashion.

The book sales from this date become so very numerous, that it is impossible in the space at our disposal to register more than a few of the most important, and these must be recorded quite succinctly.

The sale of Edmond Malone's library at Sotheby's in 1818 occupied eight days, and brought £1649.

The great sale by Evans of James Bindley's

library, which was particularly rich in early English literature, was spread over several years. Part 1, December 1818, twelve days, 2250 lots, amount of sale £3046. Part 2, January 1819, twelve days, 2588 lots, amount realised £4631. Part 3, February 1819, eleven days, 2321 lots [amount not given in Evans's sale catalogues in the British Museum.] Part 4, August 1820, books, six days, 1132 lots, amount £2253. [Part 5] omissions, January 1821, five days, 1092 lots [no totals given].

Bindley's portraits, prints and drawings, and medals were sold by Sotheby in 1819. Part 1, Bindley Granger. Part 2, portraits. Part 3, prints and drawings. [Part 4], medals. These realised £7692.

John North's library was sold in 1819 by Evans in three parts. Part 1, nine days, 1497 lots, £4285. Part 2, twelve days, 2175 lots, £5679. Part 3, four days, 842 lots, £2842. Total, £12,806.

Evans sold George Watson Taylor's library in 1823. Part 1, six days, 965 lots, £3850. Part 2, eight days, 1207 lots, £4926.

The great Fonthill Abbey sale (Beckford's collection) occurred in 1823. The sale occupied thirty-seven days, of which twenty were taken up with the disposal of the library of 20,000 volumes. The auctioneer was Mr. Phillips of New Bond Street, and the place of sale was the Abbey.

George Nassau's library was sold by Evans in 1824. Part 1, twelve days, 2603 lots, £4894. Part 2, eight days, 1661 lots, £3611.

A still finer library than this was sold in the same

year by Evans, that of Sir Mark Masterman Sykes, Bart. Part 1, eleven days, 1676 lots, £9505. Part 2, six days, 825 lots, £4580. Part 3, eight days, 1190 lots, £4644, making a total of 3691 lots, which realised £18,729.

Almost a rival to this was the sale by Evans in 1827 of the library of John Dent, F.R.S. Part 1, nine days, 1502 lots, £6278. Part 2, nine days, 1474 lots, £8762. Totals, 2976 lots, and £15,040.

In 1827 the library of the Duke of York was sold at Sotheby's for £5718.

The Earl of Guilford's library was sold by Evans in seven parts in the years 1828, 1829, 1830, and 1835. There were forty days and 8511 lots, and the total amount realised was £12,175. These totals were made up as follows :—Part 1 (1828), nine days, 1788 lots, £1665. Part 2 (1829), six days, 1459 lots, £1757. Part 3 (1829), three days, 740 lots, £880. Manuscript (1830), five days, 679 lots, £4441. Library from Corfu : Part 1 (1830), five days, 1124 lots, £998. Part 2 (1831), four days, 722 lots, £678. Remaining portion (1835), eight days, 1999 lots, £1756.

The great sale of George Hibbert's library by Evans was commenced in 1829, forty-two days' sale, 8794 lots, £6816.

Evans sold in 1831 the small but fine library of the Duchesse de Berri, who is described on the catalogue as an " Illustrious Foreign Personage." There were five days, and 846 lots, which realised £5160.

In 1832 Evans sold the library of Philip Hurd

for £5545. There were 1464 lots, which occupied eight days in selling.

In this same year the choicer portion of John Broadley's library was sold, also by Evans. There were 589 lots in three days' sale, which realised £2052. The second portion was sold during six days in 1833, 1225 lots, which realised £3707.

Joseph Haslewood's library was sold by Evans in 1833. This was an eight days' sale, consisting of 1855 lots, which realised £2471. The amount was probably more than the late proprietor expected, as he said he would refuse a thousand pound cheque in exchange for his books. Dibdin remarks in his "Reminiscences" on the fact that Haslewood always intended that his books should be sold by Sotheby. He was in the habit of saying, "What will Sam Sotheby make of this or that after I am gone?"

In 1833 and 1834 the library of P. A. Hanrott was sold by Evans in five parts, and during forty-seven days, for £22,409. There were 10,826 lots. These totals are obtained as follows :—Part 1 (1833), twelve days, 2504 lots, £7487. Part 2 (1833), twelve days, 2574 lots, £5161. Part 3 (1834), twelve days, 2753 lots, £5727. Part 4 (1834), six days, 1489 lots, £2845. Part 5 (1834), five days, 1506 lots, £1189.

The great sale of the library of Richard Heber took place during the years 1834, 1835, and 1836. Mr. H. Foss has written the following totals for the twelve parts in a copy of the catalogue in the British Museum. Two hundred and two days of sale, 52,676 lots, 119,613 volumes, which sold for £56,774. The proportionate total cost to Mr. Heber of the library is put at £77,750. The following are the particulars of the various parts :—Part 1, April and May 1834, sold by Sotheby & Son, twenty-six days, 7486 lots, £5615. Part 2, June and July (Sotheby), twenty-five days, 6590 lots, £5958. Part 3, November (Sotheby), seventeen days, 5055 lots, £2116. Part 4, December, sold by R. H. Evans, fifteen days, 3067 lots, £7248. Part 5, January and February 1835, sold by B. Wheatley, twenty days, 5693 lots, £2623. Part 6, March and April (Evans), twenty days, 4666 lots, £6771. Part 7, May and June (Evans), twenty-one days, 6797 lots, £4035. Part 8, February and March 1836 (Evans), twelve days, 3170 lots, £3955. Part 9, April (Sotheby), fourteen days, 3218 lots, £6463. Part 10, May and June (Sotheby), fourteen days, 3490 lots, £2117. Part 11, manuscripts (Evans), ten days, 1717 lots, £8964. Part 12, July (Wheatley), eight days, 1727 lots, £894. Part 13 (and last) was sold in February 1837 by Wheatley, six days, 1558 lots, £780. This amount must be added to the totals of the twelve parts given above.

In 1835 the remarkable collection of Dr. Kloss of Frankfort was sold by Sotheby & Son. It contained many original and unpublished manuscripts and printed books, with MS. annotations attributed to Philip Melancthon. There were 4682 lots, which took twenty days to sell, and realised £2261. The catalogue was the work of Samuel Leigh Sotheby, and he expended much labour upon it.

Evans sold in 1835 the fine library of the Comte de Noailles, who is described in the catalogue as "a distinguished collector." There were 952 lots, sold in five days for £3188.

The Hon. Baron (Sir William) Bolland's library was sold by Evans in 1840. The sale consisted of 2940 lots, and occupied thirteen days, realising £3019. In the next year was sold, also by Evans, the library of Thomas Hill (supposed to be the original of Paul Pry), during seven days. There were 1684 lots, which brought £1424.

The library of George Chalmers, F.R.S., was sold by Evans in 1841 and 1842, and the catalogue was divided into three parts. Part 1, September and October 1841, nine days, 2292 lots, £2190. Part 2, March 1842, six days, 1514 lots, £1918. Part 3, November 1842, eight days, 1966 lots, £2081.

Horace Walpole's collections were sold at Strawberry Hill by George Robins in April and May 1842, during twenty-four days. The first six days were devoted to the sale of the library, which consisted of 1555 lots, and realised £3900. It was very badly catalogued, and the books and books of prints, collection of portraits, &c., forming the seventh and eighth days' sale, were withdrawn, re-catalogued, and extended to a ten days' sale.

The library of Lord Berwick was sold at Sotheby's in April and May 1843 for £6726.

The great sale of the years 1844 and 1845, at Evans's, was that of the extensive library of the Duke of Sussex, which occupied sixty-one days in selling, and consisted of 14,107 lots. The total amount realised was £19,148. The sale was divided into six parts, as follows :—Part 1, July 1844, theology, twenty-four days, 5551 lots, £8438. Part 2, July and August 1844, manuscripts, four days, 510 lots, £3126. Part 3, August 1844, history, topography, voyages and travels, six days, 1523 lots, £2096. Part 4, January and February 1845, Greek classics, foreign history, &c., eleven days, 2641 lots, £2121. Part 5, April and May 1845, poetry, drama, polygraphy, Latin classics, belles-lettres, &c., twelve days, 2956 lots, £2649. Part 6, August 1845, four days, 926 lots, £718.

The library of Mr. B. H. Bright was sold at Sotheby's in three divisions in 1845, and the total amount realised was £8997.

In 1849 Messrs. Southgate & Barrett tried the experiment of selling the library of the Rev. H. F. Lyte and J. W. M. Lyte in the evening, but the new departure (or rather, revival of an old practice) did not meet with approval, and the practice was not followed. There were 4368 lots, and the sale occupied seventeen evenings.

In this same year the world was startled by the dispersion of the Duke of Buckingham's property at Stowe House, and Messrs. Sotheby sold the library during twenty-four days. There were 6211 lots, and the total amount realised for library and prints was £14,155. The Stowe MSS. were sold by private contract to the Earl of Ashburnham for £8000.

Since this time the sale of great libraries from the old family mansions have been so numerous, that little surprise is felt when another is added to the long list.

Messrs. Sotheby sold in 1851 the library of Granville Penn, during six days, for £7845 ; in 1851 the library of E. V. Utterson, during eight days, for £5494 ; in 1853 the library of Dawson Turner for £4562, and that of Baron Taylor for £4087; in 1854 the private library of William Pickering for £10,700 ; in 1857 the library of the Earl of Shrewsbury for £3250.

Between 1859 and 1864 were sold at Sotheby's the various portions of the library of Mons. Gulielmo Libri. The 1176 lots of manuscripts were sold in eight days of March and April 1859, and realised £6783. The "choicer portion" of the library was sold in August of the same year, thirteen days, 2824 lots, £8822.

In 1861 the mathematical and general library was sold. Part 1, A to L, twelve days, 4335 lots, £1349. Part 2, M to Z, eight days, lots 4336 to 7268, £877.

The "reserved portion" was sold in July 1862, during four days. The number of lots was 713, and these sold for the immense sum of £10,328, or an average of over £14 per lot.

The library of Miss Richardson Currer was sold at Sotheby's in 1862, during ten days, for £5984.

In July 1864 was sold by Sotheby, Wilkinson, and Hodge the extremely interesting library of George Daniel, which was specially rich in old English literature, and remarkable for the superb collection of Shakespeare folios and quartos. The sale occupied ten days, and realised £15,865.

At the same auction rooms were sold in 1865 the

library of J. B. Nicholl, in two parts, for £6175 ; in 1867 the library of Sir Charles Price for £5858 ; and in 1868 the library of Macready, the actor, for £1216.

In 1868, 1869, 1870, 1871, and 1873 were sold at Sotheby's eight portions of the unique poetical library of the Rev. T. Corser, which realised £19,781.

The library, engravings, and autographs of John Dillon were sold by the same firm in 1869, during twelve days, for £8700.

The library of Lord Selsey was sold in 1872 for £4757.

The sale in 1873 by Messrs. Gadsden, Ellis & Co., at Hanworth Park, of the grand library of Henry Perkins created a sensation. The late owner had been a purchaser at the time of the bibliomaniacal fever after the Roxburghe sale, and for years the library was practically forgotten, so that the opportunity afforded to book-collectors of purchasing its choice rarities came as a surprise. The four days' sale realised £25,954.

In 1874 the choice library of Sir William Tite was sold at Sotheby's, during sixteen days, for £19,943.

The same firm sold the library of the Rev. C. H. Crauford, during five days, in July 1876 for £6229.

In 1878 Messrs. Sotheby sold the very choice collection of books and miniatures formed by Mr. J. T. Payne, of the firm of Payne & Foss, which realised £2843, or about £16 per lot, the day's sale consisting of only 117 lots.

In 1879, 1880, and 1881 the fine library of Dr. David

Laing, of the Signet Library, Edinburgh, was sold
at Sotheby's in four portions, which realised a total
of £16,536, the first part alone making £13,288.

A portion of the library of Cecil Dunn Gardner
was sold in June 1880 at Sotheby's, during six days,
for £4734. The same firm sold in 1881 a portion
of the Earl of Clare's library for £2130, a portion
of Lord Hampton's library for £3539, and a portion
of the library of G. L. Way for £2324; Daniel
Gurney's library, four days, £1687 ; library of a
collector (Mr. Gulston), £1173.

Never before has there been, and probably never
again will there be, two such remarkable sales as
those of the Sunderland and Beckford libraries at
the same time.   The Sunderland library, the sale
of which was commenced by Messrs. Puttick and
Simpson in December 1881, was formed by Charles,
third Earl of Sunderland, who died on 19th April
1722, and was transferred from the Earl's house
in Piccadilly in 1733, when Charles, fifth Earl of
Sunderland, became Duke of Marlborough.   Suc-
cessive Dukes of Marlborough added a few books
to the library, but it is noteworthy, as we turn over
page after page of the catalogue, how seldom we
come upon a book published since 1722.   On the
1st of December a large company was gathered in
the famous auction-room in Leicester Square, to
watch the progress of what promised to be one of
the most remarkable sales of modern times.   Some
of those who formed this company were to become
duellists in the fight over the treasures arranged
upon the shelves round the room, for the fight for the

chief lots always resolved itself into a duel in the end.
Those who expected the books to make a distinguished external appearance were disappointed, for
more than a century's occupation of the great library
at Blenheim, with a scorching sun beating down upon
the backs of the books from the huge windows, had
destroyed a large proportion of the bindings. When
the sale opened it was seen that prices would rule
high ; but at the same time, the character of the
library, which contained many books now hopelessly out of fashion, was marked by the sudden
drop in the prices from hundreds of pounds to a
shilling or so, soon again to rise to hundreds of
pounds. Mr. Quaritch was the hero of the sale,
and after him the chief combatants were Mr. F. S.
Ellis and M. Techener, while Mr. Henry Stevens,
Mr. Pearson, Messrs. Pickering, Messrs. Morgand
and Fatout, and some others made a good fight for
the lots they required. As the bids of £10 and
upwards went on rapidly till £1000—in some cases
more—were reached, the excited faces of those
around formed a sight worth seeing, for few could
resist the excitement, which found vent in applause,
when the lot was knocked down.

Part 1, December 1881, realised £19,373. Part 2,
April 1882, £9376. Part 3, July, £7792. Part 4,
November, £10,129. Each of these parts consisted of ten days' sale. Part 5 (and last), March
1883, contained eleven days' sale, and realised £9908.
The lots were numbered throughout the parts, and
amounted to 13,858. The total amount realised by
the sale was £56,581, 6s.

When the sale was concluded Mr. Quaritch made a short speech appropriate to the occasion, and said that "This was the most wonderful library that had been sold by auction in the present century. Fine as the Hamilton library was he could form another like it to-morrow, but nothing like the Sunderland library would be seen again as a private collection. He held its founder in the highest respect and gratitude."

On the 30th of June 1882 the sale of the beautiful library of William Beckford was commenced at Sotheby's by Mr. Hodge. The books were in the finest condition, and in consequence they fetched very high prices. Mr. Henry Bohn, writing to *The Times* at the commencement of this sale, said that Beckford was the greatest book enthusiast he ever knew. He was a great collector of "Aldines and other early books bearing the insignia of celebrities, such as Francis I., Henri et Diane, and De Thou, and especially of choice old morocco bindings by Deseuil, Pasdeloup, and Derome." Mr. Bohn further said that after Beckford's death, and while the books were still at Bath, the Duke of Hamilton, Beckford's son-in-law, wished to sell the whole library. Mr. Bohn offered £30,000, payable within a week; but although the Duke would willingly have accepted the offer, the Duchess would not agree to the sale of her father's books. Mr. Bohn estimated that the library was now worth £50,000. It actually sold for £73,551. Part 1, June and July 1882, consisted of twelve days' sale and 3197 lots, which realised £31,516. Part 2,

December, twelve days, 2732 lots, £22,340. Part 3, July 1883, twelve days, 2781 lots, £12,852. Part 4 (and last), November, four days, 1127 lots, £6843. The total number of lots in the forty days' sale was 9837.

The library collected by the Duke of Hamilton (when Marquis of Douglas) at the same time as Beckford was adding to his own, was sold by Messrs. Sotheby, Wilkinson & Hodge during eight days of May 1884. There were 2136 lots, which realised £12,892. The most valuable portion of the Hamilton library was the collection of matchless manuscripts, which were kept distinct from the printed books, and sold to the German Government.

During the years that the Blenheim and Hamilton Palace libraries were selling many valuable sales took place, and since then there have been a great number of fine libraries dispersed. We have only space to mention shortly a few of these ; but with respect to the last ten years there is the less need for a full list, in that a valuable record of sales is given in the annual volumes of Slater's " Book Prices Current," and Temple Scott's " Book Sales."

The important topographical library of James Comerford was sold by Sotheby, Wilkinson, and Hodge in 1881. There were 4318 lots, in thirteen days' sale, which realised £8327.

In 1882 the library of Frederic Ouvry, P.S.A., which consisted of 1628 lots, in a six days' sale, was sold at Sotheby's for £6169 ; and the choice library of a gentleman, £3366.

In March 1882 was sold a portion of the Right
Hon. A. J. B. Beresford-Hope's library (two days,
£2316), and further portions were sold in 1892.

The Stourhead heirlooms (Sir Richard Colt
Hoare) were sold at Sotheby's in July 1883, eight
days, 1971 lots, £10,028.

The Towneley Hall library, consisting of 2815 lots,
in an eight days' sale, realising £4616, and the
Towneley Hall manuscripts (two days, 235 lots,
£4054) were both sold in June 1883 at Sotheby's,
as was also the Drake library (four days, £3276).

In 1884 were sold at Sotheby's the library of
Francis Bedford, bookbinder (five days, 1551 lots),
for £4867, and the Syston Park library of Sir
John Hayford Thorold, Bart. (eight days, 2110 lots),
£28,001.

The Earl of Gosford's library was sold by Puttick
and Simpson in 1884, eleven days, 3363 lots,
£11,318.

It is curious to compare the sale of a library such
as Beckford's with one like James Crossley. Both
were great collectors, and possessed many dainties;
but whilst the former was particular as to condition,
with the consequence that his books fetched high
prices, the latter was regardless of this, and necessarily his sold for small sums.

One portion of Crossley's library was sold at
Manchester by F. Thompson & Son (seven days,
2682 lots), but other two parts were dispersed in
London by Sotheby, Wilkinson & Hodge. Part 1
(1884), seven days, 2824 lots. Part 2 (1885), nine
days, 3119 lots, £4095.

The fine library of the Earl of Jersey at Osterley Park was sold by Sotheby's in May 1885 for £13,007; where also was sold, in the following month, the library of the Rev. J. F. Russell for £8682.

In 1885 the sale of the miscellaneous but valuable library of Leonard Lawrie Hartley was commenced by Messrs. Puttick & Simpson. Part 1 (1885) consisted of 2475 lots, occupying ten days in the selling, which realised £9636. Part 2 (1886), ten days' sale of 2582 lots, £5258. Part 3 (1887), eight days' sale of 2937 lots, £1635.

In January 1886 was sold the library of Mr. Wodhull, £11,972; and in November of the same year Edward Solly's, F.R.S., £1544.

A selection from the magnificent library of the Earl of Crawford was sold at Sotheby's in 1887 and 1889. Portion 1 (1887), ten days, 2146 lots, realised £19,073. Portion 2 (1889), four days, 1105 lots, £9324.

Messrs. Sotheby, Wilkinson & Hodge in 1887 and 1888 sold the almost equally fine library of Mr. James T. Gibson-Craig. First portion (1887), ten days, 2927 lots, realised £6803. Second portion (1888), fifteen days, 5364 lots, £7907. Third portion (1888), three days, £809. The total amount realised for the three portions was £15,509.

A choice portion of Baron Seillière's library was sold in February 1887 (1440 lots, £14,944). A second portion was afterwards sold in Paris.

In 1888 Messrs. Christie, Manson & Woods sold the library of the Earl of Aylesford (£10,574); and

the Wimpole library, which formerly belonged to
Lord Chancellor Hardwicke (£3244).

In the same year the beautiful library of Mr. R.
S. Turner was sold at Sotheby's. Part 1, June 1888,
twelve days, 2999 lots, £13,370. Part 2, November
1888, fourteen days, £2874. The total amount
realised for the whole library was £16,244.

Mr. Turner sold in Paris in 1878 a previous collection of books in 774 lots, which realised the large
sum of 319,100 francs (£12,764).

In February 1889 were sold at Sotheby's the Earl
of Hopetoun's library of 1263 lots for £6117, and
that of R. D. Dyneley, £3084. At the same auction
rooms, and in the same year, were sold the library
of John Mansfield Mackenzie of Edinburgh, remarkable for a large number of illustrated editions of
modern authors, 2168 lots, in an eight days' sale,
£7072; and that of J. O. Halliwell Phillipps, four
days, 1291 lots, £2298.

Also at Sotheby's in 1889 were sold the libraries
of Frederick Perkins (2086 lots, £8222); the Duke
of Buccleuch (selection), 1012 lots, £3705; W. D.
Salmond, £2557.

In the following year Thomas Gaisford's library
was sold at Sotheby's (eight days, 2218 lots, £9236);
also that of Frederick William Cosens (twelve days,
4995 lots, £5571); that of Sir Edward Sullivan
(choicer portion), £11,002; that of Frank Marshall
(six days, 1937 lots, £2187); that of Alexander
Young, £2238; and that of T. H. Southby,
£2241.

In 1891 were sold the libraries of Cornelius Paine

(£3677); Edward Hailstone of Walton Hall:—Part
1, ten days, 2728 lots, £4738. Part 2, eight days,
2904 lots, £4252 (total, £8991); W. H. Crawford
of Lakelands, county Cork, twelve days, 3428 lots,
£21,255; J. Anderson Rose, £2450; and Lord Brabourne, four days, 1149 lots, £2042.

The remainder of Lord Brabourne's library was
sold by Messrs. Puttick & Simpson in 1893 (three
days, 995 lots, £1058).

In 1892 were sold the libraries of John Wing-
field Larking (three days, 946 lots, £3925); of
Edwin Henry Lawrence (four days, 860 lots,
£7409); of Joshua H. Hutchinson (832 lots,
£2377); of Count Louis Apponyi, £3363; and of
"a gentleman deceased" (418 lots, £2411)—all at
Sotheby's.

In 1893 were sold at Sotheby's the Bateman
heirlooms (W. & T. Bateman), six days' sale, 1840
lots, £7296; of Howard Wills, £8204; and of H.
G. Reid, £3466; of Fred Burgess (dramatic library),
£1558; also selected portion of the Auchinleck
library, £2525. At the same rooms the sale of the
Rev. W. E. Buckley's library was commenced.
Part 1, ten days, 3552 lots, £4669. The second
part was sold in April 1893, twelve days, 4266 lots,
£4751. The total amount realised by the two sales
was £9420.

A choice collection of books was sold by Sotheby
in 1894, viz., the library of Birket Foster, 1361 lots,
£5198.

In 1895 were sold at Sotheby's the libraries of
Mons. John Gennadius, eleven days, 3222 lots,

£5466; of Baron Larpent, £2630; of T. B. F.
Hildyard, £4165; of the Earl of Orford, two days,
340 lots, £2609; of the Rev. W. J. Blew (liturgical),
£2220; and of Dr. Hyde Clarke, £2598.

The library of the Rev. W. Bentinck L. Haw-
kins, F.R.S., was sold at Christie's in the same
year. First portion, three days, 747 lots, £1176.
Second portion, two days, 471 lots, £833. Third
and final portion, one day, 252 lots, £894. At the
same rooms the library of William Stuart, 215 lots,
£4296.

The sales at Sotheby's in 1896 which realised
£2000 and upwards were those of John Tudor
Frere, £3747; Sir W. Pole, £4343; Adrian Hope,
£3551; Lord Coleridge, £2845; Sir Thomas
Phillipps (MSS.), £6988; Sir E. H. Bunbury,
£2965, Lord Bateman, £2151; Alfred Crampton,
£2492; fine bindings of a collector, £3613;
books and MSS. from various collections, £8554.

The chief sales at Sotheby's in 1897 have been as
follows :—Sir Charles Stewart Forbes and others,
five days, £5146; Beresford R. Heaton and others,
three days, £4054; Sir Cecil Domville and others,
four days, £5289.

The great sales, however, of 1897 were those of
the first and second portions of the library of the
Earl of Ashburnham. In the first part 1683 lots
were sold for £30,151, and in the second part 1208
lots for £18,649.

LIST OF BOOK SALES IN THE NINETEENTH CENTURY
WHICH HAVE REALISED OVER £10,000.

1812.	Duke of Roxburghe.	.	£23,397
1813.	Ralph Willett (Merly)	. .	13,508
1818–21.	James Brindley	. . over	17,522
1819.	John North . . .	.	12,806
1825.	Sir Mark Masterman Sykes	.	18,729
1827.	John Dent . . .	.	15,040
1828–35.	Earl of Guilford	. .	12,175
1833–34.	P. A. Hanrott .	. .	22,409
1834–36.	Richard Heber	. .	56,774
1844–45.	Duke of Sussex	. .	19,148
1849.	Duke of Buckingham (Stowe) .		14,155
1853.	W. Pickering (private library) .		10,700
1859–64.	Gulielmo Libri	. .	28,159
1864.	George Daniel	. .	15,865
1868–73.	Rev. T. Corser	. .	19,781
1873.	Henry Perkins	. .	25,954
1874.	Sir William Tite ..	. .	19,943
1878.	R. S. Turner (Paris)	. .	12,764
1879–81.	David Laing . . .	.	16,536
1881–83.	Sunderland (Blenheim) .	.	56,581
1882–83.	William Beckford .	. .	73,551
1884.	Duke of Hamilton .	. .	12,892
1883.	Stourhead (Hoare) .	. .	10,028
1884.	Earl of Gosford .	. .	11,318
1884.	Sir J. H. Thorold (Syston Park)		28,000
1885.	Earl of Jersey (Osterley Park) .		13,007
1885–87.	L. L. Hartley . . .	.	16,529
1886.	F. C. Severne, M.P. (Michael Wodhull) . . .	.	11,972
1887.	Baron Seillière	. .	14,944
1887–89.	Earl of Crawford .	. .	26,397
1887–88.	J. T. Gibson-Craig .	. .	15,519

1888.	Earl of Aylesford . . .	£10,574
1888.	R. S. Turner	16,244
1889.	MSS. from the Duke of Hamilton's collection (bought privately by the Berlin Government) .	15,189
1890.	Sir Edward Sullivan . . .	11,002
1891.	W. H. Crawford (Lakelands) .	21,255
1897.	Earl of Ashburnham. Part 1 .	30,151
1897.	Earl of Ashburnham. Part 2 .	18,649

It is worthy of notice in the above list that the amounts realised for the Heber and Sunderland sales were almost identical, while the totals of the Hamilton Palace libraries were larger than those for any other English sale, viz., £86,543 (Beckford, £73,551 ; Duke of Hamilton, £12,892).

In these totals the sales of booksellers' stocks have not been recorded, because they do not sell so well as private libraries, owing to a rather absurd impression in the minds of buyers that the rarer books would have sold out at the shops had they been of special value ; but it may be noted here that the stock of Messrs. Payne & Foss was sold in three portions in 1850 for £8645 (certainly much less than its worth) by Sotheby, who sold in 1868–70–72 Mr. Henry G. Bohn's stock, in three parts, for £13,333, and Mr. Lilly's in 1871 and 1873, in five parts, for £13,080. In 1873 Mr. T. H. Lacy's stock of theatrical portraits and books were sold at Sotheby's for £5157.

Mr. F. S. Ellis's stock was sold in November 1885 for £15,996, and Mr. Toovey's in February 1893 for £7090. The latter's sporting books realised £1031.

It is very much the fashion now to average the amounts realised at auctions, and to point out that at such a sale the amount obtained was about £10 or more per lot. This is a useful generalisation so far as it goes, but further information is required to enable the reader to obtain a correct idea of value. The generalisation is useful in regard to a mass of sales ; thus we may say broadly, that in the last century the ordinary large and good libraries averaged about £1 per lot, while in the present century they average at least £2 per lot.

A small and select library will naturally average a much higher amount than a large library, in which many commonplace books must be included. These averages, however, will not help us very much to understand the relative value of libraries.

For instance, at the Sunderland sale some lots sold for enormous sums, while a large number fell for a few shillings ; but at the Hamilton Palace sales (William Beckford and the Duke of Hamilton) nearly every lot was of value, and although individual lots did not reach the sums realised at the Sunderland sale, the total was much larger. As an instance of what is meant, we may quote from the notice of the Ashburnham sale in the *Times*—

"The 1683 lots realised a grand total of £30,151, 10s., which works out at an average of as nearly as possible £18 per lot. Hitherto the highest average was obtained by the disposal in 1884 of the Syston Park library, where 2110 lots brought £28,000, or £13, 5s. per lot, the next highest average being that of the Seillière library, sold in

M

1887, 1140 lots realising £14,944, or about £13, 2s. per lot. It is scarcely fair, however, to compare the Ashburnham collection with either of these two libraries, as the Seillière was admittedly only the choice portion of the assemblage of the baron, whilst nearly every lot in the Syston Park library was of importance. Eliminating from the Ashburnham collection the hundreds of lots which realised less than £1 each, the average would be nearer £40 than £18."

This is all very well in its way, but one lot fetched £4000, and such an amount would de- moralise any average. Let us therefore see what are the particular points worthy of notice in the sums making up this large total of £30,151. We find that five lots realised £1000 and over each, and including these five lots, forty-two were over £100 each. Now the total for these forty-two lots is £20,348, which, if we deduct from the grand total, leaves 1641 lots for £9803, bringing our average down considerably.

This is not perhaps a quite fair system of strik- ing an average, but it shows better how the prices of the books are distributed.

CHAPTER VIII

PRICES OF EARLY PRINTED BOOKS

IT is impossible in the following chapters to do more than select some of the chief classes of valuable books in order to indicate the changes that have taken place in the prices. It will be noticed that the great enhancement of prices which is so marked a feature of the present age commenced about the beginning of the present century.

Bibliomania can scarcely be said to have existed in the seventeenth century, but it commenced in the middle of the next century, when the Mead library was sold. Still it attracted little attention until the sale of the Roxburghe library in 1812, when it had become a power. In the middle of the present century there was a dull time, but during the last quarter the succession of sales realising one, two, and three thousand pounds have been continuous, with occasional sales realising much larger amounts. Great changes have occurred at different times in the taste of collectors for certain classes of books.

We may obtain a good idea of the public taste in books by analysing a list of the highest prices obtained at three such representative sales as the

Sunderland, the Hamilton Palace, and the Ashburnham libraries.

At the first of these the largest prices were obtained for the first editions of Bibles, classics, Italian poets, &c.; at the second, fine bindings took the lead; and at the third, Bibles and Caxtons, and other early literature occupied the first place.

All these classes are dealt with in the following chapters. In the present one, the most important among the early Bibles, the first editions of the classics, and early Italian literature are recorded. These are among the chief of those books which have been steadily rising for years, and now stand at enormous prices.

It is not safe to prophesy, but there is no reason to doubt that if riches continue to increase these prices will also advance. As these books are placed in great libraries they naturally become scarcer each year. We must, however, always bear in mind that the number of libraries and individuals who can afford to spend thousands of pounds on single books are few, and if they are reduced, those who remain in the field are likely to get books cheaper.

While the first editions of the classics will probably always keep up their price, later editions have experienced a fall from which they are never likely to recover. Scholarship and knowledge of manuscripts have so greatly advanced, that many of the old high-priced editions are now hopelessly out of date, and good German texts, which can be obtained at a few shillings, are naturally preferred.

The Delphin and Oxford classics, which were once so much sought after, have now sunk to a comparatively low price. The large paper copy of Dr. Samuel Clarke's edition of "Cæsar" (2 vols. imp. folio, 1712), of which only twenty-five copies were printed, was once a high priced book. The Duke of Grafton's copy fetched £64, and Topham Beauclerk's £44. There is a story connected with the latter, which should be noted. Beauclerk gave four guineas for his copy to the mother of a deceased officer, the sum she asked, but when he was afterwards told by his bookseller that it was worth seventeen guineas, he sent the additional thirteen guineas to the lady. Certainly the Sunderland copy fetched £101 in 1881, but this was a special case, owing to the connection of the great Duke of Marlborough with the book. The Duke of Hamilton's copy, which had belonged to Louis XIV., sold in 1884 for £36; but Beckford's copy, bound in red morocco, only brought £6.

Block books are of such excessive rarity that they have always been high priced, but like the earliest books printed from movable types, they have greatly increased in value of late years. This is seen in the case of the copy of the second edition of the *Biblia Pauperum*, which fetched £1050 at the Earl of Ashburnham's sale. This same copy brought £257 at Willett's sale, but at Hanrott's the price fell to the small amount of £36, 15s.

The following are some of the prices that those

magnificent books—the Mazarin Bible and the first
Bible with a date—have realised :—

Biblia Sacra Latina (Moguntiæ, Gutenberg et Fust, circa
1450–55) :—
On vellum—G. & W. Nicols, 1825, £504 (Messrs.
Arch for H. Perkins). H. Perkins, 1873, £3400.
Earl of Ashburnham, 1897, £4000.
On paper—Sykes, 1824, £199, 10s. (H. Perkins).
Hibbert, 1829, £215. Bishop of Cashel, 1858,
£595. H. Perkins, 1873, £2690. Thorold
(Syston Park), £3900. Earl of Gosford, 1884
(vol. i. in original binding), £500. Earl of
Crawford, 1887, £2650. Earl of Hopetoun,
1889 (one leaf injured, and slightly wormed),
£2000.

Biblia Sacra Latina (Moguntiæ, Fust et Schoeffer,
1462) [first Latin Bible with a date] :—
On vellum—
Duc de la Valliere, 4085 francs.
Count MacCarthy, 4750 francs.
Watson Taylor, 1823, £215.
Dent, 1827, £173.
H. Perkins, 1873, £780.
Earl of Crawford, 1887, £1025.
} Same copy.
The Lamoignon copy, bought by Mr. Cracherode for
250 guineas, is now in the British Museum.
Sunderland, 1881, £1600. Thorold, £1000.

The Latin Version of the Psalms, in its second edition,
by Fust and Schoeffer, 1459 (printed on vellum),
sold at Sykes's sale for £136, 10s. At the Syston
Park sale (Thorold) it brought £4950, a greater
price even than has been given for the Mazarin
Bible. It has been erroneously stated that this was
the MacCarthy copy, which was sold in 1815 for

3350 francs. The MacCarthy copy was bought by Hibbert, and at his sale in 1829 it became the property of Baron Westreenen.[1]

Biblia Latina, folio Venetiis (N. Jenson), 1476, printed on vellum, capital letters illuminated, in red morocco, sold at the Merly sale for £168. Beckford copy (supposed to be the same copy) sold in 1882 for £330. H. Perkins, 1873, £290.

The first edition of the Bible in English (translated by Coverdale), 1535 (with some leaves mended), was sold at the Earl of Ashburnham's sale for £820. Dent's copy £89 in 1827 (title and two leaves in facsimile). Freeling's copy, £34, 10s. in 1836. Dunn Gardner's, 1854 (with title and one leaf in facsimile), £365. H. Perkins, 1873 (title and two leaves in facsimile), £400. Earl of Crawford's (imperfect), £226.

The first edition of Tyndale's New Testament (1526) sold in Richard Smith's sale, 1682, for 6s. Ames bought the Harleian copy for 15s. This was sold at Ames's sale, 1760, to John White for £15, 14s. 6d. It was sold by White to the Rev. Dr. Gifford for twenty guineas, and bequeathed by Gifford, with the rest of his library, to the Baptists' library at Bristol.

The Complutensian Polyglot (6 vols. folio, 1514–17) is said to have cost Cardinal Ximenes £40,000. Six hundred copies were printed. The following prices have been paid for the one vellum copy in the market, and for some paper copies :—

Three on vellum—(1) Royal Library, Madrid ; (2) Royal Library, Turin ; (3) supposed to have

---

[1] F. Norgate, in *The Library*, vol. iii. p. 329.

been reserved for the Cardinal. Pinelli, 1789, £483, bought by MacCarthy. MacCarthy, 1817 £676 (16,000 francs), bought by Hibbert. Hibbert, 1829, £525.

On paper—Harleian copy, sold by Osborne for £42. Maittaire's imperfect copy sold for 50s. Sunderland, £195. Earl of Crawford, 1887 (general title wanting), £56. Beresford Hope, 1882, £166. W. H. Crawford (Lakelands), 1891, £100.

The vellum copy sold in the Pinelli sale was, according to Dibdin, taken to Dr. Gosset when on a bed of sickness, in the hopes that the sight might work a cure on that ardent book-lover.[1]

John Brocario, son of Arnoldus Brocario, the printer of this polyglot, when a lad, was deputed to take the last sheets to the Cardinal. He dressed himself in his best clothes, and delivered his charge into Ximenes' hand, who exclaimed, " I render thanks to Thee, O God, that Thou hast protracted my life to the completion of these biblical labours." He told his friends that the surmounting of the various difficulties of his political situation did not afford him half the solace which arose from the finishing of his Polyglot.[2] A few weeks after the noble enthusiast died.

Plantin Polyglot Bible, 1569–72, 5 vols. Five hundred copies printed ; greater part lost at sea. Earl of Ashburnham, 1897, on vellum (wanting the " Apparatus "), £79.

---

[1] Dibdin's " Reminiscences," vol. i. p. 206 (note).
[2] *Gomecius (Gomez) de rebus gestis a Francisco Ximinis Cisnerio*, 1569, quoted in Dibdin's " Reminiscences," vol. i. p. 211.

Walton's Polyglot Bible, 6 vols. folio, 1657 (with Castell's Lexicon), does not keep up its price. Seaman, 1676, £8, 2s. Bernard, 1698, £10. Duke of Grafton (without Castell), £38, 13s. Edwards, £61. Heath, £73, 10s. (bought by the Earl of Essex). H. Perkins, 1873, £19, 15s. At the Wimpole library sale (Lord Chancellor Hardwicke), 1888, a copy of Walton without Castell fetched £9, 5s. The Ashburnham copy, which had belonged to Henry, Duke of Gloucester, fourth son of Charles I., with his name on the binding, which was in blue morocco, sold in 1897 for £28.

EDITIONES PRINCIPES OF THE CLASSICS

ÆSOPUS. Fabulæ Latine et Italice. Neapoli, 1485; first 'edition of Æsop with the Italian version. Hibbert's, £17; Libri, 480 francs; Earl of Ashburnham, £203.

ANACREON. Lutetiæ, 1554, on vellum. Sunderland, 1881, £221.

ARISTOTELES. Opera varia. Venetiis, 1483, 2 vols. Earl of Ashburnham, 1897 (printed on vellum), each volume decorated in the highest style of Italian art of the period, fifty-nine beautiful historical and ornamental initials, £800.

CICERO. Opera Omnia *Mediolani*, per Alex. Minutianum et Gulielmos fratres, 1498–99 [first edition of the collected works], four vols. in two, folio, old yellow morocco. Sunderland, £30, 10s.

—— Epistolæ ad familiares. Romæ (Sweynheym et Pannartz), 1467, folio, the first edition and the first book printed in Rome and in Roman letters. Sunderland, £295.

CICERO. Epistolæ. Venetiis, a Nicolao Jenson, 1471, folio. Mead, £3, 3s.; Askew, £11, 16s.; Sunderland, £12.

—— Orationes. Adam de Ambergau, 1472, folio. Askew gave £3, 5s. for his copy, which was bought by Dr. Hunter at his sale for £12. It is now at Glasgow University. Sunderland, £18.

CLAUDIANUS. Opera. Venetiæ, 1482, first edition. Mead, £2, 2s.; Askew, £7, 15s.; Pinelli, £9, 9s.; Sunderland (broken binding), £4.

GELLIUS (AULUS). Noctes Atticæ. Romæ (Sweynheym et Pannartz), 1469, folio, first edition. Pinelli, £58, 16s. (printed on vellum); Sunderland, £790.

—— Noctes. Venetiis, per Nicolaum Jenson, 1472, folio. Mead, £2, 12s. 6d.; Askew, £11, 10s.; Sunderland, £13, 10s.

HOMERUS. Opera Omnia. Florentiæ sumpt. Bern. et Nerii Nerliorum, 1488, two vols. folio, first edition. The British Museum copy was purchased for £17; Wodhull, £200; Sunderland, £48.

—— Homeri Odyssea Græce. Florentiæ, 1488, first edition. Duke of Hamilton, 1884, very large and fine copy, red morocco, by Clarke & Bedford, £25.

—— On vellum (one of the four known to exist). Dent, part 1, 1827, £142, 16s.

HORATIUS. Opera. 1470, small folio, first edition, with a date. Sunderland, £29. The Naples edition of 1474 is called by Dibdin "the rarest classical volume in the world," and it was chiefly to possess this book that Earl Spencer bought the famous library of the Duke of Cassano.

JUSTINUS. Venetiis, per Nicolaum Jenson, 1470, small folio, first edition. Mead, £3, 3s.; Askew, £13, 13s. (sold to the British Museum); Pinelli, £18, 7s. 6d.; Sunderland, £15.

JUVENALIS ET PERSIUS. Editio Princeps. Dr. Askew
gave £3 for his copy; at his sale it was purchased
by the British Museum for thirteen guineas.

LIVIUS. The first edition, printed at Rome by Sweynheym and Pannartz, as is supposed, in 1469. The
only copy printed on vellum which is known to
exist is now in the Grenville Library (British
Museum). It was for years in the possession of
the Benedictine Library at Milan. It was bought
by Sykes at J. Edwards's sale (1815) for £903.
At Sykes's sale (1824) it was bought by Payne and
Foss for £472, 10s. These booksellers sold it to
Dent, and at Dent's sale (1827) bought it again for
Grenville for £262, 10s., a remarkable instance of
depreciation in price of a unique book.

The editor of this series contributed an article on
this copy to *The Library* (vol. i. p. 106). The arms
of the Borgia family are beautifully painted on the
first page of the text, and it has usually been supposed that Cardinal Roderigo Borgia (afterwards
Pope Alexander VI.), to whom it belonged, was
Abbot of the monastery of Subiaco (where the
first productions of Sweynheym and Pannartz were
executed) at the time the book was printed. It is
proved in the article, however, that the abbey was
not conferred upon Borgia by Sixtus IV. until 1471,
so that the connection is merely a coincidence.
This magnificent volume was probably executed for
Borgia, whose character, as delineated by Raphael
Volaterranus, is evidently imitated from Livy's
character of Hannibal.

—— Venet. Vindelin de Spira, 1470, two vols. folio,
printed on vellum. Sunderland, £520.

LUCANUS. Pharsalia. Romæ (Sweynheym and Pannartz),
1469, folio; fine edition, of which only 250 copies

were printed. Askew gave £6, 16s. 6d. for his
copy, which was bought at his sale by De Bure for
£16; Sunderland, £38.

LUCIANUS. Opera. Florentiæ, 1496, folio, first edition.
Askew gave £2, 12s. 6d. for his copy, which was
sold at the sale of his library for £19, 8s. 6d.;
Pinelli, £8, 18s. 6d.; copy on vellum in the Sunderland library, £59.

MARTIALIS Epigrammata. Ferrara, 1471, quarto, first
edition of Martial, and the first book printed at
Ferrara. Mead, £4, 14s. 6d.; Askew, £17;
Combes, £60, bought for the Bodleian.

OVIDIUS. Opera. First edition. Mead, £2, 12s. 6d.;
Askew, £10, 15s.

—— Romæ (Sweynheym et Pannartz), 1471, three vols.
folio, probably second edition. Sunderland, £85.

—— Venet. in ædibus Aldi, 1502-3, three vols. 8vo,
first Aldine edition. Sunderland, £9; copy on
vellum (Askew, £63) sold to Lord Spencer.

PLATO. Omnia Platonis Opera. Venet. in ædibus
Aldi, 1513, folio, first edition. Sunderland, £31.
Copy on vellum, Lord Orford gave £105 for it;
Askew purchased it for one-fifth of that price. At
his sale it was bought by Dr. William Hunter for
£52, 10s. It is now in the library at Glasgow
University.

PLINIUS. Venetiis, Joannes de Spira, 1469, first edition. The British Museum copy was purchased in
1775 for £43; Sunderland, £82; another copy, £70.

—— Venetiis, Nicolaus Jenson, 1472. The British
Museum copy was bought at Askew's sale for £23;

—— Parmæ, 1476. Sunderland, £7, 15s. Douce gave
Payne & Foss three hundred guineas for his copy
on vellum. It is now in the Bodleian Library.

QUINTILIANUS. Institutionum Oratoriarum lib. xii. Romæ, 1470, folio, printed on vellum. Sunderland, £290.

—— Institutiones Oratoriæ. Romæ (Sweynheym et Pannartz), circa 1470, folio. Paris library, £26, 5s., now in Cracherode library (British Museum); Sunderland, £26.

SALLUSTIUS. Venetiis, Vindelin de Spira, 1470, quarto or folio. Mead, £5, 17s.; Askew, £14, 3s. 6d.; Sunderland, £19, 10s.

SILIUS ITALICUS. Romæ (Sweynheym et Pannartz), 1471, folio, first edition. Askew gave three guineas for his copy, which was bought for the British Museum at his sale for £13, 2s. 6d.; Pinelli, £48; Sunderland, £20, 10s.

VALERIUS MAXIMUS. Moguntinæ, per Petrum Schoyffer de Gernsheim, 1471, folio, first edition, with a date. Askew gave £4, 14s. 6d. for his copy, which sold at his sale for £26; Sunderland, £32.

—— Another copy, printed on vellum, sold at the Sunderland sale for £194.

VIRGILIUS. Romæ (Sweynheym et Pannartz), 1469 (?). Most valuable of all the first editions. Hopetoun House, 1889, slightly damaged and slightly wormed, £2000. The previous occasion on which a copy was sold was at the La Vallière sale, 1784, when an imperfect copy fetched 4101 francs.

—— Venet. Vindelin de Spira, 1470, folio, first edition with a date, printed on vellum. A copy sold for twenty-five guineas at Consul Smith's sale, 1773; Sunderland, £810. A copy on paper was sold in 1889. Hopetoun, £590.

—— Venet. in ædibus Aldi, 1501, 8vo, first Aldine edition, and the first book printed with the italic type invented by Aldus. Sunderland, £65; copy printed on vellum (Askew, £74, 11s.) now in the Althorpe library.

ITALIAN CLASSICS

ARIOSTO. Orlando Furioso. Ferrara, 1516, with William
　　Cecil's (Lord Burghley) autograph. Sunderland,
　　1881, £300.
BOCCACCIO. In the catalogue of the Sunderland library
　　(1881) eight pages are devoted to the description of
　　various editions of his works. One of these, "De
　　la Ruine des Nobles Hommes et Femmes," Bruges
　　Colard Mansion, 1476, realised £920. An im-
　　perfect copy of the celebrated first edition of the
　　"Decameron" (C. Valdarfer, 1471) fetched £585.
　　This was the copy possessed by Lord Blandford
　　when he bought the complete Roxburghe copy.
　　The imperfect copy was afterwards sold in the
　　Lakelands sale (W. H. Crawford) for £230, and
　　is now in the British Museum.
　　　　The latter book will always hold a high position
　　in the annals of bibliography, from the fact that
　　when a perfect copy in the Roxburghe library was
　　sold in 1812, it was bought by the Marquis of
　　Blandford after a hard struggle with Earl Spencer
　　for £2260, the highest price ever paid for a book
　　up to that date, and for many years afterwards. It
　　had originally been added to the Roxburghe library
　　at a cost of one hundred guineas. Seven years after-
　　wards Messrs. Longman bought this same book at
　　the White Knights sale for £918 for Lord Spencer.
DANTE. First edition of Landino's Commentary,
　　Firenze, 1481; very large copy, with twenty rare
　　engravings, purple morocco, by Lewis. Duke of
　　Hamilton, 1884, £380.
　　　　W. H. Crawford, 1891, with the engravings by
　　Bacio Baldini from designs of Botticelli, £360.

PETRARCA. I Triumphi. Venetia, per Bernardino da Novara, 1488, with two sets of six illustrations, one on metal and one on wood. Sunderland, 1882, £1950.

—— Second Aldine edition, printed on vellum, 1514. Hanrott, £73; Beckford, 1883, £66.

POLIPHILI Hypnerotomachia. Venetiis (Aldus), 1499. Sykes, part 2, beautiful copy, in yellow morocco by Roger Payne, £21; Watson Taylor (on vellum), £82, 19s.; Sir C. Price, £53, 10s.; Howell Wills, £30; Luke Price, £49; Beckford, 1883 (Crozat's copy, red morocco, richly tooled), £130; Duke of Hamilton, 1884, £80; Earl of Crawford, 1887, £86; W. H. Crawford (Lakelands), 1891 (some of the woodcuts partially coloured, wanting leaf with imprint, £19; Earl of Ashburnham, 1897 (Emperor Charles V.'s copy, in stamped calf, with his figure in medallion), £151.

—— Hypnerotomachie, 1561. [French translation.] F. Hockley, 1887, £8; W. H. Crawford (Lakelands), 1891, £6, 10s.; Earl of Ashburnham, 1897, £15.

A copy bound with "Le Roy, De la Vicissitude des Choses," 1577, in blue morocco, magnificently tooled by Nicolas Eve for Louise de Lorraine, realised £220 at the Beckford sale, 1897.

An English translation of the first book by R. D. was published in 1592, which is excessively scarce. Mr. Andrew Lang reprinted this in Mr. Nutt's Tudor Library, 1890, from the copy in the Bodleian Library. There is no copy in the British Museum, and in the introduction to his reprint Lang tells a story against himself. He bought at Toovey's a poor copy of this book for £1, but shortly afterwards he found that it wanted the last five pages, and exchanged it for "Les Mémoires de la Reine

Marguerite," Paris, 1661, in yellow morocco. He regretted his exchange when he discovered its great rarity. M. Claude Popelin, who had long been lying in wait for this book, bought this copy at a London sale-room "à un de ces prix qu'on n'avoue pas à sa ménagère."

VIGILLES des Mors. Paris, par A. Verard, printed on vellum, with thirty miniatures finely illuminated in gold and colours, blue morocco by De Rome. This copy sold for 150 francs in the La Vallière sale, for 220 francs in the MacCarthy, and for £20 in Hibbert's. In the fourth portion of the Beckford library Mr. Quaritch bought it for £345.

TRISTAN. Chevalier de la Table Ronde. Two parts in one. Second edition, by Verard. Fine copy, with rough leaves, morocco super extra by Thouvenin. Duriez, 560 francs; same copy, Prince of Essling, 505 francs; same copy, Duke of Hamilton, 1884, £108.

AUGUSTINUS. De Civitate Dei. Venet. Nic. Jenson, on vellum, first page elaborately painted, and illuminated initials. Sunderland, 1881, £1000—bought by Mr. Quaritch amid shouts of applause.

CHAPTER IX

No class of books has advanced in value of late years to so great an extent as the chief examples of old English literature, and of this class the books printed by our earliest printer, Caxton, stand in a foremost position. It is proposed in this chapter to give a general idea of the variations in price of all the books printed by Caxton which have been sold by public auction. The number attached to each entry is that given by Mr. Blades in his great work, and it is hoped that few sales of these books have been left unmentioned.[1]

We learn from Mr. Blades that there was no fixed published price for these books, but the sellers obtained the best price they could for them. In 1496 the churchwardens of St. Margaret, Westminster, were possessed of fifteen copies of "The Golden Legend," bequeathed by Caxton. Ten of

---

[1] Mr. Blades has given full particulars of all the sales in his "Life and Typography of William Caxton" (1863); but there have been many sales since the publication of his great work, and particulars of these are given chiefly from two valuable articles, entitled *Caxtoniana*, by Mr. Frederic Norgate, which were published in *The Library*, Nos. 8 and 9 (August and September 1889). That accurate bibliographer has kindly allowed the author to see and use his manuscript corrections and additions to these articles.

these took five years to sell. In 1496 one copy was
sold for 6s. 8d., and in 1500 the price had gone
down to 5s. In 1510 R. Johnson, M.D., bought
five Caxtons ("Godefroy of Boleyn," "Eneydos,"
"Faytes of Arms," "Chastising," and "Book of
Fame") for a total expenditure of 6s. 8d.   These
are now in the University Library, Cambridge.
In the sale of 1678, to which the name of Voetius
is attached, three Caxtons sold for 7s. 10d.   At the
sale of Secondary Richard Smith's library (1682)
eleven Caxtons realised £3, 4s. 2d.; at Dr. Francis
Bernard's sale (1697), ten for £1, 15s. 4d.   There
were a considerable number of Caxtons in the Harleian Library, and several of these were duplicates.
They do not appear to have sold very readily, and
they occur in several of Osborne's catalogues at a
fairly uniform price of one guinea for the folios and
15s. for the quartos.   At the Hon. Bryan Fairfax's
sale (1756) nine Caxtons sold for £33, 4s.   At James
West's sale (1773) the price had considerably advanced, and thirty-four Caxtons realised £361,
4s. 6d.   John Ratcliffe's forty-eight Caxtons brought
£236, 5s. 6d.   At Dr. Richard Farmer's sale (1798)
five sold for £19, 11s. 6d.   An astonishing advance
in price is found at the Duke of Roxburghe's sale
(1812), where fourteen fine Caxtons brought £3002,
1s.   At the sale of Stanesby Alchorne's library in
1813 nine fetched £666, 15s.   Ralph Willett's seven
brought in 1813 £1319, 16s.   John Towneley's nine
sold in 1814 for £1127.   The Marquis of Blandford's
(White Knights) eighteen Caxtons brought in 1819
£1316, 12s. 6d.   At Watson Taylor's sale in 1823

nine brought £319, 14s. 6d. ; John Inglis (1826), thirteen for £431, 15s. 6d. ; John Dent (1827), four for £162, 16s. 6d. ; George Hibbert (1829), five for £339, 13s. 6d. ; P. A. Hanrott (1833), six for £180, 16s. ; R. Heber (1834), six for £219, 16s. ; Thomas Jolley (1843–51), six for £325, 15s. ; E. V. Utterson (1852), three for £116 ; J. D. Gardner (1854), seven for £739.

It will be seen from these totals that the present high prices did not rule at the sales in the middle of the present century.

In 1897 the total for the ten Caxtons in the first portion of the Ashburnham library reached £5622, and the six in the second portion fetched £4264.

The following list contains particulars of the sale prices of some of the chief issues of Caxton's press :—

The Recuyell of the Histories of Troy (1).

Dr. Bernard (1698), 3s. ; Bryan Fairfax (1756), £8, 8s. This perfect copy was bought by Francis Child, and at the sale of the Earl of Jersey's library in 1885 it was sold to Mr. Quaritch for £1820.

J. West's imperfect copy was sold in 1773 to George III. for £32, 11s., and it was perfected afterwards.

J. Lloyd of Wygfair (1816), £126. This copy was bought by G. Hibbert, and at his sale in 1829 J. Wilks bought it for £157, 10s. ; at Wilks's sale in 1847 E. V. Utterson bought it for £165 ; at Utterson's sale in 1852 the Earl of Ashburnham bought it for £55—not £155, as stated by Blades. This was described in Hibbert's and Wilks's catalogues as having " six whole leaves and parts of four others supplied in facsimile," but at Utterson's sale it was

stated to want no less than forty-seven leaves. At
the Ashburnham sale (part 2), 1897, it was said
to want forty-nine leaves. It fetched £950.

The Game and Play of the Chess, first edition (2).
R. Smith (1682), 13s. 2d.; J. West (1773), sold
to George III. for £32, os. 6d.; S. Alchorne (1813),
£54, 12s.—J. Inglis. J. Inglis (1826), £31, 10s.
—Lord Audley. Lord Audley (1855), £60, 10s.
—H. Cunliffe.

White Knights (1819), £36, 15s.—Duke of
Devonshire. This copy, sold for £42, was found
on collation after the sale to want three leaves
instead of only two, as stated in the catalogue;
it was therefore returned, and sold for £36, 15s.

Sir H. Mainwaring (1837), £101—J. Holford.
This may be the same copy as R. Smith's, as it
has on a fly-leaf in manuscript, "Ex dono Thomæ
Delves, Baronett, 1682."

Old Essex library (Lord Petre), 1886, £645—
Quaritch (perfect, excepting only the blanks). Earl
of Hardwicke (1888), wanting the Prologue and
three other leaves, £260—Quaritch.

It is necessary to quote from Scott's "Antiquary"
a well-known passage, because, as Mr. Blades says,
"not a single statement is founded on fact." The
particulars are so circumstantial, that they have
possibly deceived many readers, more especially as
Scott himself vouches for the anecdote as literally
true. "Snuffy Davy bought the 'Game of Chesse,'
1474, the first book ever printed in England, from
a stall in Holland for about 2 groschen, or twopence of our money. He sold it to Osborne for
£20 and as many books as came to £20 more.
Osborne resold this inimitable windfall to Dr. Askew

for 60 guineas. At Dr. Askew's sale this inestimable treasure blazed forth in its true value, and was purchased by Royalty itself for one hundred and seventy pounds." It may be added that Askew never had a copy.

Chesse, second edition (34).

Dr. Bernard's copy (1698) sold for 1s. 6d.

J. Ratcliffe's (1776) was bought for £16 by R. Willett; and at his sale in 1813, the Duke of Devonshire bought it for £173, 5s.

Le Recueil des Histoires de Troyes (3).

James (1760), £2, 12s. 6d.—Jacob Bryant. This copy was presented by Bryant to George III., and made perfect with a few leaves presented by the Duke of Roxburghe. It was retained by George IV. when the Kings' Library was presented to the nation, and is now at Windsor Castle.

Payne, bookseller (1794), £5, 5s.—sold to the Duke of Roxburghe, at whose sale in 1812 it fetched £116, 11s. It has been sold several times since, each time for less money. Among Lord Spencer's duplicates (1823), for £73, 10s., to J. Dent; at Dent's sale in 1827, for £36, 10s., to P. A. Hanrott; at Hanrott's sale in 1833, to the Earl of Ashburnham, for £27. Second part of Ashburnham sale (1897), £600. Wanting thirty-three leaves.

G. Watson Taylor (1823), £205, 16s.—Earl Spencer (perfect, and uncut).

G. Libri (1844), £200 (a perfect and unusually fine copy)—sold to British Museum.

The copy, slightly imperfect, in the National Library, Paris, was purchased at Brussels in the early part of the century by M. de la Serna for 150 francs.

Les fais du Jason (4).

The perfect copy in the National Library, Paris, was purchased in 1808 by M. de la Serna for 2 louis from a stranger, who had obtained it for half that sum.

Propositio Johannis Russell (7).

The Althorpe copy formerly belonged to John Brand, and at the sale of his library the Marquis of Blandford bought it for £2, 5s. At the White Knights sale in 1819 Lord Spencer bought it for £126. The Earl of Leicester has the only other known copy. Both copies are perfect.

Infancia Salvatoris (8).

The only existing copy known is in the Royal University Library, Göttingen. It was from the Harleian Library, and was purchased from Osborne in 1746 for 15s.

The History of Jason (9).

Richard Smith (1682), 5s. 1d.; Dr. Bernard (1698), 3s. 6d.

J. West's copy was sold in 1773 for 4 guineas to J. Ratcliffe, at whose sale in 1776 it fetched £5, 10s.

John Erskine's copy was bought in 1817 by G. Watson Taylor for £162, 15s., but at his sale in 1823 it only brought £95, 11s., Richard Heber being the purchaser. At Heber's sale (1834) it was bought by Payne the bookseller for £87. This uncut copy, which is the finest known, came afterwards into the possession of the Earl of Ashburnham. It sold at the second part of the Ashburnham sale (1897) for £2100.

The White Knights copy (Marquis of Blandford)

was sold (1819) for £85, 1s. At W. S. Higgs's
sale (1831) it was bought by J. Wilks for £87, 3s.,
and at his sale (1847) it was bought by J. Dunn
Gardner for £121. This copy was returned as
wanting a leaf, and resold for £105. Gardner
bought it afterwards from Pickering, who had in the
meantime supplied the leaf from another copy. At
Gardner's sale (1854) it was bought for Mr. Lenox
for £105.

The Dictes and Sayings of the Philosophers, first edition
(10).
Francis Child bought his imperfect copy at Bryan
Fairfax's sale (1756) for £6. It was bound with
"Moral Proverbs," and was one of the copies from
the Harleian Library. At the Earl of Jersey's sale
(1885) it brought £141.
John Ratcliffe's copy was bought by Ralph
Willett in 1776 for 15 guineas, and at his own sale
in 1813 it brought £262, 10s.
Sales since the publication of Blades's book :—
Rev. T. Corser (1868), £100. C. H. Crawford
(1876), £87 (Corser's copy). Duke of Buccleuch
(1889), £650. Earl of Ashburnham, 1897 (one of
four complete copies), £1320—Quaritch.

—— Second edition (28).
James West (1773), £21—George III. John
Towneley (1814), £189 — Duke of Devonshire
(erroneously described in the catalogue as "first
edition").

—— Third edition (83).
John Munro (1792), £16, 16s. Dr. Vincent
(1816), £99, 15s.—Singer, for Marquis of Blandford. In 1840 some books were turned out of the

Blenheim Library, and sent for sale at Oxford. The
Bodleian Library bought this copy at that sale for
£50. Blades was misled into saying that the Bodleian gave £199, 15s., by the fact, in this copy some
irresponsible person has altered the price it fetched
at Vincent's sale to £199, 15s. by the addition of
the figure 1. Fuller Maitland (1885), £165—
Quaritch (described as a second edition in the catalogue, three leaves in facsimile).

Chaucer's Canterbury Tales, first edition (12).
  J. West (1773), £47, 15s.—George III. J.
Ratcliffe (1776), £6. White Knights supplementary
sale (1820), £31, 10s.—T. Payne (imperfect); not
recorded by Blades.
  The highest price recorded by Blades is £300,
given by Mr. Huth at Lilly's sale, 1861. In 1896
two copies (both imperfect) were sold for over
£1000; Mrs. Corbet's (Barlaston Hall), wanting
nineteen leaves, £1020; R. E. Saunders (wanting
only two leaves, a few wormed, lower margins in
Melibeus mended), £1880. Earl of Ashburnham
(1897), £720—Pickering & Chatto (imperfect, also
some leaves from a shorter copy).

—— Second edition (57).
  Brand's imperfect copy (1807) was bought by
Heber for 10 guineas; it was sold at his sale in
1834 to the Earl of Ashburnham for £78, 15s.
Lord Ashburnham (1897), £300—Pickering and
Chatto (wanting twenty-eight leaves).

Boethius de Consolacione Philosophiæ, translated by
Chaucer (25).
  B. Worsley (1678), 5s. J. West (1773), £5, 10s.
—G. Mason. J. Ratcliffe (1776), £4, 6s.—George

III. S. Alchorne (1813), bought by the Marquis of Blandford (Spencer duplicate, imperfect) for £53, 11s.; sold to Watson Taylor, at his sale in 1819, for £22, 11s. 6d.; at Taylor's sale (£1823) Thorpe bought it for £13, 5s.

Thorpe bought a copy in old Oxford calf from Browne Willis's library, " without the slightest defect or repair," for £59 in July 1849, and he sold it in December of the same year for £105.

The Grenville (very fine, clean, and perfect) copy was purchased for £52, 10s.; Duke of Hamilton (1884), £160 (perfect, stained and mended); nobleman (Earl of Westmoreland), 1887, £156 (perfect, excepting the blank); Earl of Ashburnham (1897), £510 (two leaves in facsimile).

Cordyale, or the four last things (26).

Osborne (1748), £2, 2s. J. West (1773), £14— W. Hunter. Stanesby Alchorne bought W. Fletewode's copy in 1774 for £6, 12s. 6d., and at his sale in 1813 George III. bought it for £127, 1s. Dr. Valpy's copy, bought in 1832 by Henry G. Bohn for £26, 15s. 6d., is not mentioned by Blades; Valpy is said to have given £87 for it. Earl of Ashburnham (1897), £760—Pickering & Chatto (wanting eight leaves).

The Mirrour of the World, first edition (31).

R. Smith (1682), 5s. F. Child bought Bryan Fairfax's perfect copy in 1756 for £3; this was sold to Mr. Quaritch at the Earl of Jersey's sale (1885) for £195. J. West had two copies, which were sold in 1773—a perfect one to George III. for 12 guineas, and a very imperfect one to Richard

Gough for £2, 13s.   The latter sold at Gough's sale (1810) for £4, 14s. 6d.   Mr. Cracherode's perfect copy (now in the British Museum) was bought by him at Ratcliffe's sale (1776) for £2, 15s. The Duke of Roxburghe's fine and perfect copy, for which he gave 9 guineas, was sold at his sale (1812) to the Duke of Devonshire for £351, 15s.

The following copies (in addition to the Earl of Jersey's, mentioned above) have been sold since the publication of Mr. Blades's book :—

In 1877 Mr. Quaritch had a copy for sale with a vi, a viii, and the last leaf in facsimile, which he priced £200.

Sir John Thorold (1884), £335—Quaritch (perfect, excepting the blanks).   Earl of Hardwicke (1888), £60—Quaritch (very imperfect).   W. H. Crawford (1891), £160 (perfect, with the exception of one blank).   Earl of Ashburnham (part 2, 1897), £225 (leaves in facsimile).

The Mirrour of the World, second edition (84).

West's perfect copy was bought by Willett in 1773 for £9, 15s. ; at his sale (1813) it was bought for Lord Spencer for £136, 10s.

A perfect copy, very clean and large, was sold in 1844 with the library of Calwick Hall, Staffordshire, to Rodd for £41.   Thorpe gave Rodd £94 for it, but sold it to Mr C. Hurt for £90.   At Hurt's sale in 1855 Sir William (then Mr.) Tite bought it for £105.   At his sale in 1874 it realised £455.

A perfect copy in the original binding of oak, covered with stamped leather, and almost uncut, is in the library of the Baptist College at Bristol, having been presented by A. Gifford, D.D.   It has the following notes on a fly-leaf in Dr. Gifford's autograph :—

<pre>
"Memoranda.   Pd. Simco . . £2 12   6
      Another at Mr. Ratcliffe's
      sales to perfect y^s .   .   2 16   0
   Repairing and gilding, &c. .   0   2   6
                                 ─────────
                                  5 11   0
</pre>

Mem. Mr. White gave for another perfect
      one at Ratcliffe's sale £8, 8s.
Mem. 2. No copy of this in Museum."

The following sales, in addition to Sir William Tite's, mentioned above, have taken place since the publication of Blades's book :—

Sale at Puttick & Simpson's (1884)—a very poor copy, wanting eleven leaves, was sold for £8. Rev. Fuller Russell (1885), £265 (Hibbert's copy, which sold in 1829 for £36, 4s. 6d. ; Hibbert had given £55, 13s. at the Marquis of Blandford's sale in 1819). Hardwicke (Wimpole), 1888, £60 (with "Cicero de Amicitia"). F. Perkins (1889), £100 (two leaves of Table in MS.). Birket Foster (1894), £77 (wanting eighteen leaves).

The History of Reynard the Fox, first edition (32).

J. Ratcliffe (1776), £5, 10s.—George III. J. Inglis (1826), £184, 16s.—T. Grenville. J. D. Gardner (1854), £195—Duke of Newcastle. (All three copies are perfect.)

—— Second edition.

One copy only—that in the Pepysian Library, Cambridge—is known to exist.

Tully of Old Age, etc. (33).

Dr. Bernard (1698), 4s. 2d. Francis Child bought Bryan Fairfax's perfect copy in 1756 for 2 guineas.

In 1885 this was sold at the Earl of Jersey's sale (1885) for £350.

Dr. Askew bought T. Rawlinson's perfect copy in 1756 for £1, 5s., and at Askew's sale (1775) Willett gave 13 guineas for it. At Willett's sale (1813) it was sold to the Marquis of Blandford for £210. At the Marquis's sale (1819) T. Brockett gave £87, 3s. for it. At Brockett's sale (1823) Watson Taylor bought it for £47, 5s. Thorpe bought it at Watson Taylor's sale (1823) for £47, 15s. 6d. The "Merly" copy turned up again in 1857, when it was sold to Mr. F. Huth for £275.

The Duke of Roxburghe's imperfect copy was bought in 1812 by the Duke of Devonshire for £115.

Since Blades's book was published—the Rev. T. Corser (1868), £96 ("Old Age" only); Mr. Severne (1885), £250 (perfect); Earl of Crawford (1889), £320 (perfect); Earl of Ashburnham (1897), £102 —Pickering & Chatto (*Declamatio* only).

The Chronicles of England, first edition (39).

R. Smith (1682), 3s. 6d. ; Dr. Bernard (1691), 4s. ; J. Ratcliffe (1776), £5, 5s. ; S. Alchorne (1813), £63—Duke of Devonshire.

J. Roberts's copy (1815) was bought for £105 by John Milner, at whose sale in 1829 W. S. Higgs bought it for £70, 7s. ; at Higgs's sale (1830) it realised £73, 10s.

The following sales have taken place since the publication of Blades's book :—

Mr. Rainy, Bath (1883), £160—British Museum (poor copy, and imperfect). J. Hirst (1887), £67 (imperfect). Duke of Buccleuch (1889), £470— Quaritch (perfect blanks excepted).

The Chronicles of England, second edition (43).

Bryan Fairfax's imperfect copy was sold in 1756 to Francis Child for £5. In 1885 it sold for £40 at the sale of the Earl of Jersey's library.

J. Ratcliffe's imperfect copy was sold (1776) to George III. for £4, 5s.

An imperfect copy was bought by the Earl of Ashburnham in 1860 for £180. It was added to the sale after the library of E. A. Crowninshield, of Boston, U.S., had been brought to England. This copy, bound in new brown morocco, with " Description of Britain " (three leaves in facsimile), sold at Lord Ashburnham's sale (1897) for £610—Pickering & Chatto.

Mr. Quaritch bought the Duke of Buccleuch's copy in 1889 for £45. This was wrongly described in the catalogue as wanting only "fourteen leaves, of which two are blank," whereas it not only wanted the first fourteen printed leaves as well as the two blanks, but also the last six.

The Description oj Britain (40).

J. Towneley's imperfect copy was bought by George III. in 1814 for £85, 1s.

The Duke of Buccleuch's copy was bought by Mr. Quaritch in 1889 for £195. It was made up from two imperfect copies, with some leaves inlaid, but otherwise complete.

The History of Godfrey of Boloyne (42).

R. Smith (1682), 18s. 2d.—Earl of Peterborough. Dr. Bernard (1698), 4s. J. West (1773), £10, 10s. —George III. J. Ratcliffe (1776), £6, 16s. 6d.— W. Hunter. Dr. Vincent (1816), £215, 5s., bought by Singer, but Blades says the Marquis of Blandford; but Mr. Norgate thinks this is a mistake, as there was no copy in the White Knights sale. Mr. Holford's copy and that in the British Museum were the only known perfect copies until 1884, when Mr. Quaritch announced in his catalogue (No. 21,842) a "very fine copy, quite perfect, with all the blanks, and in the original binding," priced £1000. Mr. Norgate suggests that this may be Dr. Vincent's copy.

Polycronicon (44).

R. Mead (1755), £3, 13s. 6d. Joseph Ames (1760), two copies; one sold for 7s., and the other for 14s. J. West (1773), £16, 5s. 6d.

There were three copies in Ratcliffe's sale (1775); one sold for 3s. 3d., another for 2s. 3d., and a third for £5, 15s. 6d.

Heber bought S. Tyssen's copy in 1801 for £5; at his own sale it fetched £10, 15s.

The White Knights perfect copy was bought by Payne in 1819 for £94, 10s. It is now in the Grenville Library. (Blades overlooked this.)

Dent's perfect copy was bought by Perkins in 1827 for £103, 19s.; at the latter's sale (1873) it was bought by Mr. Quaritch for £365.

Lord Charlemont (1865), £477—Walford (wanting two leaves). This copy went to New York, and was sold immediately for 6750 dollars (= about £1380). T. Edwards (1871), wanting seven leaves, £34—Quaritch. This copy was sold at the Earl of Aylesford's sale (1888) for £110, also to Mr. Quaritch. The seven leaves were supplied in facsimile. Ten were mounted, and a few others mended.

Sir W. Tite's copy, with a 2, 3, 4, 8 in facsimile,

realised in 1874 £150. Ashburnham copy (1897), wanting forty-six leaves, £201.

Other copies sold since the publication of Blades's book were mere fragments, and only realised small sums.

The Pilgrimage of the Soul (45).

R. Smith (1682), 5s.   J. West (1773), £8, 17s. 6d. J. Ratcliffe (1776), £3, 17s. At the Marquis of Blandford's sale (1819) Earl Spencer bought it for £152, 5s. He perfected it with three leaves from a copy formerly belonging to Heber, and sold it in 1821, when Heber bought it again for £26, 15s. 6d., but at his sale in 1834 it only realised 18 guineas.

The Festial, first edition (47).

J. Ratcliffe had two copies : J. Edwards bought one for £3, 2s., and Dr. Farmer the other for £3. In 1796 the latter bought Herbert's copy for £2, 2s., and made a perfect copy from the two. Lord Spencer bought this at Farmer's sale in 1798 for £5.

—— Second edition (88).

The Duke of Roxburghe's copy was bought by Earl Spencer for £105. Only one has occurred for sale since, viz., Rev. E. James (1854), £27, now in the British Museum.

Confessio Amantis (50).

F. Child bought B. Fairfax's beautiful and perfect copy for £3 in 1756, and at the Earl of Jersey's sale in 1885 it realised £810. It is now in the United States. George III. bought West's imper-

fect and cropped copy for 9 guineas. Topham Beauclerk's copy, wanting ten leaves, sold in 1781 for
£2, 4s.; in 1881 it was sold at Mr. G. L. Way's sale
for £77. The Duke of Roxburghe's perfect copy
was bought by the Duke of Devonshire for £336.

Willett's copy has been sold several times, and
each time for a lower price than before. In 1813
the Marquis of Blandford bought it at Willett's sale
in 1813 for £315. At the White Knights sale
(1819) it was described as "remarkably fine and
perfect," and was sold to G. Watson Taylor for
£205, 16s. On being collated it was found to
want six leaves, and was consequently returned, and
resold to Mr. Watson Taylor for £131, 5s. At his
sale in 1823 it only realised £57, 15s.

W. Haggard (1867), £185 (wanting several
leaves). Lord Selsey's perfect copy sold in 1872
for £670. H. Perkins (1873), £245 (six leaves in
facsimile). Ashburnham (part 2, 1897), imperfect,
£188.

The Knight of the Tower (51).
R. Smith (1682), 5s. 1d. J. Brand's perfect
copy was bought by Earl Spencer in 1807 for
£111, 6s.

G. Watson Taylor bought the Marquis of Blandford's perfect copy (without blanks) in 1819 for
£85, 1s. At his sale in 1823 Jolley bought it for
£52, 10s. Rodd bought it for Corser, at Jolley's
sale in 1843, for £90. At Corser's sale (1868) Mr.
Quaritch bought it for £560.

Caton (52).
R. Smith(1682), 4s. 2d.; Dr. Bernard(1698), 1s. 10d.
The Duke of Devonshire's fine and perfect copy
has the Earl of Oxford's autograph—"I bought this

book at Edinburgh and paid for it the price of
£3, 3s. to Mr. Alex. Seymmer Bookseller in the
parliament close May 24 1725." In another hand,
"Ex Bib: Harl: £1, 1s., Feb. 1745." It was
bought from Messrs. Arch for £105.

The sale of Watson Taylor's copy (1823) to
Barclay for £30, 19s. 6d. is not recorded by Blades.

Earl of Ashburnham (1897), £295—Pickering
and Chatto (imperfect).

The Golden Legend, first edition (53).

West's imperfect copy was bought (1773) by Dr.
Hunter for £12, 15s., and is now at Glasgow.
Ratcliffe's imperfect copy was bought by George III.
(1776) for £5, 15s. 6d. The highest price recorded
by Blades at which a copy has sold is £230, bought by
the Duc d'Aumale in 1854 at J. Dunn Gardner's sale.
This copy wants the last leaf in the Table and Biiij,
the latter supplied in facsimile. Corser's imperfect
copy sold in 1869 for £147. It is now in the Huth
library. W. H. Crawford's imperfect copy sold in
1891 for £465.

—— Second edition (66).

There are no records of sales.

—— Third edition (93).

Printed by Wynkyn de Worde.

The Order of Chivalry (56).

J. West (1773), £5, 5s.—G. Mason. J. Ratcliffe
(1776), £2, 8s.—George III. (imperfect). Lord
Lovat (1852), £55, 10s.—Earl of Ashburnham
(imperfect). Lord Ashburnham (1897), £345—
Pickering & Chatto (imperfect).

O

Troylus and Creside (60).

West's perfect copy was bought by George III. in 1773 for 10 guineas. Ratcliffe's large and clean, but imperfect, copy has been sold several times at very varying prices. Herbert bought it in 1776 for £2. At Towneley's sale in 1814 the Marquis of Blandford bought it for £252, 2s. At the White Knights sale in 1819 Watson Taylor gave £162, 15s. for it. Thomas Grenville bought it for £66, 3s. at Watson Taylor's sale in 1823.

The Life of our Lady (61).

Earl Spencer gave £130 for his imperfect copy. The highest sale price recorded by Blades is £49 for the Duke of Roxburghe's copy. The Rev. T. Corser's imperfect copy, for which he gave £32 at Utterson's sale in 1852, sold for £113 in 1868. Sir William Tite's very imperfect copy (wanting thirty leaves) belonged to West, and was bought at his sale by Herbert for £2, 12s. 6d. Tite bought it in 1859 for £41, and at his sale it sold for £54. The Earl of Devon's quite perfect copy (with the blanks) was bought by Mr. Quaritch for £880 in 1883.

The Noble Histories of King Arthur (63).

The only known perfect copy was in the Harleian Library, and was sold by Osborne in 1748 to Bryan Fairfax for £5. At Fairfax's sale in 1756 Francis Child bought it for two guineas and a half, and in 1885 it was sold at the Earl of Jersey's sale to Mr. Quaritch for £1950. It is now in New York.

The Life of Charles the Great (64).

The only known copy which is perfect is now in the King's Library, British Museum. Ratcliffe bought it at West's sale (1773) for £13, and at Ratcliffe's sale (1776) George III. obtained it for 4 guineas.

The Knight Paris and the Fair Vienne (65).

The only known copy, in the King's Library, is perfect.   It was bought at West's sale by George III. for £14.

The Royal Book (67).

West's imperfect copy was bought by George III. for £10.   Gustavus Brander bought Ratcliffe's imperfect copy in 1777 for £2, 13s., but at his own sale it only brought 15s.   It was sold in 1864 to Lilly for £62.

The Althorpe perfect and beautiful copy was bought by the Marquis of Blandford at Louis Goldsmid's sale (1815) for £85, 1s.   At the Marquis's sale (1819) George Hibbert bought it for £73, 10s., and at Hibbert's sale (1829) Lord Spencer obtained it for £61, 19s.

The Duke of Buccleuch's copy (wanting a. i, with two very slight defects, both repaired) is not mentioned by Blades.   It was bought by Mr. Quaritch at the Duke's sale (1889) for £365.

Speculum Vitæ Christi (70).

West's copy was bought by Ratcliffe, who had three imperfect copies; at his sale in 1776 George III. bought one for £3, 3s., Dr. Hunter another for the same amount, and the third sold for £3, 10s. Earl Spencer bought two copies—one at J. Allen's sale (1795) for 11 guineas, and the other at the Roxburghe sale for £45; he completed the latter with two leaves taken from the former.   The duplicate was sold and came into the possession of Sir Francis Freeling : at his sale in 1836 Mr. Corser bought it for £25, 10s.. and at Corser's sale (1868) it realised £67.

Two copies are known on vellum—one, in very poor condition, is in the Royal Library at Windsor ;

the other, in the British Museum, was bought in
1864 for £1000.

The Doctrinal of Sapience (71).

The Duke of Devonshire gave £78, 15s. for the
Spencer duplicate (perfect) in Alchorne's sale (1813).
Dawson Turner's copy (wanting six leaves) was
bought by T. Bateman in 1859 for £28; at his
sale in 1893 it realised £58. Earl of Ashburnham's
copy (first and last leaf in facsimile), 1897, sold for
£660—Quaritch (for the British Museum).   The
last Earl gave £150 for this copy.

Servitium de Transfiguratione Jhesu Christi (73).

The only known copy was bought for the British
Museum at a sale at Puttick's in 1862 for £200.
It was found in a volume of Theological Tracts
presented to the Congregational Library, Blomfield
Street, by Joshua Wilson of Tunbridge Wells in 1831.

The Fayts of Arms (74).

The largest amount paid for a copy at a public
sale is £336, which the Duke of Devonshire gave
for the Roxburghe copy (with a few lines of the last
leaf in facsimile).

Bryan Fairfax's imperfect copy was bought by
Francis Child for £1, 11s. 6d. At the sale of
Lord Jersey's library in 1885 it sold for £71.

Libri's perfect, but mended and washed, copy,
which he had bought in very poor condition from
Mario the great tenor, was sold in 1862 to Mr. F.
Huth for £255.

Mr. Corser's perfect copy was bought in 1868 by
Mr. Quaritch for £250.

Sir W. Tite's copy (with the first two leaves in
facsimile) sold in 1874 for £190. This copy was

bought by Tite at the Rev. C. H. Crauford's sale in 1854 for £77. Crauford bought it at Wilks's sale (1847) for £54.

The Earl of Crawford's perfect copy, with Table inlaid, sold in 1889 for £235. R. Lindsay, in Philadelphia, had this copy in his catalogue (June 1893) for £425.

The History of Blanchardin and Eglantine (78).

The only known copy, which is imperfect, is in the Althorpe library. This copy was bought at Ratcliffe's sale by G. Mason for £3, 6s.; at Mason's sale (1799) the Duke of Roxburghe bought it for £21. Earl Spencer gave £215, 5s. for it at the Roxburghe sale.

Eneydos (81).

R. Smith (1682), 3s. Walter Rea (1682), 1s. 6d.

F. Child gave 30s. for B. Fairfax's perfect copy, which sold at the Earl of Jersey's sale (1885) for £235.

Hanrott's imperfect copy was bought in 1833 by Lord Auckland for £43, 1s.; at his sale two years afterwards H. Holland bought it for £24. At Holland's sale (1860) Mr. H. Huth bought it for £84.

Mr. Quaritch had a copy in 1875 with two leaves in facsimile, otherwise a fine copy, which he marked £300.

The Art and Craft to Know Well to Die (86).

West's perfect copy was bought by Ratcliffe for £5, 2s. 6d.; at Ratcliffe's sale George III. bought it for 4 guineas.

Mr. C. Tutet's copy was bought in 1786 by Payne for 2 guineas; probably this is the perfect copy which Payne sold to the National Library, Paris, for 10 guineas.

The Chastising of God's Children (90).

R. Smith (1682), 5s.   Dr. Bernard (1698), 1s. 10d. Osborne (1751), 15s.

The Roxburghe copy (perfect) was bought by Lord Spencer for £140.

The Earl of Aylesford bought the Marquis of Blandford's copy (bound with "'Treatise of Love," No. 91) for £32, 10s., and at his sale in 1888 it realised £305.   F. Perkins (1889), £100.

S. Alchorne's copy sold in 1813 for £94, 10s.; Valentine's copy in 1842 for £5.   Blades describes this last in his catalogue list as Alchorne's; but this is probably a mistake, as Valentine bought J. Inglis's copy (1826) for £17, 10s.

Sex perelegantissimæ Epistolæ (1483).

24 leaves.   The only copy known of this tract was discovered in 1874 by Dr. G. Könnecke, archivist of Marburg, in an old volume of seventeenth-century divinity in the Hecht-Heinean Library at Halberstadt.   The discovery was described by Mr. Blades at the time in the *Athenæum* (Feb. 27, 1875).   This copy was bought by the British Museum in 1890 for £250.

Almost as scarce and valuable as Caxtons are the books printed at St. Albans :—

The Chronicle of St. Albans (circa 1484), the second book printed at St. Albans, and the first edition of the Chronicle, was sold at the Earl of Ashburnham's sale (1897) to Messrs. J. & J. Leighton for £180.   It was imperfect, but no absolutely perfect copy is known.

In Quaritch's catalogue, 1884 (No. 355), a copy with five leaves in facsimile and twenty-two others deficient, was marked £300.

The Boke of St. Albans (1486), a copy perfected in MS., was sold at the Roxburghe sale for £147. It was resold at the White Knights sale for £84. In March 1882 Mr. Quaritch bought it at Christie's for 600 guineas. The Grenville copy now in the British Museum has gone through many vicissitudes, which were graphically described by Dr. Maitland in 1847. It appears that at the end of the last century the library of Thonock Hall, in the parish of Gainsborough, the seat of the Hickman family, was sorted out by an ignorant person who threw into a condemned heap all books without covers. A gardener who took an interest in heraldry begged permission to take home what he liked from this heap, and he chose among other books *The Book of St. Albans.* This remained in his cottage till June 1844, when his son's widow sold 9 lbs. of books to a pedlar for 9d. The pedlar sold the lot for 3s. to a chemist in Gainsborough, who was rather struck by *The Book of St. Albans*, and tried to sell it, but the neighbours did not wish to buy it. Eventually he obtained £2, 2s. for it from a man who expected to sell it to advantage. The purchaser sold it to Stark the bookseller for £7, 7s. Stark took it to London and sold it to the Right Hon. Thomas Grenville for seventy or eighty guineas. Mr. Blades communicated this account to *Notes and Queries* (3rd Series, iv. 369).

A copy was sold at the Earl of Ashburnham's sale (1897), which was stated to be the Roxburghe copy, completed by the Earl from another copy. Mr. Quaritch bought this for £385.

Still rarer than this is one of the treatises in a
separate form, and printed in the next century :—

Juliana Barnes's *Treatyse of Fysshynge with an Angle.*
London : Wynkyn de Worde (1532). First separate
edition, unique.
In the Harleian Library, afterwards in Gulston's
collection, who sold it to J. Ratcliffe, bought at
his sale by White the bookseller, sold by him to Mr.
Haworth, at whose sale it sold for 19 guineas (unbound). Earl of Ashburnham (1897), green morocco,
£360.

A few prices may now be given of some of the
most interesting publications of the old English
press, consisting of the works of poets, travellers,
&c., all of which have greatly increased in value,
and will probably increase still more :—

King Arthur, W. Coplande, 1557.
Dent, £20, 9s. 6d., fine copy, in olive morocco
by Lewis. H. Perkins (1873), £120 (same copy).
Bancroft's (T.) *Two Bookes of Epigrammes and Epitaphs,*
1639. *Rare Books and MSS.* (Sotheby, March
1897), fine uncut copy, £42.
Barnfield's (Richard) *Encomion of Lady Pecunia,* 1598.
Malone bought Farmer's copy for 19s. Ouvry
(1882), £105.
Bradshaw's (Henry) *holy lyfe and history of Saynt Wer-
burghe* (Pynson, 1521, 4°, pp. 294).
Only three copies known : (1) Gough's, now in
the Bodleian ; (2) Heber's, sold in 1834 for £19, 5s.;
(3) copy in Longman's catalogue (Bibl. Anglo-
Poetica), 1815, marked £63.

The prices of Caxton's two editions of Chaucer's "Canterbury Tales" are recorded on a previous page of this chapter. Imperfect copies of Pynson's first and second editions were marked £25 in Longman's catalogue (1815). The first edition (fifty-four leaves inlaid and two leaves in facsimile) fetched at the Heber sale £60,18s., and at the Earl of Ashburnham's, £233. The second edition (1526) sold at the Roxburghe sale for £30, 9s., and an imperfect copy at the Ashburnham sale for £26.

Wynkyn de Worde's edition is as valuable as a Caxton, and a fine and perfect copy sold at the Ashburnham sale for £1000.

> Cutwode's (T.) *Caltha Poetarum; or, Bumble Bee*, 1599.
> Three copies only known: (1) Malone's, now in the Bodleian; (2) Heber's, from which the Roxburghe Club reprint was made, sold in 1834 for £3, 18s.; (3) a copy which belonged successively to Steevens, Caldecott, and Freeling. Steevens' sale (1800), £2, 12s. 6d.; Freeling (1836), £11, 15s.
>
> According to Ritson, this book "was staid at the press by order of the Archbishop of Canterbury and Bishop of London; and such copies as could be found or were already taken were to be presently brought to the Bishop of London to be burnt." Dibdin gives an amusing account of the Roxburghe Club reprint (1815) in his "Reminiscences" (vol. i. p. 465, note):—"A bet was laid (the winner of the bet to give the Roxburghe Club a dinner) between Sir M. M. Sykes and Mr. Dent whether the anniversary meeting of 1815 was the third or fourth of the club. Mr. Dent was the loser, when Mr. Heber promised to present the club with a reprint of the

above poem at the extra dinner in contemplation. Only nine days intervened, but within that period the reprint was transcribed, superintended at the press by Mr. Haslewood (without a single error), bound by Charles Lewis, and presented to the members on sitting down to dinner. Mr. Haslewood was reported to have walked in his sleep with a pen in his hand during the whole period of its preparation."

Drummond of Hawthornden's *Forth Feasting*, 1617, bought by Ouvry at Sotheby's in 1858 for £8, 15s. (bound in morocco), fetched £60 at Ouvry's sale in 1882.

Fabyan's *Chronicles* (Pynson, 1516), first edition.
    Dr. F. Bernard (1698), 4s. 8d.
    Roberts (1815), £84—North. John North (1819), £92. (Perfect.)
    Samuel Lysons (1820), £35—Lord Aylesford. Lord Aylesford (1888), £250—Christie Miller. (Completed by leaves from another edition.)

Foxe's *Acts and Monuments* (John Daye, 1562–63), first edition, complete.
    Earl of Ashburnham (1897), £150.

Frobisher's *Three Voyages of Discoverie*, 1578, with Keymis's *Second Voyage to Guiana*, 1596, in one vol., calf gilt, by Kalthoeber.
    Beckford (1882), £300.
    Ouvry's copy of Frobisher, wanting the maps, sold for £68.

Froissart's *Cronycles* (Pynson, 1523–25), two vols. folio.
    G. Mason (1798), £36, 15s. Roxburghe (1812), £63. Towneley (1814), £42 (title of vol. i. a reprint). W. H. Crawford (Lakelands), 1891, £25.

Hakluyt's *Principal Navigations, Voiages and Discoveries of the English Nation*, 1589, with rare map, fine copy, in pigskin.
Jadis, £26, 5s. Same copy, Duke of Hamilton (1884), £23.

Hariot (T.), *Merveilleux et estrange Rapport* . . . Francofurti, 1590.
Duke of Hamilton (1884), fine copy, in morocco by Lewis, £97.

Linschoten's *Voyages into the Easte and West Indies*, 1598, maps and plates from the Dutch edition, title inlaid, and last leaf mended.
Roxburghe, £10, 15s. Same copy, Beckford (1882), £14. Colonel Stanley, £22.

Lodge's (Thomas) *Rosalynde*, 1598.
Longman (1815), £20 (imperfect). Heber, £5, 10s. Ouvry (1882), £63.

Lok's (Henry) *Ecclesiastes* (London: Richard Field, 1597).
Longmans (1815), £28. Sotheby's (March 1817), £6, 16s. G. Daniel, £38, 10s.

The first editions of Milton's works have greatly increased in price. Not many years ago a copy of the first edition of the "Paradise Lost" could be obtained for about five pounds, but now a good copy is worth at least four times as much. The prices vary considerably with the date of the title-page, of which there are several issues. G. Daniel's fine copy sold in 1864 for £28, 10s.

Milton's *Maske* (*Comus*), 1637.
> Loscombe, £25.   G. Daniel, £36.

—— *Poems*, 1645, first edition, with portrait by Marshall.
> G. Daniel, £5, 15s.   *Rare Books and MSS.*
> (Sotheby, March 1897), fine uncut copy, £24, 10s.

Purchas his Pilgrimes, five vols., 1625–26.
> Digby (1680), £3, 5s. 6d.   H. Perkins, 1873,
> fine copy, £86.   Beckford, 1883, fine copy, £63.
> Earl of Gosford (1884), £82 (crimson morocco).
> Earl of Crawford (1887), £60.

Rhodes (Hugh), *Boke of Nurture*, 1577.
> Steevens (1800), £2, 2s.   Longmans (1815),
> £15.

Ricraft's *Peculiar Characters of the Oriental Languages*,
sm. 4to.
> Bindley, £19, 19s.   Same copy, bound afterwards
> in russia extra by Lewis, who charged £1, 5s. for
> the binding, sold in Beckford sale (1883) for £8,
> 17s. 6d.

Scot's *Discoverie of Witchcraft*, 1584.
> Boswell, £3, 3s.   Comerford (1881), £25, 10s.
> (citron moroeco).

It is interesting to notice that in the old sales of
the seventeenth century the folios of Shakespeare,
Beaumont and Fletcher, and Ben Jonson all sold
for about the same price. Those of the first now
sell for one hundred and two hundred times what
they brought then, while those of the second and
third do not bring ten times.

Beaumont and Fletcher's Works, 1647.
>Sir Edward Bysshe (1679), 13s. 6d. Smallwood
(1684), 8s. A. Young and others (Puttick's), 1875,
£5. Alfred Crampton (1896), 10 guineas.

Jonson's (Ben) Works, 1640.
>Benj. Worsley (1678), £1, 13s. 6d. Sir Edward
Bysshe (1677), £1, 10s. Lord Bateman (1896),
£8, 5s.

Spenser's *Faerie Queene*, 1590–96, first edition.
>Sir Edward Bysshe (1679), 6s. 2d. Lloyd and
Raymund (1685), 1s. Ouvry (1882), £33. Alfred
Crampton (1611), 1896, with additional leaves, £85.

Weever's *Funeral Monuments*, 1631.
>Two copies on large paper in Beckford's sale,
part 4 (1883), olive morocco, index inlaid, £25;
blue morocco, £38.

Wycliffe.
>Mr. Addington bought at the Dix sale four unique
tracts of Wycliffe for £400, and expressed his opinion
that they would have been cheap at any price, but
at his own sale (1886) they only realised £133—
viz., Crede, &c., £37; Consolation, £27; Testament of Moyses, £36; Small Prayers to Common
People, £33.

Americana is a class of book which has grown
enormously in price. Anything published in America in the seventeenth and eighteenth centuries
now fetches a price.

Smith's *Virginia*, 1624.
>Dr. F. Bernard (1698), 4s. 2d. Hunter (1813),
£27, 6s.

A large paper copy sold at the Beckford sale (1883) for £605 (dedication copy to the Duchess of Richmond, in old brown morocco, covered with gold tooling, with the Duchess's arms forming the centre ornaments).

Eliot Bible of 1661–63.

Dr. L. Seaman (1676), 19s.   Wimpole library (Lord Chancellor Hardwicke), 1888, £580— Quaritch.

At this Wimpole sale (Christie's) a volume of twelve tracts of the sixteenth and seventeenth centuries relating to America sold for £555.

A curious incident occurred at Messrs. Sotheby's in July 1897, during the sale of the library of Mr. Cyril Dunn Gardner. A volume of Sermons, which included "A Sermon preached at Plimmoth in New England, Dec. 9, 1621," was put up, and the biddings, commencing at 5s., were carried on till £1, 17s. was reached, when the lot was knocked down at that amount. A dispute arising, it was put up again, and was eventually bought by Messrs. H. Stevens and Son for £87.

CHAPTER X

PRICES OF SHAKESPEARE'S WORKS

THE first edition of Shakespeare's Plays (folio, 1623) has been rising in price from the commencement of the nineteenth century; but the enormous prices now paid do not date further back than 1864, when a specially fine copy was bought by the Baroness Burdett-Coutts at George Daniel's sale for £716, 2s. This amount was paid on account of the height of the book and of its great beauty, and possibly the circumstance of the year being the tercentenary of Shakespeare's birth had something to do with it, but this sale had the effect of raising the price of all copies permanently.

Beloe, writing in 1807 ("Anecdotes," vol. i. p. 36), said, "Perhaps there is no book in the English language which has risen so rapidly in value as the first edition of the works of our great national poet. I can remember a very fine copy to have been sold for five guineas. I could once have purchased a superb one for nine guineas." This statement can be corroborated; for the Cracherode copy in the British Museum, one of the few really fine copies, has the price £8, 18s. 6d. marked in it. Richard Wright's copy sold in 1787 for £10, Allen's in 1795 for 18 guineas. Farmer's copy (wanting title, and with the last leaf in MS.) sold for £7. Garrick bought his copy from Payne for £1, 16s. Jolley obtained it at Garrick's sale in 1823 for £34, 2s. 6d., and at Jolley's sale in 1844 it realised £84. Lord Denbigh's fine copy sold in 1825 for £89, 5s., and Broadley's in 1832 for £51 ; William Combes's copy (wanting title-page and all prefatory leaves, but with the text of the Plays complete) fetched 8 guineas in 1837 ; Bright's copy (1845), with title repaired, verses from another edition, and some leaves inlaid, brought £31, 10s. The Stowe copy (1849), with verses inlaid, £76 ; Hawtrey's (1853), with some leaves mended, £63. In 1824 Mr. Thorpe the bookseller advertised a set of the four folios— first, £65 ; second, 10 guineas ; third, £25 ; and the fourth, 6 guineas, or the four for £100. About the same time Mr. Pickering marked a similar set £95.

Copies of the first folio are so constantly sold that one might suppose it to be a common book, but this may be accounted for by the fact that they are constantly changing hands. There are only a few copies absolutely perfect, but others are made up from various copies, or with pages in facsimile. This makes the most imperfect copies of value, because they can be used to perfect others.

Dibdin described thirty copies of the first folio in his " Library Companion," and these he arranged in three classes. In the first class he placed three copies, belonging respectively to Mr. Cracherode, the Right Hon. Thomas Grenville, and Mr. Daniel Moore. The first two are now in the British

Museum, and the third is the Daniel copy, for which Lilly the bookseller offered £300.

"These have size, condition, and the genuine properties of a true copy. They are thirteen inches in height, eight and a half in width, have the true portrait and title-page, with the genuine verses in the centre of the leaf facing the title-page. They have no spurious leaves foisted in from other editions. . . . Of these three copies, that in the Cracherode collection is the most objectionable, as the commendatory verses of Ben Jonson, facing the title-page, are, although genuine, inlaid."

Mr. Grenville's copy was bought at Saunders's sale in 1818 for £121, 16s., which was then thought to be a great sum, and Dibdin makes the unfortunate prophecy that this was "the highest price ever given, or likely to be given, for the volume." Mr. Grenville told Dibdin that an ancestor of Sir Watkin Williams Wynn possessed an uncut copy of the first folio. "It was lying on the table in that condition when, in a luckless moment, a stationer in the neighbourhood of Wynnstay came in. The book was given to him to be bound, and off went not only the edges, but half of the margins." Another piece of vandalism was the inlaying the leaves of the book and binding them in three volumes. This was Henderson the actor's copy, which sold at Reed's sale for £38. In the second class were included some very good copies.

"Lord Spencer's copy had every leaf picked by the experienced hands of the late George Steevens. The verses opposite are genuine, but inlaid, and there are many tender

P

leaves throughout. There are also in the centre of some of the pages a few greasy-looking spots, which might have originally received the 'flakes of pie-crust' in the servants' hall, as notified by Steevens.[1] But it is a beautiful and desirable copy."

The price mentioned by Steevens is that which the Duke of Roxburghe gave for his copy in 1790, respecting which Dibdin relates an anecdote that took his fancy so much, that he tells the story both at the beginning and at the end of his *Bibliomania*.

"A friend was bidding for him in the sale-room: his Grace had retired to a distance to view the issue of the contest. Twenty guineas and more were offered from various quarters for the book: a slip of paper was handed to the Duke, in which he was requested to inform his friend whether he was 'to go on bidding.' His Grace took his pencil and wrote underneath, by way of reply—

'Lay on, Macduff;
And d—d be he who first cries, "Hold, enough!"'

Such a spirit was irresistible, and bore down all opposition. His Grace retired triumphant, with the book under his arm."

[1] Steevens's remarks, given in another page of Dibdin's "Library Companion," are worth quoting here, more particularly as that Shakesperian commentator gives his opinion of what was a high price for the first folio: "I have repeatedly met with thin flakes of pie-crust between the leaves of our author. These unctuous fragments, remaining long in close confinement, communicated their grease to several pages deep on each side of them. . . . Most of the first folios now extant are known to have belonged to ancient families resident in the country. Since our breakfasts have become less gross, our favourite authors have escaped with fewer injuries. . . . I claim the merit of being the first commentator on Shakespeare who strove with becoming seriousness to account for the present stains that disgrace the earliest folio edition of his plays, which is now become the most expensive single book in our language; for what other English volume without plates, and printed since the year 1600, is known to have sold, more than once, for £35, 14s. ?"

A rather different version of this story of Nicol's purchase for the Duke is given in Martin's "Privately Printed Books."

This copy sold at the Roxburghe sale for £100, and is now in the Duke of Devonshire's library. Dibdin had a commission from Sir Mark Masterman Sykes to give £75.

Hibbert's copy was pronounced by Mr. Amyot to be the best copy he had seen after those placed in the first class. It belonged to "Dog" Jennings, and was purchased of Mr. Payne for 70 guineas. At Hibbert's sale it fetched 81 guineas, and was resold in 1847 at Wilks's sale for £155. It again occurred at Dunn Gardner's sale (1854), when it was bought by Mr. H. Huth for £250.

Dent's copy was a tall copy, identical in measurement with Daniel's, and with some rough leaves, but the title and verses were pasted down. It was bought by H. Perkins for £110, 5s., and at Perkins's sale it realised £585, 10s.

John Kemble's copy was inlaid on large paper, and bound by Mackinlay. It was purchased by Mr. Boswell for £112, 7s., and at his sale it brought £105.

In the third class are the following :—

Steevens's copy was given to him by Jacob Tonson in 1765, and it had passed through the hands of Theobald and Dr. Johnson, the "latter not having improved its condition." It wants the title and portrait, the latter being supplied by a facsimile drawing by Steevens. The verses are from the second edition. Dr. Charles Burney bought this

at the sale of Steevens's library for £22. It is now
in the British Museum. Nassau's copy was perfect,
with the exception that the verses were from the
second edition. It was bought by Mr. Thorpe for
£49, 7s.

E. V. Utterson's copy was fair, with title and
portrait mounted, verses inlaid, and several leaves
mended. It sold for £49 in 1852.

Colonel Stanley's copy was in fair condition, but
wanted the original verses and title-page. It was
bought at Stanley's sale by Mr. North for £37, 16s.,
and at North's sale it realised £39, 18s.

Heber gave 10 guineas for his copy, which wanted
verses, list of actors, &c., title a reprint from the
second edition, some leaves stained, and others
mutilated. This sold at Heber's sale (1834) for
£57, 15s.

A copy of the first folio is now looked upon as a
necessary addition to a first-class library, but there
was no copy in the libraries of the Earl of Oxford,
Dr. Mead, West, Askew, Crofts, Beauclerk, Heath,
Willett, Bindley, or in the Sunderland or Hamilton
Palace libraries.

Mr. Robert Holford is said to have given £250
for his tall copy.

The following is a list of some of the copies which
have been sold since the famous Daniel copy :—

> In 1882 Beresford-Hope's copy, with verses inlaid,
> title repaired, in morocco by Clarke, fetched £238 ;
> and Ouvry's sound copy, in red morocco by Clarke
> and Bedford, sold for £420.
>
> The Earl of Gosford's copy, perfect, with title

and verses mounted, and margins of leaves slightly mended, was sold in 1884 for £470.

Hartley's copy was in poor condition, although very tall (13⅜ by 8¾), title with portrait wanting, page with verses mutilated, and some leaves mended. It sold in 1887 for £255. Hartley gave £500 for it to those who had bought it at a knock-out for £75.

The Earl of Aylesford's copy, wanting title, with verses from second edition, and five leaves stained, sold in 1888 for £200.

In 1889 F. Perkins's copy, with title and verses mounted, sold for £415; and Halliwell Phillipps's poor copy, with portrait, verses, preliminary and last leaf in facsimile, for £95.

W. H. Crawford's imperfect copy, with title, verses, prefatory matter, and "Cymbeline" reprinted in facsimile, sold in 1891 for £16, 10s.

In this same year Brayton Ives's copy, perfect, but rather short, was sold in New York for 4200 dollars (£840).

Addington's copy, with verses inlaid, in good condition, but short (12⅝ by 8¼), fetched £280.

A copy, with title in facsimile, leaf containing verses, last leaf and a few others mended in the margin, was sold in a sale of Early English Poetry (Sotheby, 1892) for £208.

Birket Foster's copy sold in 1894 for £255; and Mr. Toovey's, with title and verses in facsimile, for £169.

SECOND FOLIO, 1632.

The most interesting copy of the second folio is
in the King's Library. It belonged to Dr. Mead, at
whose sale it was bought by Askew for £2, 12s. 6d.
At Askew's sale it was bought by Steevens for £5,
10s., an amount which he styled enormous. At
Steevens's sale this copy was bought for George
III. for eighteen guineas. It formerly belonged to
Charles I., who wrote in it, " Dum spiro spero, C.R."
The King presented it the night before his execu-
tion to Sir Thomas Herbert, who had written, " Ex
dono serenissimi Regis Car. Servo suo Humiliss.
T. Herbert." Steevens mistook the identity of
this Herbert, and wrote, " Sir Thomas Herbert
was Master of the Revels to King Charles the
First." George III. wrote beneath Steevens's
note, " This is a mistake, he (Sir Thomas Herbert)
having been Groom of the Bed-Chamber to King
Charles I., but Sir Henry Herbert was Master of
the Revels."

Dibdin made the same mistake with respect to
this price that he did with respect to the price of
the Grenville first folio. He wrote, " £18, 18s.—the
largest sum ever given, or likely to be given, for the
book." Now in 1895, at the Earl of Orford's sale,
the largest and finest copy known of the second
folio, in the original calf binding, sold for the
enormous sum of £540. This is out of all proportion to the price of the first folio, and a ridiculous
amount to pay for a volume of little interest by

itself, and only of value as one of the four original editions.

The next largest price realised for a second folio was £148 for Daniel's copy, which has some rough leaves, and was bought by Daniel from Thorpe, who bought it at the Nevill Holt sale for £28, 1s. The Earl of Aylesford's copy, with title laid down, and without verses (13¾₁₆ in. by 8¾ in.), sold in 1888 for £140. Brayton Ives's perfect copy was sold in New York in 1891 for 400 dollars (£80). Birket Foster's copy sold in 1894 for £56.

It is only lately that such high prices have been obtained for this edition. The following is a list of some of the prices given at an earlier date :—

> B. Worsley (1678), 16s.   Digby (1680), 14s.
> Richard Wright, M.D. (1787), £2, 9s. and £1, 6s.
> Allen (1795), £4, 4s.   Stanley (1813), £13, 2s. 6d.
> Heber, Part 1, £10, 5s. ; Part 4, wanting verses opposite title-page, and last leaf inlaid, £3, 7s. Valpy (1832), £18 ; resold to Broadley (1832), £12, 5s.   Stowe (1849), £11, 5s.

Copies Sold within the Last Twenty-five Years :—
> H. Perkins (1873), £44 (fine copy). Well-known collector (Sotheby's), 1880, £12, 15s. (verses from fourth edition printed, part of title in facsimile reprint). Ouvry (1882), £46. Beresford-Hope (1882), £35, 10s. (title mended). Standard English Works (Puttick's), 1886, £19. F. Perkins (1889), large copy, but worm-hole through half the volume, £47. W. H. Crawford (1891), wanting verses, £19, 10s. Smithson and others, 1896 (Puttick's), £18, 5s. (verses and several pages

wanting, and a few worm-holes).   Jack, Halliday,
&c. (Sotheby, July 1897), £55 (fine copy, portrait
and verses mended).

Sir Henry Irving gave £100 for Dr. Johnson's
copy of the second folio, which contains many notes
in the margin by Theobald and Johnson.   Osborn
the bookseller bought it at Theobald's death and
presented it to Johnson.   Samuel Ireland gave £1
for it at Johnson's sale in 1785.   It wants title and
part of another leaf.[1]

THIRD FOLIO, 1664 (some copies dated 1663).

This edition is scarcer than the second, owing to
the copies having been destroyed in the Fire of
London.   The title-page of 1663 has the portrait,
and that of 1664 is without it.   Mr. Thorpe, in one
of his catalogues, said that he had "refused £10
for the title of 1663."   Mr. Quaritch gave £11 for
one in 1895 at Sotheby's.

The following is a list of the prices that some
copies have realised :—

> B. Worsley (1678), £1, 8s. 6d.   Smallwood (1684),
> 15s. 6d.   Richard Wright, M.D. (1787), £1, 1s.
> Allen (1795), £6, 6s.   Steevens (1800), £8, 8s.
> Roxburghe (1812), £35.   Stanley (1813), £16, 16s.
> Broadley (1832), £11, 5s.   William Combes (1837),
> £5, 7s. 6d. (some leaves inlaid).   Stowe (Duke of
> Buckingham), 1849, £35 (margin of portrait mended,
> title lined).   Lord Stuart de Rothesay, £50 (tall

----

[1] "Talk about Autographs," by George Birkbeck Hill, London,
1896, p. 69.

copy, with duplicate titles). Miss Currer (1862), £43, 10s. (original calf). Addington, £130 (large and fine copy). S. Daniel (1864), £46. H. Perkins (1873), £105 (⅛-inch taller than Daniel's copy). Beresford-Hope (1882), £72, 10s. (portrait and title inlaid). Ouvry (1882), £116. Earl of Aylesford (1888), £93 (13½ in. by 8 in.). F. Perkins (1889), £100. Halliwell Phillipps (1889), £24 (title mounted, portrait, verses, and last leaf mounted). Brayton Ives (1891), 950 dollars (£190), portrait from fourth edition. Hawley (1894), £205. Hildyard, 1895 (with two title-pages), £280. Misc. Coll. (Sotheby's), 1895, original calf, £350.

FOURTH FOLIO, 1685.

Dibdin says of this that it "has little to recommend it, either on the score of rarity or intrinsic worth." Even now the prices are not very high, and it is only required to complete the set of folios.

The following are some of the prices that this volume has realised :—

Richard Wright, M.D. (1787), £1, 1s. Steevens (1800), £2, 12s. 6d. Roxburghe (1812), £6, 6s. Broadley (1832), £2, 2s. William Combes (1837), £2, 5s. Stowe (Duke of Buckingham), 1849, £4, 6s. Daniel (1864), £21, 10s. H. Perkins (1873), £22. Beresford-Hope (1882), £24. Ouvry (1882), £28. Choice library of a gentleman (1882), £17, 10s. Chevalier de Chatelain (1882), £7, 5s. (imperfections supplied in MS.). Addington (1886), £23, 10s. (good tall copy). Old Essex library

(Lord Petre), 1886, £31, 10s. (old calf).   Earl of
Aylesford (1888), £29 (14¼ in. by 9¼ in.).   F. Perkins
(1889), £14 (portrait and last two leaves slightly
repaired).   Halliwell Phillipps (1889), £30 (perfect
copy, in original calf).   Brayton Ives (1891), New
York, 210 dollars (£42).   Early English Poetry
(Sotheby, 1892), £31.   Birket Foster (1894), £25.
Alfred Crampton (1896), £42 (14⅜ in. by 9⅛ in.).

SEPARATE PLAYS.

*All's Well that Ends Well, Antony and Cleopatra, As
You Like It, Comedy of Errors, Coriolanus, Cymbeline,* first editions in first folio.

Hamlet (Printed for N. L. and John Trundell), 1603, two
copies known.
  (1) Duke of Devonshire, purchased of Payne and
Foss, 1825 (in vol. containing twelve early editions
of this play), for £250 (wanting last leaf).
  (2) British Museum, wanting title-page.   Bought
by Mr. Rooney of Dublin in 1856 for small sum,
sold to Boone for £70, purchased of them by Halliwell Phillipps for £120.   It was sold subsequently
to the British Museum.

—— (L. R. for N. L.) 1604.
  (1) Duke of Devonshire.   (2) Earl Howe.   (3)
H. Huth.

Henry IV., Part 1 (P. S. for Andrew Wise), 1598.

—— (S. S. for Andrew Wise), 1599.
  Steevens, £3, 10s.   Roxburghe, £6, 6s.   White
Knights, £18, 7s. 6d.   Utterson, £14.   Halliwell
(May 1857), £75.   G. Daniel (1864), £115, 10s.

Henry IV., Part 2 (V. S. for A. Wise and W. Apsley), 1600.

Steevens, two copies (Dibdin, "Library Companion," 805), £3, 13s., £2, 15s. Smyth (1797), £8, 8s. Roxburghe, £2. 4s. Heber (Part 2), £40. Utterson (1852), £17, 10s. Halliwell Phillipps, £100 — sold to Mr. Huth. F. Perkins, 1889 (Heber's copy), £225.

Henry V., "Chronicle History" (Thomas Creede for T. Millington & J. Burby), 1600.

Steevens (inlaid), £27, 6s. Kemble, resold (Sotheby, April 1821), £18, 7s. 6d. Heber (Part 2), £24, 3s.—bought by Mr. Daniel. Bought at Daniel's sale (1864) for 220 guineas by Lilly. (Fine copy.)

Henry VI., Parts 1 and 2, first editions in folio. Part 3 ("The true Tragedie of Richard, Duke of York"), P.S. for T. Millington, 1595.

Chalmers (Part 1), £131.

—— (W. W. for T. Millington), 1600.

Steevens, £1, 16s. Rhodes, £5, 7s. 6d. (one leaf MS.). Jolley, £10, 10s. Halliwell (1857), £60.

Henry VIII., Julius Cæsar, King John, first editions in folio.

True Chronicle Historie of King Lear (Nathaniel Butter, St. Paul's Churchyard), 1608.

Steevens, £28. Dent, £14, 5s. Strettell, £15. Edwards (1804), £15, 4s. 6d. Heber (Part 2), £32. Halliwell (1856), £22, 10s.—bought for Mr. Huth. Birket Foster (1894), £100.

There were second and third editions published
in the same year with Butter's name, but without
place.

Love's Labour Lost (W. W. for Cuthbert Burby), 1598.
Dent, £26. Bindley, £40, 10s. Rhodes, £53,
11s. Heber (Part 2), £40 (Bindley's copy); came
into the possession of George Daniel, who valued it
at £200. It sold for 330 guineas at Daniel's sale. F.
Perkins (1859), £70 (headlines cut into, and last
leaf mended). Thomas Gaisford (1890), £140.

Macbeth, Measure for Measure, first editions in folio.

Merchant of Venice (J. Roberts), 1600.
Steevens, £2, 2s., £2 (two copies, both inlaid).
Roxburghe, £2, 14s.; resold to Jadis, £6, 6s.; re-
sold to Holland (1860), £15. Heber (Part 2), £12.
Jolley, £14. Utterson (1852), £16. Halliwell
(1859), £21. F. Perkins (1889), £121. W. H.
Crawford (1891), £111. Sir Cecil Domville, 1897,
(fine copy), £315.

—— (J. R. for Thomas Heyes), 1600.
Duke of Grafton, £9, 9s. Bindley, £22, 1s.
Roxburghe, £10. Heber (Part 2), £33, 10s.
Field, £13, 15s. Gardner (1854), £32—bought by
Mr. Tite. Halliwell (1856), £37—bought by Mr.
Huth. Daniel, £99, 15s. F. W. Cosens (1890),
£270. W. H. Crawford (1891), £111. Birket
Foster (1894), £146.

Merry Wives of Windsor (T. C. for Arthur Johnson),
1602.
Bindley, £18. Steevens, £28—purchased by
Malone; resold to Heber. Heber (Part 2), £40;

bought by G. Daniel; sold at his sale in 1864 for 330 guineas to Lilly.   Thomas Gaisford (1890), £385.

Merry Wives of Windsor, for Arthur Johnston, 1619.
Roxburghe, £1, 3s.   Steevens, £1, 4s.   Dent, £8.   Heber (Part 2), £7.   Halliwell (1856), £16 —bought by Mr. Tite.   Halliwell (1858), £14. 5s.

Midsummer Night's Dreame (Thomas Fisher), 1600.
Steevens (part of a leaf wanting), £25, 10s. Bindley, £22, 10s.   Heber (Part 2, very fine), £36—bought by Daniel; sold at his sale in 1864 for 230 guineas to Lilly.   Brayton Ives (New York), 1891, 725 dollars.   Birket Foster (1894), £122 (large copy).

——— (James Roberts), 1600.
Boswell, £2, 1s.   Roxburghe, £3, 3s.   Duke of Grafton, £4, 8s.   Dent, £4, 10s.   Heber (Part 4, fine), £7—bought by Daniel; sold at his sale for £36—bought by Lilly.   Gardner (1854), £12, 15s. Sotheby, 1857 (Berry), £21.   F. Perkins (1889), £61 (three headlines shaved).

Much Ado about Nothing (V. S. for A. Wise and W. Apsley), 1600.
Smyth (1797), £7, 10s.   Steevens, £2, 12s. 6d. Roxburghe, £2, 17s.   Broadley (1832), £2, 19s. Bindley, £17, 17s.
Heber, Part 2 (finest copy known, with rough edges), £18—bought by Daniel; sold at his sale (1864) for 255 guineas—Toovey.   Halliwell (1857), £65—bought by Mr. Huth.   Halliwell Phillipps (1889), £50 (several leaves in facsimile).   F. Perkins (1889), £75 (headlines cut into).   Thomas Gaisford (1890), £130.

Othello (N. O. for T. Walkley), 1622.

Steevens (with MS. notes), £29, 8s. Gilchrist, £19, 10s. Dent, £22. Bindley, £56, 14s.; re-sold Heber (Part 2), for £28; bought by Daniel; sold at his sale for £155 to Lilly. William Combes (1837), £15, 5s. F. Perkins (1889), £130.

Pericles (H. Gosson), 1609.

Steevens, £1, 2s. Roxburghe, £1, 15s.

Heber, Part 2, £18—bought by Daniel; sold at his sale for £84.

F. Perkins, 1889 (Steevens's copy, with his auto-graph), £60. Halliwell Phillipps (1889), £30 (title reprinted, and two leaves wanting).

J. T. Frere, 1896, £171.

Richard II. (Valentine Simmes for Andrew Wise), 1597.

Daniel's was the first copy brought to auction. Bought by Lilly (1864) for 325 guineas.

—— (Val. Simmes for Andrew Wise), 1598.

Steevens, £4, 14s. 6d. Roxburghe, £7, 7s. White Knights, £10. Heber, £4, 14s. 6d. Bright (1845), £13, 10s. Daniel (1864), 103 guineas—Halliwell.

Richard III. (Valentine Sims for Andrew Wise), 1597.

Nixon (1818), £33; resold to Heber. Heber (Part 2), £41, 9s. 6d.; bought by Daniel; sold at his sale for 335 guineas to Lilly.

Romeo and Juliet (John Danter), 1597.

Heber, Part 2 (wanting title, and cut into the text), £1, 1s.

Kemble gave Stace the bookseller £30 for his copy, now in the library of the Duke of Devon-shire.

Romeo and Juliet, second or first complete edition
(T. Crede for C. Burby), 1599.

   Steevens, £6.   Roxburghe, £7, 10s.   White
Knights, £10, 10s.   Heber, £5, 15s. 6d.   Daniel,
£52, 10s.   F. Perkins (1889), £164 (headlines cut
into, and title mounted).

Taming of the Shrew, Tempest, Timon of Athens, first
editions in folio.

Titus Andronicus (Edward White), 1611.

   Daniel (1864), £31, 10s.

   F. Perkins (1889), £35 (margin of title repaired).

Troilus and Cressida (G. Eld for R. Bonian & H.
Walley), 1609.

   Boswell, 13s.   Steevens, £5, 10s.   Roxburghe,
£5, 5s.   Heber (Part 2), £16.   Daniel (1864),
109 guineas; this fine copy, with second title,
cost him £50.   F. Perkins (1889), £30 (headlines
cut off).

Two Gentlemen of Verona, Winter's Tale, first editions in
folio.

Venus and Adonis (Richard Field), 1593.

   Malone gave £25 for his unique copy, now in
the Bodleian.

—— (Richard Field), 1594.

   Jolley (1844), £106 (close cut, and mended);
now in the Grenville Library.   Daniel (1864),
£240—Lilly; finest copy known.

Venus and Adonis (R. F. for John Harrison), 1596.
Sir W. Bolland (1840), £91—Bright; Bright's sale (1845), £91, 10s. — Daniel; Daniel's sale (1864), 300 guineas—Boóne.

Lucrece (Richard Field for John Harrison), 1594.
Baron Bolland (1840), £105. Bright, £58 (top margin repaired). Daniel (1864), 150 guineas —Lilly. W. H. Crawford (1891), £250. Mr. Holford is said to have given £100 for his copy. F. Perkins (1899), £200 (small hole burnt in two leaves).

Sonnets (G. Eld for T. T.), 1600.
Steevens, £3, 19s. ; this copy cost Narcissus Luttrell 1s. ; at Daniel's sale (1864) it realised 215 guineas. Edwards (1804), £8. Longman's Catalogue, £30. Roxburghe, £21. Chalmers (1841), £105. Halliwell (1856), £41—bought by Mr. Tite. Halliwell (1858), £154, 7s.—bought by Mr. Huth.

Poems (Thomas Cotes), 1640.
Collins (1683), 6d. Lloyd & Raymond (1685), 6d. Field, £2, 5s. Nassau, £3, 13s. 6d. Bindley, £5, 15s. Longman's Catalogue, £8, 18s. 6d. ; another copy, £10, 10s. Stowe, £7, 10s. Bright, £15. Daniel (1864), £44. F. W. Cosens (1890), £61.

CHAPTER XI

IN this chapter some account will be given of a
few of the various classes of literature which have
not previously been alluded to ; but to give a
general idea of some of these books which bring
a high price, it will be necessary to be brief.

Oldys refers to the sale of a book which he
supposes to have been erroneously valued, but
he was not quite correct in his statement. He
wrote, "The atheistical book of Giordano Bruno
sold at Paul's Coffee-house for £30 in 1709; it
has scarcely sold for so many pence since." [1]

The book referred to was — Giordano Bruno,
Spaccio de la Bestia Trionfante. Parigi (Londra :
T. Vautrollier 1584), the sale of which is com-
mented upon in *The Spectator*, No. 389. The sale
at which this book occurred was that of Charles
Bernard in 1711, and the amount was really £28.
The purchaser was Walter Clavel, and this copy
was successively in the possession of John Nichols,
John Ames, Sir Peter Thompson, and M. C. Tutet.
At the sale of the latter's library in 1786 it was
bought by Samuel Tyssen for seven guineas.

---

[1] "Memoir of William Oldys," 1862, p. 104.

Q

Another copy, which had formed part of the library of Mr. P. Le Neve, was sold at Dr. Mead's sale (1754) for four or five guineas.[1]   The price has not gone down, as Oldys supposed it would, for at the Dunn Gardner sale (1880) a copy brought £20, 15s., and another, at the Duke of Hamilton's sale (1884), sold for £18, 10s.

There is a larger circle of bibliophiles in France than in England, and they are more willing to pay high prices for out-of-the-way books.   The early editions of Molière and Rabelais, like those of Shakespeare, are sold for large sums, and early French literature generally, like our own, has greatly advanced in price of late years.

Two instances of the great advance that has occurred may be given :—

Perrault, *Contes de ma Mere Loye*, 1697, wanting leaf of errata, a fine copy, in blue morocco by Bauzonnet, sold at Charles Nodier's sale for 112 francs.   The same copy at the Duke of Hamilton's sale brought £85.

Gringoire, *Les Fantasies de Mere Sote* (Paris, 1516), a copy in blue morocco by Padeloup, sold at Hibbert's sale for nine guineas.   The same copy brought the large sum of £180 at Beckford's sale. One can understand such high prices as these, which arise from the revived interest felt in this kind of book, but the high price of *Le Pastissier François* (Amsterdam : L. & D. Elzevier, 1655) seems absurd.   Such a book can be of little

---

[1] Nichols's " Literary Anecdotes," vol. i. p. 593.

interest to English buyers, although certainly Mr.
Andrew Lang grows enthusiastic over it in his
"Books and Bookmen." In an early edition of his
Manuel (1821) Brunet wrote—

"Till now I have disdained to admit this book into my
work, but I have yielded to the prayers of amateurs.
Besides, how could I keep out a volume which was sold
for one hundred and one francs in 1819?"

The book has greatly increased in value since
then, and, as a consequence, copies not hitherto
known have come into the market. Berard only
knew of two copies. Pietiers, writing on the El-
zevirs in 1843, could cite only five, and in his
Annales he had found out but five more. Willems,
on the other hand, enumerates some thirty, not including Motteley's.[1] Mr. Lang himself calculates
the number of *Pastissiers* now existing at forty, and
gives a good many prices to show how the book
has increased in value. A copy was sold in 1780
for 4 francs. Sensièr's copy sold for 128 francs
in 1828, and for 201 francs in 1837. It was afterwards bound by Trautz-Bauzonnet, and sold with
Potier's books in 1870 for 2910 francs. At the
Benzon sale (1875) it fetched 3255 francs, and was
sold again in 1877 for 2200 francs. Mr. Lang
further says that a copy was marked in Bachelin-
Deflorenne's catalogue at £240, and that Morgand
and Fatout sold an uncut copy for £400. The
Earl of Orford's copy sold in 1895 for £100.

---

[1] Lang's "Books and Bookmen," p. 13.

This is one of the very few books that are absolutely valueless, except in regard to such value as it
gains from its rarity and association with a great
firm of printers ; yet Mr. Lang says that "there are
at least four thousand people who would greatly
rejoice to possess a *Pastissier*, and some of these
desirous ones are very wealthy." This is amazing,
but I suppose it would scarcely be polite to refer to
Carlyle's verdict as to what the mass of people are.

Another scarce book, which is stupid, and of no
interest in itself, is Horace Walpole's "Hieroglyphic
Tales" (1785). The British Museum does not possess
a perfect copy, but it has some of Walpole's own
corrected proofs bound up in a volume. The Earl
of Orford's copy, interleaved and bound in morocco
by Roger Payne, sold in 1895 for £37.

County histories vary in price, but they must
always hold their ground and sell well, on account
of the value of the information contained in their
pages, which cannot easily be found elsewhere.
They may be considered as eminently safe property.
The following are the prices of a few of these :—

Atkyns's (Sir R.) *Gloucestershire*, folio, 1712. Large paper
(first and best edition).
　　Bryant (1807), £17, 17s. Dent (1827), £14,
14s. Sykes, £16. Nassau, 15 guineas. H
Perkins (1873), £29. Comerford (1881), £41.
Beresford-Hope (1882), £38. Beckford (1882),
£52.

Aubrey's *Surrey*, 5 vols., 1719. Large paper.
　　Dent, £19, 5s. H. Perkins (1873), £32, 10s.

Blomefield's *Norfolk*, 5 vols., 1739–75.
Comerford (1881), £160 (illustrated).   Earl of
Gosford (1884), £87 (drawings by Cotman inserted).
William Brice, &c (1887), £20.

Drake's (T.) *Eboracum, History of the City of York*, 1736.
Large paper, proof-plates coloured, in red morocco
by Kalthoeber.
H. Perkins (1873), £25.   Beckford (1882), £63.

Dugdale's (Sir W.) *Antiquities of Warwickshire*, 1656.
First edition, and the only one admitted as evidence
in a court of law.
Bindley, £10, 10s.   Sykes, £11, 11s.   Comerford, £12, 10s.   Beckford (1882), £20.   Sunderland (1882), £15.

Dugdale's *Warwickshire*, 2 vols., 1730.   Large paper.
Dent, £33.   Sykes, £39, 8s.   Heath, £64, 1s.
Nassau, £33.   Willett, £52, 10s.   H. Perkins
(1873), £84 (red morocco by Derome).

Gough's *Sepulchral Monuments*, 5 vols., 1786–96.
Fonthill, £92, 8s.   Beckford (1882), £31.   (Same
copy.)

Loggan (D.), *Oxonia illustrata*, 1675.
Beckford (1882), £14 (old red morocco).

—— *Cantabrigia illustrata*, 1688.
Beckford (1882), £11 (old red morocco).

Nichols's *Leicestershire*, four vols. in eight, 1795–1815.
Large paper (original edition of vol. iv., part 1), russia
extra.
H. Perkins (1873), £260.   Earl of Gosford (1884),
£275.

Ormerod's *Cheshire*, 3 vols., 1819. Large paper.
H. Perkins (1873), plates in three states-etchings, proofs, and proofs on India paper, morocco extra by Lewis, one of six copies, £155.

Plot's *Oxfordshire*, 1677. Large paper.
Beckford (1883), £8, 15s. (old red morocco).

—— *Staffordshire*, 1686. Large paper.
Beckford (1883), £40, 10s. (old black morocco).

Thoroton's *Nottinghamshire*, 1677.
Heber (part 9), £11, 5s. Beresford-Hope (1882), £11. Beckford (1883), £14, 10s.

First editions of our English classics have increased greatly in price of late years. Many of Defoe's works are very scarce, and bring good prices. The late Mr. James Crossley had a fine collection of these, but his library was in such poor condition that the books did not sell well. The British Museum bought at his sale, June 20, 1885, the autograph manuscript of Defoe's "Compleat English Gentleman," which had never been printed until Mr. Nutt issued it to subscribers in 1890. The manuscript remained in the possession of Defoe's relations, the Baker family, for more than a hundred years, as Dawson Turner bought it in 1831 from the Rev. H. D. F. Baker, the descendant of Henry Baker, son-in-law of Defoe, for £69. In 1859, at the sale of Turner's MSS., Crossley bought the book for £75, 8s.

Robinson Crusoe, first edition, 2 vols., 1719.
Roxburghe (1812), £1, 4s. Sotheby's (1846), £4, 16s. (with " Serious Reflections," 3 vols., 1719-20).
Alfred Crampton, 1896 (3 vols.), £75.
Sir Cecil Domvile, 1897 (part 1), £45, 10s.

Walton's *Angler*, 1653, first edition.
> Rev. J. Brand (1807), £3, 3s. (fine copy). Hunter (1813), £7, 10s. Utterson (1852), £11, 15s. Beckford (1883), fine copy, in green morocco, £87—Bain. Gibson-Craig (1887), £195 (morocco). Gibson-Craig (1888), £23 (imperfect, sold with all faults). G. Wood (Sotheby, 1891), £310 (clean, in original sheepskin). Sotheby (December 1895), £415.

Goldsmith's *Vicar of Wakefield*, 1766, first edition.
> Mansfield - Mackenzie (1889), £67. T. B. T. Hildyard (1895), £56 (original calf). Alfred Crampton (1896), £65 (morocco extra by Bedford). Rare Books and MSS. (Sotheby, March 1897), £60 (original calf).

BOOKS ON VELLUM

Collectors have always had a fancy for these very choice books, and that the taste has not yet died out is seen from the fact that the late William Morris printed copies of the beautiful books issued from the Kelmscott Press on vellum, and was particularly careful in the selection of the skins, which he obtained at first from Italy. A complete set of all the books on vellum (including Chaucer), forty-nine volumes, were offered at the Kelmscott Press for £650, and have been sold at that price.

We can understand the early printed books being struck off upon vellum, as the printers appreciated that material on account of its use by the scribes in the production of the beautiful manuscripts of a

former age, but it is surely infinitely more convenient to have a book printed on good paper
rather than on such a refractory material as vellum.
Some collectors have been so infatuated as to
confine their libraries to books printed on vellum,
and the French Marshal Junot was one of them.
Modern books were printed for him on this sub-
stance; but when they came to be sold it was found
that the public did not care much for his books, and
more than half of them were bought in. One of the
lots illustrates in a remarkable manner the advance
in prices at the present time. The book was Longus's *Pastoralia*, printed by Didot in 1802. One
copy only was pulled on vellum for the Marshal,
and this volume contained the original drawings of
Proudhon, and a set of proof impressions of the
engravings. At the Junot sale in 1816 this book
only realised £37, 10s.; at the Beckford sale it
brought £900. One of the most charming of
Junot's books was the Didot *Horace* of 1799 folio,
a volume which contained the original drawings
from which the copperplate vignettes were executed. This was bought by George Hibbert for
£140.

Of old books, mention may be made of the
dedication copy to James V. of John Bellenden's
translation of Hector Boece's "Cronikles of Scotland" (1536), which was printed on vellum, and
which, in a fine old binding, realised at the Duke
of Hamilton's sale (1884), £800.

Dibdin styled this hobby of collectors the fifth
symptom of the bibliomania, and he gave a list of

the vellum-printed books in Count MacCarthy's and James Edwards's libraries. In the latter collection was a copy of Martin Luther's German Bible (Augsburg, 1535, two vols. folio), which sold for the reasonable price of £52, 10s. These copies on vellum were printed at the charge of John Frederick, Elector of Saxony.

Edwards employed Bodoni to print for him six copies of the edition of the "Castle of Otranto" (Parma, 1791) on vellum, and his own copy, made up with a selection of the best sheets, sold at his sale in 1815 for £29, 8s.

At Watson Taylor's sale Pope's "Essay on Man" (1819), printed on vellum, sold for £10.

Mention has already been made of the grand copies on vellum of the earliest productions of the printing-press—the Mazarin Bible, &c.

ILLUSTRATED BOOKS

Good illustrated books, which are an ornament to any library, are now high priced, and are not likely to fall in value. Such books as Dibdin's bibliographical works, Rogers's "Italy" and "Poems," and many other books of a like kind, must always be a delight to the æsthetic collector.

Collections of engraved portraits have realised great prices, such as Holland's *Basiliwlogia* (1618), which sold for £600 at Christie's in 1811 ; and his *Herwologia* (1620), which sold for £17 at the Beckford sale, £28, 10s. at the Earl of Crawford's sale (1887), and £19, 15s. at W. H. Crawford's

(Lakelands) sale (1891); and the superb series of Vandyck's etchings, which sold for £2850 at the Beckford sale.

Great prices have also been paid for extra illustrated books; but it is useless to record the prices given for them, unless a list of the contents is given also. Grangerising has been ridiculed with much justice, and some of the bulky works which have been produced, such as the illustrated Bibles and Shakespeares, are instances of a very absurd mania. Dr. Hill Burton gave an amusing and by no means exaggerated sketch in his " Book Hunter" of how the compiler set about his work. Now in England Grangerising is mostly confined within the limits of illustrating topographical works with views and historical books with portraits, but in the United States the old plan is said to be still in force.

BINDINGS

In no class of books have prices more conspicuously advanced than in the case of bindings, and in many sales that have taken place of late years fine specimens have been brought to the hammer; but no sale could compare with that of the Beckford library in this respect. Good examples of the libraries of Margaret of Valois, Maioli, Grolier, Thuanus, and Canevari are eagerly sought after, and the following prices of some of the choicest of these bindings will give readers an idea of the current values of these charming books :—

Marguerite de Valois.   Carmina illustrium Poetarum
   Italorum, 1579, 2 vols.   Old brown morocco,
   covered with the arms and devices of Marguerite
   de Valois.
      Beckford (1882), £242.

Diane de Poictiers.   Le Livre des Statuts et Ordonances
   de l'Ordre de Sainct Michel (Paris, 1550), printed
   on vellum.   A beautiful specimen of the library of
   Diane de Poictiers, in old brown morocco, ornamented with the arms of Henry II. of France, the
   crescent, bows and quivers of Diana, and fleurs
   de lis.
      Beckford (1882), £155.

Grolier.   I. Aurelius Augurellus (Venetiis: Aldus, 1505).
   Brown morocco, beautiful specimen of Grolier's
   library.
      Beckford (1882), £250.

——— Lucanus cura Aldi Romani (Venetiis: Aldus, 1515).
   Grolier's copy, covered with scroll tooling.
      Beckford (1882), £290.

——— Another copy, *veau fauve*, with Grolier tooling,
   £120.

Grolier and Thuanus.   Lucanus de Bello Civili (Lutetiæ:
   R. Stephanus, 1545).   Brown morocco, covered with
   Grolier tooling; apparently bound for Grolier, and
   subsequently possessed by Thuanus.
      Beckford (1882), £135.

——— Franchini Poemata (Romæ, 1554).   Red morocco,
   covered with Grolier tooling, and monogram of the
   Marquis de Menars on back, from the libraries of
   Grolier and Thuanus.
      Beckford (1882), £230.

Grolier and Thuanus. Buchanani Psalmorum Para-
phrasis Poetica (apud H. et R. Stephanum, s.a.).
Olive morocco, sides and back covered with gold
tooling in the Grolier style, the first arms of
Thuanus forming the centre ornament.
Beckford (1882), £310.

Louis XIII. and Anne of Austria. Sainct Johan Zebedee
L'Apocalypse, Mystère (Paris, 1541). Blue morocco,
richly ornamented with gold tooling and the crowned
cyphers of Louis XIII. and Anne of Austria, by A.
Ruette.
Beckford (1882), £255.

Demetrio Canevari, Physician to Urban VIII. Tirante
il Bianco (Vinegia, 1538). A perfect specimen of
Canevari's library, in Venetian red morocco, with
his device.
Beckford (1883), £111.

Du Fresnoy. Lucanus de Bello Civili (Lugd. Bat., 1658).
Red morocco, richly ornamented with gold tooling,
with arms and monogram of H. Petit Du Fresnoy
stamped on the sides and back, by Boyet.
Beckford (1882), £84.

Marguerite de Montmorency, Dame de Fosseteau. Du-
chesne, Histoire genealogique de la maison de
Montmorency et de Laval, 2 vols. in 1 (Paris,
1624). Old olive morocco, the sides and back
covered with the MF and device (the Marguerite)
of Marguerite de Montmorency.
Beckford (1882), £120.

A few instances of the work of the great French
binders follow, and it will be seen that the work of

no binder is more appreciated by collectors than that of Monnier:—

Clovis Eve. Coloured Drawings of Maps and Plans of places in France, executed in 1602 and 1603 for Henry IV.'s own use. Olive morocco, covered with fleurs de lis, the King's arms forming the centre ornament, with his crowned H at each corner. A magnificent specimen of Clovis Eve's art. Beckford (1882), £375.

Boyet. In the second portion of the Sunderland library there was a small volume in old crimson morocco (Cicero, *De Officiis*, Amst. ex off. Elzeviriani, 1677), which was not specially described, nor the title printed in capitals. It did not look worth many pounds, but Mr. Quaritch obtained it after an exciting contest with Mr. Morgand for £120. The cause of the excitement was this: from the character of the end papers it was judged that the book had been bound by the French binder Boyet. Specimens of his handiwork are very rare, and hence the great price.

Deseuil (or *Du Seuil*). In the second portion of the Beckford library was a copy of the Leyden edition of Macrobius (1670), bound in red morocco doublé by Deseuil. This fetched £39, while another copy in vellum only realised 16s.
      Here is another instance of the increased value of a copy of a book bound by a good binder. A copy of Montaigne, *Essais*, 3 vols. 8vo (Amst.: Elzevir, 1659), bound in red morocco doublé by Deseuil, brought £200, while another copy. bound by Roger Payne in red morocco, only sold for £12, 10s.

A small duodecimo volume bound by Deseuil (Longus, Les Amours Pastorales de Daphnis et Chloe, *Paris*, 1788) was sold at G. Daniel's sale in 1864 for £92.

Monnier. Decor Puellarum (Venetia : N. Jenson, 1471). Girardot de Prefond's copy, a magnificent specimen of Monnier's binding, in blue morocco, ornamented with flowers worked on variegated leathers, and stamped in gold.

Beckford (1883), £530.

—— De l'Imitation de Jesus Christ traduction nouvelle (Paris, 1690). Large paper. Citron morocco, magnificent specimen of Monnier's binding.

Beckford (1882), £356.

—— Corneille, Rodogune. Au Nord [Versailles], 1760. Madame de Pompadour's own copy, printed under her eyes in a northern apartment of the Palace of Versailles, in yellow morocco ; fine specimen of Monnier's binding.

Beckford (1882), £325.

It has hitherto been the fine French and Italian bindings that have fetched the high prices, but now some of the beautiful English bindings of the seventeenth and eighteenth centuries are coming in for their share of consideration. At the Earl of Orford's sale (1895) R. Wood's "Essay on Homer" (1785), bound by Roger Payne by order of Wood's widow for presentation to Horace Walpole, sold for ten guineas. There is an interest in this book as having fallen into the hands of Goethe when his powers were first developing themselves, and it strongly

interested him.   Robert Wood was Under-Secretary
of State in 1762, and he related an affecting anecdote
of Lord Granville, a statesman known now only to
the few.   Wood was directed to wait upon the
President of the Council (Lord Granville) a few
days before he died with the preliminary articles of
the Treaty of Paris.   " I found him," he continued,
" so languid that I proposed postponing my business
for another time ; but he insisted that I should stay,
saying that it could not prolong his life to neglect
his duty," adding a quotation from Homer, which
may be found in Mr. Matthew Arnold's discourses
on Homeric translations.

EARLY EDITIONS OF MODERN AUTHORS

The last five-and-twenty years has seen the rise of
a new taste in early editions of the works of modern
authors, and a new class of bibliographers has arisen
to describe these books.

Mr. J. H. Slater (the editor of " Book Prices
Current ") has published a useful guide to this sub-
ject, entitled " Early Editions : a Bibliographical
Survey of the Works of some popular Modern
Authors.   London, 1894."

I have taken some particulars from this book,
and supplemented them with a note of the prices
realised at the remarkable sale of Mr. Alfred
Crampton's collection in 1896.   I have also added
a few books sold since that date.

Among the first of modern books to sell for high
prices were the illustrated novels of Dickens and

Thackeray, and to be valuable these must be in perfect condition, with the original wrappers, &c. After these come the other books illustrated by Cruikshank, "Phiz," Leech, and others, viz., Ainsworth's and Lever's novels, Surtees' Sporting novels —"Sponge's Sporting Tour," "Jorrocks's Jaunts," "Handley Cross," &c.

Of poets, Shelley's pieces were among the first to attain high prices, and Byron's among the last.

Arnold.—Matthew Arnold's "Strayed Reveller. By A.," 1849, and "Empedocles on Etna," 1852, have long been classed among the rare books. The former was published at 4s. 6d., and its usual price now is £4, but a copy has fetched £7. The latter was published at 6s., and is now valued at from £3, 10s. to £6.

Beckford, *Poetical Sketches.*
    Gaisford (1890), £40.

Blake (W.), *Songs of Innocence and of Experience* [1789]. Engraved and coloured by Blake, in green morocco by Lewis.
    Sir W. Tite, £61.   Lord Beaconsfield, £85. Beckford (1882), £146.

——— *Milton : a Poem.*   Engraved throughout, and ornamented with designs by Blake, blue morocco by Mackenzie.
    Beckford (1882), £230.

Browning.—Robert Browning's first publication, which appeared when its author was in his twenty-first year, is a great rarity.

"Pauline; a Fragment of a Confession. 'Plus ne suis ce que j'ai été, Et ne le sçaurois jamais être.' —*Marot.* London : Saunders & Otley, Conduit Street, 1833."

Mr. Slater says that there are about eight copies known, and that it was supposed to be worth £40 or £50. A copy, with an autograph note by the author, was sold at Alfred Crampton's sale for £145. Mr. Thomas J. Wise printed a facsimile reprint in 1886, which has been used by the forger to deceive. Mr. Slater had seen a "doctored" copy of this reprint, in which Wise's title and prefatory note were removed, the paper was rotted to make it porous, and the leaves were smoked to give them a mellow appearance. Mr. Wise's paper is thicker than the original, and Mr. Slater gives a hint how to distinguish the two :—

"On the final page (71) appear the words—'Richmond, October 22, 1832.' If the word 'October' is printed in *thin* italics the book is without doubt a reprint. So far as I am aware, there is no other difference between Mr. Wise's excellent reprint and the original (the paper excepted)."

Burns.—The most amazing price ever realised for a modern book was that of £572 for "Poems chiefly in the Scottish dialect. By Robert Burns. *Kilmarnock,* 1786." The original price of this octavo volume was three shillings. The history of the very fine copy sold in Edinburgh in February 1898 is traced back about eighty years by a writer in *Literature.* In 1870 it was sold for six guineas to G. B. Simpson, of Dundee, who sold it

R

in 1879, with some other books, to A. C. Lamb for
£124. The price of the Kilmarnock Burns has
steadily advanced from £3, 10s. in 1858 to £111
in 1888, and then it made the immense leap to
£572.

Byron.—"Poems on Various Occasions" (Newark,
1807, 8vo) sold at Alfred Crampton's sale for £45.
"The Waltz" (1813, pp. 27), published without a
wrapper at 3s., sold at the same sale for £55. Mr.
Slater says that an uncut copy has been sold by
auction for £86.

Meredith.—A fine uncut copy of George Meredith's Poems, 1851, sold at a sale of Rare Books
and Manuscripts (Sotheby, March 1897) for £17,
10s. Another copy with alterations in the author's
autograph (Sotheby, June 1897) sold for £25.

Morris.—The beautiful issues of William Morris's
Kelmscott Press advanced in price in many instances before publication, and are likely, now that
the supply has ceased, to advance still more ; but
they vary very much according to the literary rank
of the books. The edition of Keats, published at
30s., was sold lately for £12. Shelley's Poetical
Works, in three volumes 8vo, was sold at Sotheby's
early in 1898 for £8. Chaucer's Works, folio, is
out of print, and was marked by Messrs. J. & J.
Leighton at £30.

Rossetti. — The first printed work of Dante G.
Rossetti is of great rarity. The poet was thirteen
years old when the lines were composed, and

fifteen when they were printed. The title is "Sir Hugh the Heron: a Legendary Tale, in four parts. G. Polidori's Private Press, 15 Park Village East, 1843. Private Circulation only," pp. 24. A copy was sold at Sotheby's in 1890 for £16. Miss Christina Rossetti's first poems, privately printed at the same press, have brought seven guineas.

Ruskin.—"Poems by J. R., collected in 1850 for private circulation only," a foolscap octavo volume of 283 pages, is valued at £50 or £60. The value of his sumptuous books, "The Stones of Venice," the "Seven Lamps of Architecture," and "Modern Painters," is known to all, and when in good condition they look their value. The original editions of the first, 1851 to 1853, are valued at from £12 to £15. The first edition of the "Seven Lamps," 1849, at £4, and the second edition, 1855, at £4, 10s. The "Modern Painters," 5 vols., early editions, from £20 to £25.

Shelley.—The early editions of Shelley's Poems and Prose Treatises were amongst the first of this class of books to attain high prices. Some may be noted here in chronological order :—

"Zastrozzi : a Romance," 1810, was published at 5s. Bound and cut copies have sold for £5, 15s., and £12, 5s. An uncut copy, in calf, fetched £12, 5s. in 1890, and an uncut copy in morocco brought fifteen guineas in 1897 (Sir C. S. Forbes).

The most interesting of these pamphlets is the one which was the cause of its author being expelled from University College, Oxford.

"The Necessity of Atheism. Worthing. Printed by E. & W. Phillips. Sold in London and Oxford," n.d. [1811] f. 8vo, pp. 13.

Nearly all the copies were destroyed by the printers, and Mr. Slater values a clean copy at about £20, but probably it would realise much more than that.

"St. Irvyne," 1811, morocco uncut, Sir C. S. Forbes, 1897, £16, 10s.

"An Address to the Irish People" (Dublin, 1812) was published at 5d., and Mr. Slater values a copy at £8 to £12, but one was sold at Alfred Crampton's sale, 1896, for £42.

"Queen Mab," 1813, in the original boards, was sold in 1891 for £22, 10s.

"The Refutation of Deism," 1814, fetched £33 at an auction in 1887.

The largest price, however, given for one of these pamphlets was £130 for "Œdipus Tyrannus," 1820, at Crampton's sale. The entire impression was destroyed except seven copies, only two or three of which are known to exist, but a reprint on vellum appeared in 1876. The British Museum possesses a copy, presented by Lady Shelley.

Tennyson. — The first editions of Tennyson's Poems bring high prices, and the scarcest is the famous "Poems by Two Brothers," 1827, published for 5s., and large paper for 7s. The present value of the former is about £15 to £20.

The original MS. was sold in December 1892 to

Messrs. Macmillan & Bowes of Cambridge for £480. After a facsimile had been taken, it was resold to an American collector.

Dickens.—"Sunday under Three Heads" was one of the first of the novelist's works to sell for a high price. As it is a very small book, it is not saying much to describe it as selling for its weight in gold; in point of fact, it sells for more. Mr. F. C. Kitton gives the market value of the various novels in his "Novels of Charles Dickens," 1897. The first edition of the " Memoirs of Joseph Grimaldi" sold in July 1897 at Sotheby's (Jack, Halliday, &c.) for £8, 17s. 6d.

Thackeray.—Thackerayana is very high priced, and the following two instances of sales in 1897 show that the tendency is still upwards:—Two incomplete sets of "The Snob," ten numbers and thirteen numbers, 1829–30, fetched at Sotheby's (Parlane & Dasent) £89. The eleven numbers complete, with seventeen numbers of the "Gownsman," sold at the Mansfield-Mackenzie sale, 1889, for £25.

"The Fox and the Cat," final proof-sheets of a story apparently intended for the *Cornhill Magazine*, but never published, revised by the author, with numerous corrections and additions in his autograph, sold by Sotheby's in March 1897 (Rare Books and MSS.) for £45, bought by Messrs. Smith, Elder, & Co.

The price of the first editions of Sir Walter Scott's

novels have been long in rising, but good fresh copies fetch a good price now.

The most remarkable price for a three-volume novel was obtained in July 1897 at Sotheby's (Jack, Halliday, &c.), when the first edition of "Jane Eyre" sold for seventeen guineas.

The question naturally occurs, Will such prices as this continue? but it is a question very difficult to answer. All that can be said is, that in this class of books there is the most uncertainty as to the high prices being sustained.

Depreciation is a factor which must be taken into consideration, but it is not at present very wide-spread. It is quite easy to understand why editions of the classics and Thomas Hearne's editions of "Chronicles," &c., have gone down in price, because the publication of superior texts has partially superseded them; but one can scarcely explain why the set of "Byzantine Historians" should fall so much in price, for these ponderous volumes have not been superseded. At the Hamilton sale in 1884 a fine large paper set of these "Historians," 1645–1777, eighteen volumes in red morocco by Ruelle, and five in calf, only brought £4, 10s.

Mezeray's *Histoire de France*, 3 vols. folio, bound in blue morocco by Derome, which sold formerly for £105, only sold for £33 at the Beckford sale.

A large paper set of Hearne's Works, bound in red morocco, was bought at Mead's sale for fifty

guineas by an ancestor of Meerman the bibliographer. It continued at the Hague with Meerman's library until the sale of the latter in 1822,
when it was bought by a London bookseller for
£200. Pickering purchased it, and sold it to
Hanrott for £500; at his sale in 1836 it was bought
by the Duke of Buccleuch for £400. At Watson
Taylor's sale a set fetched £200. At the Beckford
sale, the set of Hearne's Works were all on small
paper, with the exception of "Camden," "Annales,"
1717, "Fordun's Scoticronicon," 1722, and "History
and Antiquities of Glastonbury," 1722. The twenty-
seven lots only brought altogether £41, 10s.

In conclusion, there remain two points to lay
stress upon and to reiterate—

(1) That price depends largely upon condition.
This every one connected with book-buying knows,
but the fact is almost entirely overlooked by those
who know but little of books. Constantly when a
very high price is announced in the papers some
person finds that he has a copy of the identical
book, for which he expects to obtain an identical
price, and he cannot understand when he is told
that his copy is practically valueless, because it is
in bad condition.

If a book is unique, he who wants it must take it
as it is, and make the best of the missing leaves,
the worm-holes, or the stained pages; but if several
copies still exist, it will be found that the price of
the bad copy bears no proportion to that of the
good one.

(2) The forger is abroad whenever prices rule
high.   We have seen how facsimiles have been sold
as the originals, and bindings have often been
doctored, Maioli's and Grolier's being manufac-
tured for the ever greedy demand.   Fortunately,
however cleverly the frauds may be produced, the
expert is pretty sure to notice something that makes
him suspicious, and suspicion will soon be turned
to certainty ; but the public are easily gulled by that
to which they are unaccustomed.

Groliers may be imitated to deceive even the
expert, but in respect to more elaborate toolings,
such as those of Le Gascon, we are safe, because
to imitate these successfully would cost so great
an expenditure of time, that the forgery would be
worth almost as much as the original.

INDEX

THE END

Printed by BALLANTYNE, HANSON & Co.
Edinburgh & London

For EU product safety concerns, contact us at Calle de José Abascal, 56–1°, 28003 Madrid, Spain or eugpsr@cambridge.org.

www.ingramcontent.com/pod-product-compliance
Ingram Content Group UK Ltd.
Pitfield, Milton Keynes, MK11 3LW, UK
UKHW010347140625
459647UK00010B/892